Sept. 11, 2019

Dr. Kerzner

A token of our appreciation for the excellent care & concern that you have provided for Naomi and myself over these past few years (even when you berated me about my weight) much Mazel on your new chapter of your life

Allan & Naomi Frand

ArtScroll Series®

Rabbi Nosson Scherman / Rabbi Meir Zlotowitz
General Editors

It's Never Too Little
It's Never Too Late

Published by
Mesorah Publications, ltd

It's Never Enough

and other other timeless insights for challenging times

RABBI YISSOCHER FRAND

FIRST EDITION
First Impression ... August 2009

Published and Distributed by
MESORAH PUBLICATIONS, LTD.
4401 Second Avenue / Brooklyn, N.Y 11232

Distributed in Europe by
LEHMANNS
Unit E, Viking Business Park
Rolling Mill Road
Jarow, Tyne & Wear, NE32 3DP
England

Distributed in Australia and New Zealand
by **GOLDS WORLDS OF JUDAICA**
3-13 William Street
Balaclava, Melbourne 3183
Victoria, Australia

Distributed in Israel by
SIFRIATI / A. GITLER — BOOKS
6 Hayarkon Street
Bnei Brak 51127

Distributed in South Africa by
KOLLEL BOOKSHOP
Ivy Common
105 William Road
Norwood 2192, Johannesburg, South Africa

ARTSCROLL SERIES®
IT'S NEVER TOO LITTLE, IT'S NEVER TOO LATE, IT'S NEVER ENOUGH
© Copyright 2009, by MESORAH PUBLICATIONS, Ltd.
4401 Second Avenue / Brooklyn, N.Y. 11232 / (718) 921-9000 / www.artscroll.com

ALL RIGHTS RESERVED
The text, prefatory and associated textual contents and introductions
— including the typographic layout, cover artwork and ornamental graphics —
have been designed, edited and revised as to content, form and style.

No part of this book may be reproduced
IN ANY FORM, PHOTOCOPYING, OR COMPUTER RETRIEVAL SYSTEMS
— even for personal use without written permission from
the copyright holder, Mesorah Publications Ltd.
except by a reviewer who wishes to quote brief passages
in connection with a review written for inclusion in magazines or newspapers.

THE RIGHTS OF THE COPYRIGHT HOLDER WILL BE STRICTLY ENFORCED.

ISBN 10: 1-4226-0922-7 / ISBN 13: 978-1-4226-0922-4

Typography by CompuScribe at ArtScroll Studios, Ltd.
Printed in the United States of America by Noble Book Press Corp.
Bound by Sefercraft, Quality Bookbinders, Ltd., Brooklyn N.Y. 11232

Dedicated in loving memory of
our dear mother,

Ruth Skydell ז״ל
רחל לאה ב״ר חיים צבי ז״ל

devoted daughter of the legendary
Harry and Etta Herskowitz ז״ל

She was a model of generosity and integrity who, together with our dear father,
Rabbi Adrian Skydell שליט״א,
perpetuated a legacy of devotion to Torah study and compassionate concern for the welfare of others. She eagerly sought out and responded to those in need, and performed innumerable acts of individual chesed with sublime modesty and discretion. As a professor of psychology, she enhanced the lives of countless individuals through her teaching, writing and counseling.

שֶׁקֶר הַחֵן וְהֶבֶל הַיֹּפִי, אִשָּׁה יִרְאַת ה׳
הִיא תִתְהַלָּל ... וִיהַלְלוּהָ בַשְּׁעָרִים מַעֲשֶׂיהָ.

May her good deeds be an inspiration to us all.

תנצב״ה

Myron and Laurie Goldberg and Family
Bernard Skydell and Family
Harry and Rachel Skydell and Family

In memory of
Isaac and Sylvia Forgash
and
Irving and Frances Rivkin

dedicated by
Jack and Carole Forgash and Family

Acknowledgments

While not writing a formal preface, I do feel the need to give great credit where credit is certainly due.

I have been very fortunate to have as my editor Rabbi Yehuda Heimowitz. Actually the thanks begin with our "shadchan," Rabbi Nosson Scherman, who suggested R' Yehuda originally. The Ribono Shel Olam has gifted him with tremendous talents to pursue his second love — writing and editing — so that he can pursue his first love, which is learning in the *kollel* of Yeshivas Mir Yerushalayim. It was a delight to work with him from start to finish and he made invaluable contributions that make the present volume a more readable and enjoyable work. I will miss his daily emails!

I cannot imagine a better publishing house with which to work than ArtScroll/Mesorah. They have assembled a group of gifted professionals whose talents cover the entire spectrum of the skills needed to put out a beautiful product. In particular I would like to personally thank Reb Avraham Biderman, Reb Mendy Herzberg and Reb Eli Kroen. It's been a pleasure working with each of them.

Two individuals and their families have made this work financially feasible. They are Mr. and Mrs. Harry Skydell and Mr. and Mrs. Jack Forgash. I have met them as a result of my work on behalf of the Just One Life organization — an organization, as its name suggests, that helps women in Eretz Yisrael bring their babies to term rather than the alternative. Credit here must also be given to Rabbi Martin Katz, the long-time director of Just One Life, who introduced them to me many years ago. May the One above repay them for their kindness and generosity, on behalf of so many worthy causes, with good health and *nachas* from their families.

I count myself among the many, many individuals who consider Rabbi Meir Zlotowitz one of their best friends. How can one person have so many best friends? The answer is simple — if you put yourself out for so many people, you make the "best friend" list of many people. The personal attention he paid to the publication of this volume is incredible. He treated it as though it were the first book that he was publishing. I hope to enjoy and merit his friendship and kindness for many years to come.

And one more person: my "Editor in Chief" (and in life), my wife Nechama. We pray to the Almighty that He grant us many years of good health and nachas from our wonderful children — Reb Yakov and Shuli Frand, Reb Yisroel and Avigayil Rapps, and Reb Baruch and Toby Frand — and their delicious children.

Never in my wildest dreams did I ever think that I would write even one book, let alone the six that I have written with ArtScroll. To paraphrase the words of Yaakov Avinu, *"katonti me'kol ha'chassadim,"* and I hope and pray that You, *HaKadosh Baruch Hu*, will give me the opportunity to continue for many more years in the future.

Yissocher Frand

Tu Be'Av 5769
August, 2009
Baltimore, MD

Table of Contents

IT'S NEVER TOO LITTLE — THE BASICS OF JEWISH LIVING

It's Never Too Little, It's Never Too Late, It's Never Enough	13
The Forgotten Trait	21
Shidduchim: Ending the "Crisis"	31
Sticks and Stones vs. Words and Tones	47
Keeping Faith in Troubled Times	65
My Son, Your Son … the *Eibishter's* Son	79
When Winning Isn't Everything	97

IT'S NEVER TOO LATE — FOR TESHUVAH

Paint Your Masterpiece	115
Baby Steps Toward Hashem	131
Getting Our Priorities Straight	147
The Blame Game	163

IT'S NEVER ENOUGH — STRIVING FOR MORE

Marriage: From Caterpillar to Butterfly	185
Kiruv: Not Just for Pros	201
Life, Liberty, and the Pursuit of … *What*?	217
Never Stop Davening	229

It's Never Too Little

The Basics of Jewish Living

It's Never Too Little, It's Never Too Late, It's Never Enough

Those who attended the previous *Siyum haShas* in 1997 will naturally reflect on the differences between that *siyum* and this one. Many will be struck by how much things have changed. As great an occasion as this may be, our happiness is tinged with a certain measure of sadness when we remember the *gedolim* who graced the dais at the last *siyum* and who are no longer with us to take part in this one.

There are other significant differences as well. We are living in a changed world. The sense of security most Americans felt at that time is gone. Each time we look at the New York City skyline, and each time we board an airplane, we are reminded that "Fortress America" is no longer.

But with all the changes that have occurred in the 7½-year span since the last *siyum haShas*, one thing has remained the same: the

---

These words were delivered to audiences gathered worldwide in honor of the eleventh Siyum haShas of Daf Yomi, on March 1, 2005.

Torah. The Torah remains eternal, and the way we learn it is still the same. We are once again being *mesayeim* (concluding) *Shas* with the words, "*Hadran alach tinokes u'slikah lah Maseches Niddah*," and beginning *Maseches Berachos* with the words, "*Mei'eimasai kor'in es Shema be'aravin."*

That is reassuring. It is comforting to witness the eternity of Torah, which is interconnected with the eternity of the Jewish people who study and revere it.

The Talmud (*Megillah* 16a) states that when Haman came to take Mordechai and lead him through the streets on Achashveirosh's royal horse, he found Mordechai teaching his students the laws of *kemitzah*. He asked what they were studying, and they explained that when there was a *Beis HaMikdash*, one who would bring a *minchas nedavah* (voluntary meal-offering) would place a *kometz* (handful) of the offering on the Altar, and he would thereby atone for his misdeeds.

Haman suddenly came to a startling realization — an understanding of the odds against him.

"*Asa malei kumtza kimchah didchu* — a handful of meal-offering of yours came along," he remarked, "*vedachi asarah alfei kikrei kaspi didi* — and wiped out 10,000 silver talents of mine." (Haman had offered Achashveirosh 10,000 silver talents as payment for allowing him to destroy the Jewish people.)

What was it that deflated Haman and made him realize that his plan was doomed?

Haman expected to find Mordechai and his students studying the laws of dying *al kiddush Hashem* in preparation for their imminent annihilation. The fact that, even in such ominous times, they could sit and study laws that pertained to a *Beis HaMikdash* that had been destroyed nearly 70 years earlier demonstrated to Haman the indomitable spirit of the Jews, and their enduring belief in the eternity of *Klal Yisrael* — an eternity that is nourished by the Torah and those who study it.

In May of 1962, Adolph Eichmann, *yemach shemo vezichro*, was executed by the Israeli government. The identity of his executioner was kept secret for thirty years, until the man retired. As it turned out, Eichmann's executioner was an Orthodox Jew of Yemeni descent. A German television station tracked him down and asked to interview him. He agreed on one condition: the interview would be filmed in the *kollel* where he studied.

"Why do you insist on having it done there, with all the noise and hubbub in the background?" the producer asked. "Why can't we do it in the comfort and quiet of our studio?"

"Because," the executioner-cum-*kollel yungerman* responded, "I want the German people to see why we survived. I want the German people to see Jews alive and studying Torah."

From Inspiration to Action

A memory that comes to mind from the previous *Siyum haShas* is the pervasive excitement of all those who participated in the celebration. I remember returning to Baltimore and finding the community filled with a palpable sense of euphoria. But excitement and euphoria must be harnessed and turned into something tangible.

The Ramban (*HaEmunah VeHaBitachon* §19) finds this concept expressed in a homiletic elucidation of a verse in *Shir HaShirim* that states, "Im ta'iru ve'im te'oreru es ha'ahavah ad she'techpatz." This means, says the Ramban, then when your love for Hashem is awakened and inspired, you must channel it into a *cheifetz*, into something tangible. If not, the feelings will soon dissipate, and you will be left with nothing.

Indeed, in the aftermath of the previous *Siyum haShas*, many people did turn their excitement into something concrete, as we see in the growth of the crowd that has gathered for this event. The previous *Siyum haShas* was attended by 50,000 people in various venues. The crowds that have gathered worldwide for this *siyum* come to a sum total of over 100,000 people.

More importantly, at this *siyum* there are so many more *mesayemim*, so many more individuals who have completed *Talmud Bavli*.

The growth in number of those studying *daf yomi* is nothing short of amazing. Our times offer so many ways to waste one's time. We are bombarded by a myriad of distractions. Email. iPods.

Blackberries. Real-time streaming of the stock market. Virtual-reality game systems. We live in a society engrossed in the full-fledged pursuit of pleasure and leisure, and yet, more and more people voluntarily "sign up" for the rigors of *daf yomi*.

How do you explain that?

I think that there are two factors that bring people to join *daf yomi*.

First, the inspiration that people take from this event. Seeing so many people involved in *daf yomi* proves to one and all that *daf yomi* is no longer limited to the elite. We see that it is doable. *If everyone else can do it,* people think, *then so can I.*

There is a mitzvah to blow *shofar* at the beginning of *yovel* (the jubilee year), signaling that all slaves who are Jews be set free. Why must the *shofar* be blown? Why can't masters just set their servants free at the appointed time without the sound of the *shofar*?

The *Chinuch* explains that, understandably, a master will find it difficult to part with a loyal servant who has been with him for so many years. When masters would hear the sound of the *shofar*, they would be reminded that they are not the only ones releasing their servants. *Everyone* is freeing their servants. "Nothing strengthens the heart," writes the *Chinuch*, "like actions that are common to the general public." Knowing that there are others in the same situation helps you do things that you might otherwise consider too difficult.

This is the picture that the *siyum* of *daf yomi* presents. It shows that *daf yomi* is a *ma'aseh harabim* — it is something that is undertaken by the general public.

Daf yomi has a ripple effect on everyone — even those who, as of yet, have not been studying *daf yomi*. It has become a great *mechayeiv* and serves as an impetus to everyone. It has raised the bar by several notches. When a man walks into shul at 6:30 for the early *minyan* and finds a group that has been studying *daf yomi* since 5:30, it sends a message to him. It reminds him that daily learning is something that we must all do.

Daf yomi also raises the expectations that we have of ourselves. Thirty years ago, people were satisfied to attend a weekly *gemara shiur* on Shabbos afternoon before Minchah. *Daf yomi* has changed that. It must be said that the *kollel* system that has now produced two to three generations of *lomdei* and *ohavei Torah* is partly responsible for this change. One no longer feels comfortable with a once-a-week *shiur*. Everyone feels that he must designate times to study Torah each day.

The second reason that people are able to disregard all the distractions and join *daf yomi* is that ultimately, Torah is the only substance that will satisfy the *Yiddisheh neshamah*, the Jewish soul. Shlomo HaMelech wrote, "*Vegam hanefesh lo simalei* — the soul is never satisfied" (*Koheles* 6:7).

A Midrash (*Midrash Zuta, Koheles* 6) explains that the Jewish soul will never feel satisfied by earthly pleasures, because it is not of this world. Another Midrash (*Koheles Rabbah* 6:1) brings the analogy of a commoner who marries a princess. No matter what he brings her, he can never satisfy her. Why? Because she is a princess who has had it all. A commoner's concept of delicacies and luxuries will never compare to what she has had in the past. So too, all the physical pleasures that this world can provide will never satisfy the *neshamah*, which comes from the upper, spiritual worlds and cannot appreciate such pleasure.

Specifically in our times, when the world has become steeped in hedonistic pleasure-seeking, the Jewish *neshamah* bursts forth, searching for something to quench its thirst for meaning. All of the distractions are the equivalent of junk food for the soul. Just as the body cannot be sustained over time by chips and Coke, so the *neshamah* cannot be sustained by the junk food of material pursuits. It needs something real. It needs the Torah.

◆§ Floating Between the Extremes

The previous *Siyum haShas* inspired people to make a commitment to strengthen their connection to Torah, and this *siyum* should be no different. Each person must leave this event with a commitment to raise his personal standard of Torah study.

Those who have concluded *Shas* must increase the quality of the way they study *daf yomi*. *Daf yomi* is, *lehavdil*, like touring the world. A tourist can appreciate the beauty of this world. But there is so much more to each country than you can see by merely spending a few days viewing its main attractions. And there is so much more to *Shas* than can be gleaned through a brief perusal of its pages.

When you leave this *siyum*, harness the inspiration you have gotten by making a commitment to do more. Be it in *chazarah* (review) of the *daf*, in the preparation you invest into the *daf* before attending a *shiur*, or in plumbing the depths of a *sugya* (topic) that grabs your attention. Whatever you do, make sure not to allow the excitement to dissipate without a new, deeper commitment.

To those who have never completed *Shas*, may this event prove to you that just as the ordinary, busy people who are seated at your side managed to finish, then *so can you.*

And for others, may this event inspire you to learn your very first *daf* of Talmud.

Let me share a story about an assimilated Jew — so assimilated, in fact, that his chosen profession was none other than boxing. This man was so removed from Judaism that he didn't even make a bar mitzvah for his son. Through a series of events, however, his son became interested in *Yiddishkeit*. One thing led to another, and somehow this boy ended up in a yeshivah where he became a great *masmid* (diligent student).

During vacation, the boxer's son would come home and sit at the dining-room table studying Talmud, while his father sat in the living room with his eyes glued to the television.

One day the father walked into the dining room and told his son, "I want to learn something too. If you are so engrossed in studying

Torah that I cannot pry you away from it, then I too want to learn it."

"Daddy," the son said hesitantly, "you barely know Hebrew, and the Talmud is written in Aramaic. It is going to be so difficult for you."

"Please," the father nearly begged. "Just teach me *one page*."

And so began a long and arduous journey.

More than a year later, the boxer finally mastered his very first *daf* of Talmud. He was so thrilled with himself that he wanted to throw a party. "The party you are talking about," said his son, "is called a *siyum*. But it is reserved for a person who finishes an entire tractate."

When the father insisted, the son decided to ask the Rav of their Lower East Side neighborhood — none other than Rav Moshe Feinstein — whether his father could make a *siyum* on one *daf*. Rav Moshe responded that under those circumstances, he could make a *siyum*, and that he, Rav Moshe Feinstein, would attend.

So it was. Rav Moshe came to that *siyum* and offered words of encouragement to the *mesayeim*.

That very night, the former boxer passed away in his sleep.

Rav Moshe Feinstein delivered a eulogy at the man's funeral. "Just as the Talmud states [*Avodah Zarah* 10b] that one can acquire his portion in the World to Come in one moment," he said, "so is it possible for a man to acquire his portion in the World to Come with *one daf*."

When it comes to Torah study, it is never too late, and it is never too little.

But it is also never enough. Let me tell you a story that is the matching bookend to the previous one.

In the final months of Rav Moshe's life, Rav Michel Shurkin, a close *talmid*, once came to visit him. He writes that at that point in his life, Rav Moshe would rise each day at 3 a.m. and study Torah undisturbed until it was time for Shacharis. "How is the Rosh Yeshivah doing?" Rav Shurkin asked.

"*Nisht gut, nisht gut*," replied Rav Moshe.

"What's wrong?" Rav Shurkin asked, deeply disturbed by the pessimistic answer.

It's Never Too Little, It's Never Too Late, It's Never Enough / 19

"The doctor was here," Rav Moshe explained, "and he insisted that I must sleep an additional hour each day due to my flagging health. *Ich vell bleiben a gantzer am ha'aretz* – I will remain an absolute ignoramus."

The nonagenarian Rav Moshe, who had spent his *entire life* devoted to intense Torah study, was worried that an "extra" hour of sleep would leave him an ignoramus.

I venture to say that all 100,000 Jews participating in this *Siyum haShas* are somewhere between these two extremes. I don't think anyone here is as green as the boxer who spent his final months studying his first *daf,* and no one in attendance is like Rav Moshe, who spent nine decades studying Torah with such incredible diligence.

When it comes to Torah study, remember: *it's never too little, it's never too late, and it's never enough.*

The Forgotten Trait

Judaism is not a religion for the weak-kneed or the faint of heart. Being a Jew in past millennia meant facing too many inquisitions, expulsions, pogroms, and other iniquities too frightful for those who could not stand strong as Jews to survive. Only the *gevurah* (strength of character) of our *zeides* and *bubbes* ensured that there would be continuity to a nation under constant threat of annihilation. From where did that strength come?

Gevurah is one of the *middos* of Hashem. As we say in *Shemoneh Esrei* three times a day: *haKeil hagadol,* **hagibor***, vehanora* (the great, mighty, and awesome God); *Atah* **gibor** *le'olam Hashem* (You are eternally mighty, my Lord). Each one of us has a *neshamah* that is a *cheilek Eloka mima'al* — a portion of Hashem Himself. Since Hashem has *gevurah,* so do we.

Gevurah has been coursing through the veins of the Jewish people from the very beginning. Those millions of brave Jews who perished throughout the generations were *gibborim* who honed the *middas hagevurah* first exemplified by Avraham Avinu when he opted to be thrown into the fire at Uhr Kasdim rather than capitulate to Nimrod. The *middas hagevurah* hit its peak, perhaps, during the Holocaust, of which we have heard hundreds or thousands of stories of simple *Yidden* who went to the gas chambers or the killing fields with a song of faith in Hashem on their lips. The strength to do that was derived from the knowledge that our nation is strong enough to prevail no matter how determined the world was to rid itself of us.

And those who emerged from that *gehinnom* with their *emunah* intact were *gibborim* beyond belief.

There was a fellow by the name of Dr. Shield who lived in Philadelphia. In his later years, Dr. Shield became ill, and a rav came to visit him. Dr. Shield asked the rav if he could be *mattir* a *neder* (annul a vow). "What is the *neder*?" asked the rav.

"I want to be allowed to sit in shul," said Dr. Shield.

"Why shouldn't you be able to sit in shul?" asked the rav incredulously.

"When I was in Dachau," said Dr. Shield, "we were forced to stand up when the SS officers walked into the room and were required to remain standing. I made a *neder* that if I would get out of that place and no longer be forced to stand up for those swine, I would never sit down in a shul. I would stand before Hashem in appreciation of being saved from the disgrace of standing for those sub-humans."

From that day on, Dr. Shield had never sat down in shul. That is but a glimpse of the *gevurah* of those who emerged from the camps.

On a deeper level, can we even begin to comprehend the *gevurah* of those who saw their entire families wiped out in the war, and still had the strength to start life anew and raise a second family? Can we fathom the *gevurah* it took not to become bitter and abandon the faith that has sustained the Jewish people through the generations?

Those of us who hail from American stock also have stories

of the *gevurah* displayed by our parents and grandparents. Jews who came to America in the first half of the 20th century faced the dilemma of dealing with the threat, "If you don't come in on Saturday, then don't come in on Monday." It was an overwhelming challenge, and yet many Jews refused to work on Shabbos despite not knowing how they would pay the rent the following week.

My father came to America from Frankfurt am Main in 1939. He brought two suitcases. One held all of his worldly possessions, and the other contained a *Sefer Torah* that he managed to salvage from the Hofman yeshivah in Frankfurt am Main and risked smuggling out of Europe. He was once stopped by a guard who asked, "What is in that suitcase?" to which my father responded, "A copy of the Five Books of Moses." Thankfully, the guard did not insist on opening the suitcase.

When my father reached America, he went into the HIAS agency in New York and said, "I have one goal in life: I want a Shomer Shabbos job in order to earn enough to bring over my mother, wife, and son."

"What sort of work can you do?" the clerk asked.

"I am a bookkeeper," my father responded.

"I have two positions available that meet your requirements," the clerk said. "One is in Charleston, South Carolina, and the other is in Seattle, Washington."

"Where is Seattle, Washington?" my father asked.

"It is outside of New York City," the man responded.

When my father said that he would take that job, they put him onto a Greyhound bus, and five days later he alighted at the other end of America.

My father was a soft-spoken, *eideleh* person. He was a *gibbor* nonetheless, because Shabbos meant more to him than anything else, and he was willing to go anywhere for the cause.

Such was the *gevurah* of Jews in previous generations.

But then the Holocaust ended, and we moved on to a new existence, in a world that seems, at least superficially, to be much kinder. In His overwhelming kindness, Hashem placed us into a wonderful country, a *malchus shel chesed* (kingdom of kindness) —the United States of America. America is an indulgent, tolerant

The Forgotten Trait / 23

country, in which we are free to serve Hashem without fear of reprisal. But the freedom to live as one chooses makes America a dangerous place for a Jew. The fact that we need not exercise the *middas hagevurah* the way our *zeides* and *bubbes* did has turned us into a soft, flabby People that is lax to stand up for its ideals. We no longer use strength to make the tough decisions that are required at times. We prefer the easy way out.

The *middas hagevurah* has become dormant, mostly because we believe that we no longer face the challenges that require us to display that *middah*. In truth, we are making a dreadful mistake. Jews must still exercise *middas hagevurah,* albeit in a very different way. We cannot allow it to become a forgotten trait.

Hashem granted me the great gift of being able to teach in a yeshivah, where I don't face many challenges. Those of you who are out in the workplace face *nisayon* after *nisayon*. But how many of us promised ourselves when we left yeshivah that we were going to stay true to our ideals? We promised ourselves that we wouldn't act or speak like the masses around us. We were going to avoid socializing with those whose *weltanschauung* differs so sharply from ours.

As time passes, however, we slip. We begin to compromise and make concessions. We rationalize that we cannot be the pariah in the office and avoid all small talk — even as we are aware how corrosive that chatter is to us.

The *yetzer hara* has appealed to our soft side, capitalizing on the fact that we no longer need to be *gibborim* in the conventional sense. *Chazal* foresaw this *yetzer hara* and said, "*Eizehu gibbor? Hakovesh es yitzro* — Who is mighty? He who conquers his [evil] inclination" (*Avos* 4:1). Indeed, we no longer need to display our *gevurah* to those who threaten our physical existence, but we must display it to that ever-present force within us that seeks to destroy us spiritually. We must reassess our ideals every once in a while and make sure that we are sticking to them with the very same *gevurah* that Jews throughout the generations displayed.

The Case of the Missing Shoes

There is another area in which we must rediscover what it means to apply the *middas hagevurah*. An overwhelming majority of our decisions as parents are rendered with the *middas hachesed* (Attribute of Kindness) — and rightfully so. We want to give and do for our children, and not disappoint them or make them feel unloved. But there are times when we must speak to them with *gevurah*. If we cannot say "No" to them when the situation calls for it, then we are endangering them. We must learn to say, "No, you can't go there" and "No, you can't wear that."

It's tough. We feel as though we are not giving them what they want and need. In truth, by saying *no*, we are giving them something much more valuable than what they asked for. We are giving them core values, something to strive for.

Rabbi Ephraim Wachsman related that Rebbetzin Schorr, wife of the *Ohr Gedalyahu*, Rav Gedalyah Schorr, grew up in Detroit. Her father was Rabbi Isbee, whom she remembered as a loving and compassionate father. But her father felt that the streets of Detroit in the earlier part of the 20th century would be detrimental to his daughter. He was worried about the impact the streets might have if she played outside on Shabbos. So every Shabbos, he would hide her shoes so that she could not go outdoors.

I'm sure that it was difficult for Rabbi Isbee to hide his daughter's shoes, and that he did so only because he knew that his daughter was confident of his love for her. Only in that context, and out of overwhelming concern for her spiritual safety, was he able to bring himself to do something so extreme. It is probably not a good idea for us to attempt this, and in many communities it is not necessary. But there are other instances when we must show our children this type of tough love.

When my wife was growing up in Baltimore, the "in thing" to do was to go to an Orioles game. My father-in-law, Rabbi Yaakov Blumenkrantz, felt that going to a baseball game was a form of *avodah zarah*. One day she came home from school and asked him for permission to go to a baseball game.

"It's *avodah zarah*," my father-in-law responded.

"But all the other girls in my class are going," his daughter protested, utilizing the time-honored invocation that every child tries on his or her parents. You must realize, though, that my wife had classmates who were daughters of *chashuvah rabbanim*.

"*Avodah zarah!*" my father-in-law insisted.

My wife begged, and pleaded, and cried, but the answer remained "no."

Right or wrong, by standing firm, my father-in-law instilled a value into this young girl: there is no compromise when you feel strongly about something.

On a more superficial level, a fellow who owns a pizza shop told me that he keeps a box of huge lollipops on display at his checkout counter. A woman walked in one day and ordered a slice of pizza for her child. Before she let the child approach the counter, however, she said to the owner in a hushed tone, "Can you take away the box of lollipops so my child does not insist on having one?"

"Madam," he responded, "there is a word in the English language called 'no.'"

We must learn how to tell our children "no" — whether in regard to insignificant matters, such as lollipops, or important ones, such as playing with friends who might have a harmful influence on them — so that they can learn to say no to themselves later on in life.

✥ Gevurah for the 21st Century

Our wives and daughters are faced with *nisyonos* in the area of *tznius* (modesty in dress) day in, day out. The entire world dresses one way, and they must dress another way. It is not easy to stand out, obviously different from the world around you. My wife was once in a Seattle shopping mall during the summer. A salesperson innocently — albeit moronically — remarked, "You look like someone out of *Fiddler on the Roof.*" To dress like that is not easy. It takes *gevurah*.

In *Eishes Chayil*, Shlomo HaMelech describes the mode of dress of a woman of valor: *Oz vehadar levushah* — Strength and splendor are her raiment (*Mishlei* 31:25). We can understand the use of *hadar*/splendor as an adjective to describe clothing, but what is the word *oz*/strength doing there? What does it mean to dress with strength?

It means exactly what it says. It takes *strength* to dress like an *eishes chayil*. You must be able to look at yourself in the mirror and say, "I know that this is different, but it is correct."

It takes even more strength when many others in our community are wearing clothing that don't match up to our standards, and we must instruct our wives and daughters to look different from those in our own circles. But ultimately, they will be better for it, as Shlomo HaMelech concludes that very verse, "*Vatis'chak leyom acharon* — she will laugh on the Final Day."

Frum men face a steady bombardment of salaciousness that emanates from billboards, magazine stands, and newspapers — not to mention the Internet — threatening us with a one-way trip into spiritual oblivion. Each Yom Kippur we promise not to slip this year, but as time goes by the onslaught overwhelms us and we lapse. Because we need to exercise *gevurah*, and we are not accustomed to doing so.

It takes *gevurah* when someone says something unkind or cutting and insults you, and a fitting response is on the tip of your tongue. But if you remember that *Chazal* (*Yoma* 23a) teach us that those who hear themselves being insulted and do not respond are compared to the mighty sun at the height of its power, and are beloved by Hashem, then you might just succeed in restraining your retort.

It can even take *gevurah* to go out to shul for Maariv. On many cold, icy nights, I think to myself, "Maariv is a *reshus*. It is so cold outside. I'll just *daven* at home."

Every time that happens, I remember Rav Elozor Isbee. I was once at his house toward the end of his life, when he could still walk, but with great, painstaking effort. He walked an entire block to Maariv that night. He exercised *gevurah*, and it is that *gevurah* that keeps me going out to *daven* Maariv on those impossible winter nights.

Rabbi Nosson Friedman of Baltimore has been giving a *shiur* on Monday nights from 8-10 p.m. for approximately 25 years. One evening in May he looked at one of the participants and said, "You look weak. Is everything okay?"

"I'm just a bit weak from fasting," the man responded.

"Why are you fasting?" Rabbi Friedman asked.

"It's *bahab*," he answered. (*Bahab* is observed on one of the first sets of Monday-Thursday-Monday following Pesach and Succos. Many communities recite *Selichos* on those days, and some exceptionally righteous people fast as well.)

"You fast on *bahab*?" Rabbi Friedman asked wondrously.

"Yes," the man responded. "I have to do something for *Klal Yisrael*."

"But the fast is over in 40 minutes," Rabbi Friedman responded. "Why don't you *daven* in the first *minyan* and go home to eat?"

"I have a *seder* [a designated time to study Torah]," the participant responded. "I'm not going to miss a *shiur* just because I am hungry."

Rabbi Friedman finished his *shiur* early that night to allow this man to eat. But then he realized that the previous Monday night had also been *bahab*, and this man had sat through the *shiur* until 10 p.m., then *davened* Maariv, and only arrived home to eat at 10:30. That is *gevurah*. He wouldn't miss his *seder* for anything.

Mrs. Miriam Blumenkrantz once sent me an email with memories of the *gevurah* of her father, Rabbi Binyomin Steinberg, whose spirit permeates the Bais Yaakov of Baltimore, which he served as principal. When I read that email, I could not stop myself from crying. I want to share one small incident with you.

> One Yom Kippur, as *Kol Nidrei* was about to begin, my father was so weak from his round of chemotherapy, but was so thankful for the opportunity to be in shul. He took my brother's

hand and said, "Remember, no matter what happens, '*Tzaddik Hashem bechol derachav, vechasid bechol maasav* — righteous is Hashem in all of His ways, and magnanimous in all his deeds' (*Tehillim* 145:17). We cannot question the ways of Hashem."

Imagine the *gevurah* necessary to accept such *yissurim* (suffering) and still be able to encourage your son to have faith in Hashem.

I would like to conclude with one more story.

At the age of 20, Rav Yechezkel Abramsky was already the Rav of Slutzk. He was arrested by the Bolsheviks for teaching Torah in violation of their ban against it, and sent off to Siberia. To give you an idea of the greatness of this man, Rav Elchonon Wasserman recounted that when news of his arrest reached the Chofetz Chaim, the latter sent a message to all yeshivos in Lithuania instructing them to recite five chapters of *Tehillim* each day to merit the release of, "the Rav of Slutzk and all other *rabbanim* arrested by the Bolsheviks."

Rav Elchonon asked the Chofetz Chaim why he didn't say simply, "to pray for the release of all the *rabbanim*."

"The Rav of Slutzk is special," said the Chofetz Chaim, "because he is entirely immersed in Torah. He breathes Torah, he eats Torah, and he sleeps Torah."

While in Siberia, Rav Abramsky refused to do anything that violated halachah. His refusal did not sit well with the communist officers, who had no compunctions whatsoever in regard to killing a Jew. At one point, a Russian commissar pointed a gun at him and threatened to shoot him for ignoring orders.

Rav Abramsky faced him calmly and said, "You have numerous gods and one world, so you are afraid to die. I have One God and two Worlds, so I am not afraid to die."

Throughout the generations, Jewish *gevurah* has fortified us and enabled us to remain true to our One God, even if it meant losing our lives. In the 21st century, at least in the United States, we no longer face the threat of physical annihilation. But that does not obviate the need to prefer life in the Next World over life in this fleeting one.

With *gevurah* that parallels that of Rav Yechezkel Abramsky and all who came before and after him, each of us must rise to the occasion and ensure our place in the World to Come by standing firm against the enticements of our own *yetzer hara*.

Shidduchim: Ending the "Crisis"

While the *shidduch* crisis — as it has come to be known — is an issue that primarily affects the young (and not-so-young) men and women who are actively seeking *shidduchim*, it actually cuts across age barriers and generational lines. Along for the ride on the bumpy *shidduch* roller-coaster are not only the parents of young adults, but also the grandparents. It is not uncommon for an individual to approach me and ask whether any of the boys who attend my *shiur* in yeshivah might be appropriate for his granddaughter.

It is an issue, then, that we must all deal with in one way or another. For some it has become an overwhelming, time-consuming endeavor. Someone told me that his daughter has become his night *seder*. He used to set aside a few hours for Torah study each night, but he now finds that time occupied by phone calls investigating and pursuing leads toward a *shidduch* for his daughter.

I would like to present several ideas that might help to ameliorate the situation.

❦ Expectation Modification

We will discuss some quick-fix solutions later, but first I would like to focus on several solutions that, because they involve reeducation of both children and parents in the *parashah* of *shidduchim*, may take years to implement.

The first area in which we require reeducation is what I would call "expectation modification," with the emphasis on the word *expectation*.

Expectations lead to unhappiness. People become unhappy, or even depressed, when their expectations are not met.

Let's illustrate this point with an example. When is a woman happier — when she receives a large bouquet of flowers from her husband each Friday as a matter of course, or when he surprises her in the middle of the week with a single rose? (I am not talking about an instance in which he is trying to make up for a recent argument.)

Why does the single rose in the middle of the week elicit more happiness than the bouquet on Friday? Because the woman has come to expect her Friday bouquet, and when there are expectations, the happiness is diminished. A single rose in the middle of the week is unexpected, so it makes her happy.

Perhaps this is what the Torah is imparting to us by recording Leah Imeinu's reaction to the birth of her fourth son, Yehudah. "*Hapa'am odeh es Hashem* — *this time* I will gratefully praise Hashem" (*Bereishis* 29:35). *Rashi* explains that the *Imahos* (Matriarchs) knew that Yaakov Avinu was destined to father twelve tribes, and since he had four wives, each expected to bear three children. Leah's first three children did not elicit so much gratitude from her, because she saw it as her rightful share. Only upon the birth of her fourth child, whom she had not expected to have, did Leah say "*this time* I will gratefully praise Hashem."

Although the correlation is not immediately apparent, this lesson applies to *shidduchim* in great measure. Many young people — and often their parents as well — enter the *shidduch* market with unrealistic expectations. And those unrealistic expectations are guaranteed to diminish happiness. Let me offer a few examples.

✡ First Comes Marriage, Then Comes Love

One of the areas in which expectations are most damaging to the *shidduch* process is the area of feelings.

As much as we would like to convince ourselves that we have insulated our *frum* communities from secular influences, some residual impact has implanted itself into the psyches of many young men and women of marriageable age. They feel — and sometimes even express the feeling — that when the right one comes along, something "special" is going to happen. In other words, they are expecting to fall in love.

Why do I consider this an unrealistic expectation? It is well known that the Hebrew word for love, *ahavah*, contains the root word *hav*, which means *to give*. It does not take many years of marriage for people to realize that true love is derived from each person's willingness to give to his or her spouse. We find that couples who are happily married for 20 or 30 years keep deepening their love for one another, because they have had — and continue to have — more opportunities to give to each other. They will do anything for their spouse, and they cannot imagine living without each other.

How can a young couple who have spent a few weeks dating intermittently expect to have true feelings of love for each other? Neither one has done anything substantial for the other party.

Yet many young men and women in *shidduchim* are waiting to be swept off their feet. Boys in yeshivah have asked me, "I can eat, I can sleep, and I can learn — does that mean that I do not have true feelings for the girl that I am seeing?"

They are waiting to feel lost in a surreal feeling of "love," to hear bells and whistles, to become starry-eyed ... to experience some of the tired clichés that secular society has surreptitiously slipped into our subconscious. And chances are that they will be waiting for those magical feelings for a long time, because they rarely happen.

In Chassidic circles, the *chasan* and *kallah* hardly know each other before they are married. Thorough, in-depth research is conducted, the parents meet, they find that since the boy is a fine, upright young man and the girl is an exemplary *baalas middos,* and the families share the same background and similar goals, the children can meet briefly and then become engaged.

I am not suggesting that the *litvishe* and *yeshivishe* communities should change course and embrace the *Chassidishe* model. I don't think that we are willing to accept that approach so readily. Moreover, many of our *litvishe gedolim* felt that there *must* be some level of attraction between *chasan* and *kallah* in order for them to become engaged. Nevertheless, the decision in choosing a mate must be primarily based on a cerebral process, not on feelings or emotions. The decisions must be contingent on the fact that the girl and boy have common values and goals, that they respect each other, and that they are compatible with each other

Many times I ask a boy who comes to discuss a *shidduch* with me these questions: Do you share common values? Do you like her? Do you enjoy spending time with her? And do you have fun when you spend time together?

If the answer to all of these questions is *yes,* I ask, "Can you see yourself growing to love this person *eventually?"*

If the answer to all these questions is positive, then I guide him to become engaged, because that is all a boy can rationally expect to feel before he gets married. People generally do not "fall in love" through the *shidduch* process, and furthermore, when they do, it is often not a good sign. In most cases, when people say they fell in "love," they are not talking about true, lasting love that will withstand the trials of life. They are referring to infatuation — whether physical infatuation or infatuation with some other factor in the *shidduch.* Infatuation tends to fade with time, and if it was mistaken for love, then there may not have been any effort to build real love in its place.

If it sounds as though I am suggesting that the *shidduch* process requires a person to take a "leap of faith," it is because that is *exactly* what I am suggesting. Marrying someone to whom you feel compatible, who is physically appealing to you, and with whom you share life goals — with that being the extent of your feelings — *is* a leap of faith. Our *shidduch* system merely narrows the gap so that the leap is not a foolhardy one — that we are not attempting to jump over the Grand Canyon on a motorcycle. But it does not guarantee success. Cars come with 100,000-mile warranties, marriages do not. Even those who do feel as though they are swept off their feet by their *chasan* or *kallah* cannot be sure that they will be happily married. To build a successful marriage, you must be willing to invest hard work, to be ready to give unconditionally, and to compromise. If you are ready to do that, then you can get married, whether or not you feel that you are "in love."

While I have addressed this message to the young people who are on the "front lines" of the *shidduch* scene, it is equally important for parents — and *rebbeim*, Bais Yaakov teachers, and other mentors as well — to be aware of the problem of young adults who expect to fall in love. It is common for young men and women to come to those guiding them through the *shidduch* process and express concern over their lack of feelings for the person they are meeting. Sometimes they may not express it clearly because they are embarrassed to admit it. They realize that it is not *"frum"* to say that they are waiting to fall in love. It may be on their minds nonetheless. It is important for parents and *mechanchim* to reassure those seeking guidance that there is no reason to expect such feelings, and to encourage them to take the plunge without those powerful feelings, as long as they feel compatible with the person and attracted to them.

◆§ Steak, Air-conditioning, iPods … but Not a Shidduch

There is another expectation that we must eradicate — one that is even more insidious and damaging to one's *shidduch* prospects than the expectation of falling in love: the expectation of perfection.

We live at a time and in a country that has managed to achieve perfection in many areas.

Have you ever eaten in an upscale restaurant and ordered a three-inch Delmonico steak? When the waiter brings it, he hovers around while you take your first few bites, and then asks, "How is your steak, sir?"

"I'm sorry," you respond, "this is too rare. I ordered *medium-rare*."

"I apologize," he says. "Let me take it back to the kitchen."

He reappears a few minutes later with a freshly grilled steak. You cut in a second time, and he asks once again, "How is your steak?"

"Perfect. This steak is perfect."

You go out to your car on an extremely hot day, and you turn on your air-conditioner. It is still not cool enough, so you adjust it to 66-degrees Fahrenheit. Now your air-conditioning is perfect.

I don't mean to suggest that in my generation we had to walk five miles to school, up hill (both ways) in the snow, but we were not raised with cars that had air-conditioning. Our first car was a 1972 Dodge Dart without air-conditioning. I hate the heat, but I had to live with it because we couldn't afford the air-conditioning option, and we certainly couldn't afford the extra gas to fuel the air-conditioner. We kept that car for ten years. In 1982 we bought a used Chevy Caprice station wagon — with air-conditioning. We felt so fortunate to have air-conditioning. But that was not perfection.

Perfection is what we experienced one summer. My wife and I went on a vacation, and the rental company did not have the mid-size Ford I had reserved in stock. The clerk gave me an upgrade to a Nissan Murano, an SUV, at no extra charge. This car was perfect. Why?

Because when it comes to *shidduchim*, one of the most frequently-overlooked factors is temperature control. It has long been my observation that most men are always hot, and most women are always cold. Until this summer, each time we took a vacation, my wife wore a sweater in the middle of August. The Nissan Murano came with dual-control air conditioning, so that we could drive through Wyoming and Montana with my air-conditioning set at 60 degrees, and my wife's set at 72 degrees. That was perfection.

I'm not suspecting anyone in my reading audience of doing such a thing, but when others in my generation wanted to listen to music, they would turn on the radio and hope that something they liked would be on the air. Our children can choose from 10,000 songs stored on their miniscule iPods and MP3 players. They can choose the perfect song for their mood.

The steak is perfect, the air-conditioning is perfect, and you can choose the perfect song. Should it come as a surprise that when it comes to a *shidduch*, young people today expect nothing less than perfection?

Unfortunately, we cannot expect perfection when it comes to choosing a spouse. And even more unfortunately, it is human nature to narrow one's focus to the one or two aspects of another person that are not perfect.

Boys will often approach me the day after a date and say, "I now know that the most important quality is *middos* (good character traits). The girl I met last night did not have such great *middos*." The boy will then be set up with another girl, and he will come back to me and say, "I need an intellectual girl. This girl was wonderful, her *middos* were perfect, but she was not intellectual enough." With a third girl, the *middos* and the intellect will be fine, and he'll complain that her looks weren't good enough.

I know a boy who invariably made the same declaration each time he returned from a date: "Now I know what *the* most important quality in a girl is," and follow up with one of many possible choices: brains, looks, *middos*, and the like. Invariably, the girl he had just met was missing the quality he chose to mention. Once, a friend of his interrupted before he could list *the* most important quality and said, "I know what it is! It is what the girl you just met was missing."

Rav Pam related that a *bachur* once came to him for advice. He said that everything was perfect about the girl he was dating, but he just wasn't sure whether to get engaged. When Rav Pam saw that the boy could not figure out what it was that was bothering him, he took the proverbial bull by the horns and asked, "Is it the *chitzoniyus*, the looks?"

"Well, *I* have no problem with the looks," replied the boy, "but the other *bachurim* may think that she is not pretty enough."

"The entire issue of looks is *sheker*," responded Rav Pam. "*Sheker hachein v'hevel hayofi* [False is grace and vain is beauty (*Eishes Chayil*)], and you are ready to say *no* because the other boys will think that she is not pretty enough?"

Boys and girls in *shidduchim* must be reeducated and taught that they cannot seek perfection in a spouse. They must realize that they are not perfect, and that they cannot expect to find a perfect spouse. And if they do not realize that, it is the job of parents and *mechanchim* to make them realize it.

And once we mention parents, I think it is important for parents to take a step back and admit that they are often culpable in this area as well. Everyone feels that their child is wonderful, and that her or she deserves only the best. But realize that you can damage your own offspring's prospects and inadvertently condemn your child to years of painful waiting by demanding too much. Which leads us directly to our next point …

⟡§ Frivolous Preconditions

Most people enter the *parashah* of *shidduchim* with a mental list — sometimes they even commit it to paper — of what it is that they are looking for in a spouse. That is legitimate, and even recommended. It is hard to find something if you do not know what it is that you are seeking. But some people's lists contain items that are frivolous in the best circumstances, and downright moronic at worst.

There are stories that abound regarding families that turned down *shidduchim* because the grandmother walks into stores with — brace yourself — a small shopping cart. They can't do a *shidduch* with someone with such plebeian grandparents.

Or how about the person who said that he would not marry someone from a family that used the term "drumstick" to describe a certain piece of chicken instead of *"pulkeh"*?

We hear such stories, and we think, "How inane can people be?"

Well, let us look at our own lists. They may not be so arbitrary and trivial, but they do contain items that are senseless. For example — and I am going out on a limb here — but why must the boy be older than the girl? I'm not suggesting that I am an expert in all four sections of *Shulchan Aruch*, but I have yet to come across a halachah stating that the boy must be older. What if the girl is two or three years older than the boy? Is that really a reason to reject the *shidduch* without bothering to look into the details? I agree that if a boy is 21 and the girl is 25, then the maturity gap may be too wide to reconcile. But if he is 24 and she is 25, why won't people consider the *shidduch*?

Next issue: Why are the yeshivos he attended and the seminary she attended considered a primary factor in people's minds? There are great boys and wonderful girls graduating from all institutions. I understand that it is difficult to find out information and we must often rely on limited resources, one of which is the reputations that yeshivos and seminaries have developed. But when it seems that a *shidduch* prospect attended a less-favorable institution (in the eyes of the prospective in-laws), shouldn't we try to find out *why* he or she went there, and what it says about the student? Sometimes family members put pressure upon a boy or girl and they attended a school that was inappropriate for them. Few people take the time to ask such questions. Why? Because we have become obsessed with designer labels — whether on clothes, eyeglasses, shoes, or sons-in-law. We are ready to reject people because they are wearing the wrong label. Unfortunately, many who sought the best-name yeshivos and seminaries remained in the *parashah* of *shidduchim* for a long time, only to wed after years of painful waiting, when they are willing to compromise on their wish list.

And thus the list of *shidduch* needs often go on and on, ad absurdum. Nowadays it is not enough for the girl to have attended the correct schools — her brothers must also have attended the correct yeshivos. Isn't that a bit much? The Talmud advises a prospective *chasan* to investigate the girl's brothers, because their children will emulate his qualities — but nowhere does it mention which yeshivah he attended.

We must all whittle down our lists to *two or three* key items. Each boy and girl must identify *two or three* primary factors that they are seeking in a spouse. I'll repeat for a third time, just to be sure that no one missed it: *two* or *three* factors. Not more.

How do I know that I am correct? Because I learned it from no less a personage than Avraham Avinu. If there are mothers that believe that they must have Miss Perfect for their one-and-only *tzaddik'l*, and take advantage of the fact that it is unfortunately a boys' market, I have news for them. Avraham Avinu had a child who was closer to perfection than anyone around today. He was a *masmid*, a pure *tzaddik*, and his father had money. Yet, Eliezer was sent to seek a girl who would have *but one* characteristic. She had to be a *baalas chesed*. *That* is a quality that matters. A true *baalas chesed* will make a great wife and mother. She will have patience for her family, and treat them properly.

How we have evolved as a nation from Yitzchak's *shidduch* list to ours is beyond me. But I do know that the questions that are asked today cost people many years of happiness. If it makes a difference how the mother of the girl dresses when she lights candles on Friday night (*tichel* or *sheitel*), whether the tablecloth is covered in plastic at the Shabbos *seudos*, and whether they use paper napkins or cloth, then we will continue to see a lot of girls and boys waiting endlessly. Does it really make a whit of a difference whether the boy wears laced shoes or loafers? Please realize that I am *not* fabricating these examples. These are questions that people have actually asked. There are numerous inquiries regarding young women that I am embarrassed to put on paper.

I am addressing the boys and girls currently in *shidduchim*, but even more importantly, I am addressing the parents, who, being married for a minimum of 20 years by the time their children are in *shidduchim*, should know that these factors make no difference.

The list issue is one that I think is responsible for hundreds, perhaps thousands, of aging singles waiting endlessly. Before pointing fingers at others, we should ensure that we are not harming our own prospects by searching for the perfect boy or girl that has yet to be created.

❧ Opening Up

I want to move on to an issue that often occurs during the dating process.

First dates are easy: "Did you go to Eretz Yisrael, which camps were you in, how many siblings do you have …"

As things progress, however, the conversations must turn to more serious and personal topics. This is where many *shidduchim* get stuck. People are afraid to open up.

One of the most prevalent complaints from boys who have gone out several times with a girl is, "It is all perfect on paper, but I feel nothing." Inasmuch as we began by stating that expecting to feel love toward a girl or boy during the dating process is impractical, there must be *some* emotional bond between them in order to get engaged. The only way to feel anything is to open up a little. I'm not talking about expressing deep feelings toward each other. That may be lacking in *tznius*, and should be avoided. But you must open up about *who you are*. You cannot get engaged if you are just a generic yeshivah guy with a white shirt, dress pants, and glasses, or a girl who attended Bais Yaakov for twelve years and then went to seminary in Eretz Yisrael for one year.

Who are you? What makes you tick? You must reveal yourself. Let him or her know what you want in life.

I will give people the benefit of the doubt by assuming that some people avoid opening up because they associate it with rejection. Many times people go out six or seven times and become very close to the person they are dating, and then for some reason or other, the *shidduch* breaks off. They have spoken from the heart and have been left standing, feeling exposed. This causes them to become gun-shy. Others — especially girls — will feel that talking about themselves and what they want in life is a breach of *tznius*. Whatever the scenario, it is important to overcome the discomfort and open up, or the *shidduch* will sputter and stall.

We are all familiar with seemingly endless elucidations offered at *Sheva Berachos* to explain *Chazal's* comparison between *shidduchim* and *Krias Yam Suf*. Perhaps we can add a novel understanding. At

Krias Yam Suf, the sea "opened up" and it was split apart. In order for a *shidduch* to happen, you must open up — with regard to your hopes, aspirations, and dreams — as the waters of Yam Suf did.

There was once an older fellow who had been dating for years and was not getting anywhere. Finally he visited a psychologist who asked him to describe the girl he was dating at the time. He explained that the girl had recently been orphaned when her mother succumbed to a protracted illness. The psychologist suggested that he ask her about the experience. Although he felt uncomfortable, he obeyed the expert. The girl opened up to him, and then he found himself opening up to her, and before long they were engaged.

And opening up is not only necessary for dating. It is imperative that you take that ability into marriage as well.

Marriage is often described as "a merger," but that is a terrible misnomer. When Proctor & Gamble buys out Gillette, that is a merger. Marriage is a fusion. It makes two people become one unit. In order to fuse with someone, you must open up and let the other person know the real you.

◆§ We Must All Get Involved

Until now we have discussed *shidduchim* in terms of the people who are dating and their family members. Now I would like to discuss the topic as it applies to the rest of *Klal Yisrael*.

One of the questions that we will be asked by the Heavenly Court on our judgment day is *"Asakta bepiryah verivyah* — did you engage in being fruitful and multiplying?" (*Shabbos* 31a). The *Maharsha* notes that the question is not, "Did you bear children," rather, it is, "Did you *engage* in multiplying." He explains that Hashem will not ask us whether we bore children, because, as the *Aruch LaNer* (*Niddah* 70a) points out, He is the One Who ultimately decides whether we are going to bear children. Rather, the question is whether we helped populate the world *by enabling others to marry.* The *Maharsha* offers the example of marrying off orphans who do not have the means to get married, but we can extrapolate to making *shidduchim*, which also helps fulfill the mitzvah.

I once suggested — perhaps impractically — that in the course of one's lifetime, each person should try to make three *shidduchim*. The reason it may be impractical is because not everyone knows boys and girls in the *parashah*. But there are several things that we can all do to minimize the *shidduch* problem.

Several organizations have been founded to help with this problem. Some of them provide financial assistance to *shadchanim* so that they can free themselves from *parnassah* issues and concentrate on making *shidduchim*. If you cannot make *shidduchim* on your own, at least contribute to the process by enabling others to do so.

Another thing you can do is to listen. I am in the fortunate position of having access to boys who are of age. I get many phone calls regarding *shidduchim*, on every day of the year — including Erev Yom Kippur. It shakes me up to receive phones calls at such times, because it shows how desperate people are to marry off their children.

Many times, there is nothing I can do. But I try to listen. I recently received a phone call regarding a *shidduch* from a woman living outside my metropolitan area. When we finished the conversation she said, "Thank you for listening." Apparently people feel that they need a listening ear.

Another thing you can do is return your phone calls. You may be privy to information that another person needs in order to go ahead with a *shidduch*. Someone once told me that the verse, "*Veha'ish Moshe anav meod mikol ha'adam* — Now the man Moshe was exceedingly humble, more than any person" (*Bamidbar* 12:3) means that Moshe Rabbeinu would return his phone calls. While I cannot vouch for this interpretation of the verse, I took the underlying message to heart, and I try to return *all* phone calls. But when someone leaves a message regarding a *shidduch*, I will spare no effort in returning the call. I know that people in this *parashah* are in pain. And even if I cannot provide the information they need, I can listen.

∽§ Daven

It goes without saying that *tefillah* is our most potent tool. We should all *daven* for those who have not yet found their *shidduch*, but I want to point out that *shidduchim* is an area in which *tefillah* seems to be inordinately effective.

The Talmud (*Taanis* 4a) states that three people made improper requests from Hashem; two received what they requested, and one did not. What were the requests?

Eliezer, Avraham Avinu's servant, said that he would take the girl who would offer him water as a wife for Yitzchak. Shaul said that he would give his daughter in marriage to the one who would kill Goliath. Yiftach vowed that if he was successful in fending off the Ammonites, he would consecrate the first thing to walk out of the door of his house.

The Talmud explains why these requests were improper. What would Eliezer have done had the girl who offered water been incapacitated? What would Shaul have done had the person who killed Goliath been a slave or a *mamzer* (person born through a forbidden relationship)? And what would Yiftach have done had the first animal to walk out of his door been blemished?

Tosafos suggests that a fourth person should be added to the list. When the Jewish people were conquering Eretz Yisrael, Calev offered his daughter to the person who would conquer Kiryas Sefer. *Tosafos* points out that his offer was as dangerous as King Shaul's, because the one to conquer it could have been a slave or illegitimate.

The Talmud concludes that Hashem answered Eliezer by sending Rivkah to offer water, and Shaul by sending David to kill Goliath. In Calev's case, too, Osniel ben Kenaz conquered Kiryas Sefer and married Calev's daughter. Only Yiftach was punished for asking improperly. The first one to walk out of his house was his daughter, who was then sent away to live in solitude because she was consecrated.

What is the common denominator between the three people

who asked improperly and nonetheless received what they wanted? All three involved *shidduchim*. Apparently when it comes to *shidduchim*, Hashem is willing to accept any request, even one that is seemingly thoughtless or dangerous.

Let me add one more ingredient that you can put to work in your quest for your *shidduch* or your child's *shidduch*.

It is difficult to imagine that there is any *frum* family that does not have at least one single member in *shidduchim*. We are all in this problem together. The Talmud (*Bava Kamma* 92a) states that a person who begs for mercy for his friend, and he needs mercy in the same area, he is answered first. Let us put that teaching to work. Don't limit your *tefillos* to your own family members. Take down the names of some friends or some of your neighbors' children, and *daven* for them too.

∽§ Mashiach: An End to the Shidduch Crisis

Finally, when we are *davening* for *shidduchim*, let's not forget to *daven* for Mashiach. What does Mashiach have to do with *shidduchim*?

In *Eichah* we read, "*Besulosehah nugos, vehi mar lah* — her maidens are afflicted, and she too is embittered" (1:4). At the time of the destruction of the *Beis HaMikdash*, the young maidens were afflicted. Why? The *Targum* explains that they were lamenting the fact that they were no longer able to go out and dance in the vineyards on the 15th of Av and on Motza'ei Yom Kippur.

Do you know how *shidduchim* were made in the times of the *Beis HaMikdash*? On these two special days of the year — days that the Talmud describes as the *greatest* Yamim Tovim of the year — the girls would borrow clothing from one another to make sure that each one had something special to wear, and, mind-boggling as this may seem, they would dance in the vineyards, and the boys would choose their mates on those days. Could you imagine such a simple system? When they came of age, they would wait for Tu B'Av or Motza'ei Yom Kippur, and before long there was a *mazel tov*.

Wouldn't it be great if we could go back to this simple system? Nowadays, it would never work. We are in *galus* (exile), and in *galus* nothing is simple. Life is full of crises and anguish. Sometimes we start to feel that things are great in *galus* — we have our glatt-kosher Delmonico steaks and our air-conditioning and our iPods and our beautiful houses. We don't neglect spirituality either. We have yeshivos and Bais Yaakovs and *kollelim* and *kiruv* institutions. We begin to wonder what is missing. And sometimes Hashem has to remind us that *galus* is still *galus*.

The *shidduchim* crisis is just another reminder that we need Mashiach. As we wait for him, we need to mitigate the factors that are exacerbating the problem, and we need to *daven*.

If we come together as *frum* people to help all the unfortunate young men and women — and their families — who are suffering so much, it seems that Hashem would respond in kind and return us to a time when we will have a *Beis HaMikdash*, and the word *shidduchim* will no longer be associated with the word *crisis*, but with the happiness and joy that prevailed on those two holy nights of the year.

Sticks and Stones vs. Words and Tones

B*aruch Hashem,* we live in times in which there is much awareness of the terrible effects of *lashon hara* (harmful speech). Thanks to the work of several wonderful organizations, we have international awareness campaigns to teach us the pertinent halachos, and thousands upon thousands now learn *Sefer Chofetz Chaim* on a daily schedule. This is a tremendous accomplishment in which we can rightfully take pride.

But Rav Avrohom Pam once bemoaned the fact that not enough emphasis is placed on another aspect of speech that can be just as damaging, and in certain cases even worse than *lashon hara*.

Among your childhood memories, you probably recall at least one instance in which you complained to an adult that someone insulted you, and they responded with the trite poem:

Sticks and stones,
Can break my bones,
But words can never hurt me.

I hate to dispel a myth that you have been carrying with you for so long, but that rhyme holds approximately as much veracity as the story of the tooth fairy. The Torah teaches that words can inflict far greater damage than sticks and stones. Words can hurt, and words can heal. They can encourage, and they can destroy. Words are so potent, in fact, that there is a Torah-level prohibition against speaking hurtful words, just as there is a prohibition against stealing or eating *treifah* (nonkosher).

In *Parashas Behar*, the Torah states, "*Velo sonu ish es amiso, veyareisa mei'Elokecha, ki ani Hashem Elokeichem* — Each of you shall not aggrieve his fellow, and you shall fear your God; for I am Hashem, your God" (*Vayikra* 25:17). The word *ona'ah* (which shares a root with the word *sonu*/aggrieve that appears in this verse) is often used in the Talmud to denote monetary grievances caused by one to another, but the Talmud (*Bava Metzia* 58b) infers that in this verse the Torah is referring to *ona'as devarim* — the use of words to hurt someone.

The *Chinuch* (Mitzvah 338) defines this prohibition as follows:

> One may not aggrieve another Jew with words — i.e., one should not say to another Jew words that will hurt and pain him and render him helpless.

Left to our own devices, we might assume that one has to say something exceedingly obnoxious or downright horrible to another person in order to be considered a transgressor of *ona'as devarim*. But the Talmud (Ibid.), cited by the *Chinuch*, lists several examples of *ona'as devarim* that we might have considered perfectly normal forms of speech.

- One should not say to a *baal teshuvah*, "Remember your earlier days."
  One is not allowed to remind a *baal teshuvah* of his past. This means that if your seatmate in shul is a *baal teshuvah* who

enunciates each syllable of *davening* with feeling and shakes his *lulav* with such concentration that you find it annoying, you must not say to him, "Your *davening* is really impressive. It's hard to believe that just a short time ago you were eating shrimp salad." Such words hit in a very sensitive spot, and they therefore constitute *ona'as devarim*.

- Practical jokes can be *ona'as devarim*.

  If a person sees donkey drivers looking for hay to feed their donkeys, says the Talmud, he should not jokingly direct them to a person who does not have hay. When the hay-seekers knock on the door and ask for hay and the person turns out to be a liquor salesman, the practical joker will probably get a good laugh, but he has transgressed the prohibition of *ona'as devarim*.

In case you think that this is hyperbole, consider the following ruling that appears in the responsa of the Chasam Sofer (*Choshen Mishpat* 176).

> There was a *mohel* who would journey great distances for the privilege of performing the mitzvah of *milah*. A *shochet* in a certain village once decided to play a practical joke on him, and summoned him to his village to perform a *bris* on his son. The *mohel* spent four hours traveling to the village, and when he arrived he found out that he had been fooled: the *shochet* had a girl, not a boy. Everybody in the village had a good laugh at the expense of the *mohel*, who returned home humiliated.
>
> Great joke. But a costly one — the Chasam Sofer ruled that the *shochet* should be suspended until he receives forgiveness from the *mohel*.

Clearly, *ona'as devarim* is no laughing matter. There is a severity present that we do not find in many other prohibitions.

In *Parashas Mishpatim* the Torah exhorts us, "*Kol almanah veyasom lo se'anun* — you shall not cause pain to any widow or orphan"

Sticks and Stones vs. Words and Tones / 49

(*Shemos* 22:21). One might think that this prohibition applies only to widows and orphans, but Rashi teaches otherwise. He comments that the Torah chose widows and orphans as examples of members of society who, because they have no one to defend them, attribute any insults they receive to their vulnerability. In truth, however, the prohibition applies equally to anyone who is pained as a result of our actions.

The Torah goes on to warn us of the dire consequences that will afflict those who cause pain to another Jew: "For if he shall cry out to Me, I shall surely hear his outcry. My wrath shall blaze and I shall kill you by the sword, and your wives will be widows and your children orphans" (Ibid. vs. 22-23). While the prohibition against inflicting pain is not limited to the verbal variety, it is axiomatic that those who use words to hurt others are in danger of incurring Hashem's wrath and suffering the resultant consequences.

Perhaps this is why the Talmud states (*Bava Metzia* 59a) that all punishment for sin is meted out by Hashem's messengers, aside for the punishment for one sin: *ona'ah*. When it comes to verbal abusers, Hashem says, "I will punish you Myself."

The Talmud (Ibid.) adds that even in cases in which the gates to heaven are closed, *sha'arei ona'ah lo ninalu* — the gates of *ona'ah* are not closed. The anguish one feels when hurt by a verbal attack is so acute that when he calls out to Hashem, his cry pierces those gates.

There is a responsa titled *Amudei Ohr* written by a brilliant sage, Rabbi Yechiel Heller. Interestingly, every single *teshuvah* in his book is signed, "*He'aluv*, Yechiel Heller." *He'aluv* means, "The humiliated one." Why did Rav Yechiel Heller sign his *teshuvos* with this strange appellation?

It seems that Rav Yechiel Heller's maternal grandfather owned a liquor store. When he would travel on business, his daughter Rivkah would mind the store for him. Somehow, rumors began to spread that Rivkah had behaved in a manner inappropriate for a *bas Yisrael*. Before long the unfounded rumors damaged her reputation and she could not find a *shidduch*. Realizing that his daughter could no longer find a suitor from the upper echelons of society, her father came to the conclusion that they had no choice but to consider less-suitable prospects. His search led him to a young man nicknamed Aharon der Shmeisser, the *assistant* to the town wagon driver. The wagon driver would sit up on the wagon and control the reins. As the assistant, Aharon would run alongside the wagon and whip the horses — thus the nickname *shmeisser* (one who hits). His was a most demeaning occupation.

Rivkah, a wonderful, perfectly righteous girl, who had become the butt of wagging tongues and heartless innuendo through no fault of her own, had no option but to marry Aharon der Shmeisser.

Under the *chuppah*, Rivkah said, "*Ribono Shel Olam*, You know that these rumors are unfounded. You know that I am a fine *bas Yisrael*. Due to people's maliciousness, I can no longer marry a *talmid chacham* as I had wished."

She then invoked the words of the *berachah* that we recite after the reading of the *haftarah*: *Vela'aluvas nefesh toshia bim'heirah veyameinu* — to the one who is deeply humiliated bring salvation speedily, in our days.

"Despite the fact that I cannot marry a *talmid chacham*," she wept, "please listen to my prayers and give me sons who are *talmidei chachamim*."

True to the words of the Talmud, the *sha'arei ona'ah* were pierced by her prayers, and Aharon and Rivkah merited to bring four sons into the world who were not only *talmidei chachamim* — each one was a *gadol b'Yisrael*. The *Amudei Ohr*, the *Chosen Yehoshua*, and two other great *rabbanim* were born from a union that began with this piercing *tefillah*.

In tribute to his mother's pain and suffering and the spiritual merit he and his brothers were endowed with as a result of her prayer, Rav Yechiel Heller signed each letter with the appellation *he'aluv*, the humiliated one.

⊷§ An Attack on Hashem's Protectorate

What is it about *ona'as devarim* that angers Hashem to the extent that He will always listen to those who have been hurt through

Sticks and Stones vs. Words and Tones / 51

words and punish the perpetrator Himself?

The Maharal (*Nesivos Olam, Nesiv Ahavas Harei'a* 2) explains that unlike a physical attack that affects the body, a verbal insult is an attack on a person's *nefesh*, his spirit, and the *nefesh* is the protectorate of Hashem.

The proof of this is that one cannot insult an animal. A cow does not become insulted when you call it fat. It does not have a *nefesh*, and therefore cannot be dealt a blow through *ona'as devarim*. But a human *nefesh*, which is in the "Hands" of Hashem, does get insulted, and only Hashem knows how much it is affected by those insults. Thus, the verse regarding *ona'as devarim* ends with the words, "*Veyareisa mei'Elokecha, ki ani Hashem Elokeichem* — and you shall fear your God, for I am Hashem, your God." Eating pork does not come with the warning of *veyareisa mei'Elokecha*, and neither does *sha'atnez* or eating *chametz* on Pesach. But *ona'as devarim* does, because Hashem promises to personally seek retribution for a frontal attack on the *nefesh* that He holds near and dear to Him.

Considering the severity of *ona'as devarim*, why is it so common for people to engage in hurtful speech? I would suggest that there are three types of *ona'as devarim*: deliberate *ona'as devarim*, inadvertent *ona'as devarim*, and mindless *ona'as devarim*.

☙ Deliberate Ona'as Devarim

There are cases in which a person intentionally insults his fellow. Sometimes it is due to jealousy. In other cases, a person may attempt to build his own self-image by putting down others.

There is a terrible story, cited in several works, in which a community in Europe hired a new rav, and, as was customary, on the day that he arrived they made a grand *kabbalas panim* (welcoming ceremony). The rav was escorted by the entire community to the shul, which was decorated with a large banner reading, "*Baruch atah bevo'echa*" (Blessed shall you be when you come in [*Devarim* 28:6]). Once there, he was asked to deliver his first *derashah* as rav of the city. Among the community members present was a brilliant young man who had just married a daughter of one of the congregants. The rav delivered an intricate, deep *shiur* on a Talmudic topic, and the young man, apparently seeking to impress his *shver* (father-in-law), interrupted the speech with question after question. Each answer from the new rav brought a barrage of follow-up questions, until the young man finally came up with a question that stumped the rav.

When the young man realized that he had won the debate, he rose to his feet and said, "*Efsher iz es shoin der tzeit tzu zuggen 'Baruch atah b'tzeisecha'* — Maybe it is time to say, 'Blessed shall you be when you go out'" (Ibid.).

Great line. What a *"chapp."* But in Judaism we call one-liners like that *"ona'as devarim."* Without going into particulars, suffice it to say that this young man did not have a happy life after delivering this insult.

Deliberate *ona'as devarim* can also be an attempt to exert control or intimidate someone else. The case of the *baal teshuvah* mentioned by the Talmud, for instance, is a typical case of someone locating a fellow's Achilles heel and honing in on it in order to control him.

Rabbi Samson Raphael Hirsch defines the prohibition of *lo sonu ish es amiso* as follows: "Misusing or taking advantage of a weak spot in someone else." He suggests that the root of *sonu* is connected to that of *kano*, which means to take ownership of something. A domineering person who wants to control someone else will humiliate that person repeatedly until the latter feels intimidated and subconsciously begins to kowtow to his oppressor to avoid further embarrassment.

Rav Yaakov Weinberg, rosh yeshivah of Yeshivas Ner Yisrael, suggested that the reason why *ona'as devarim* was placed — seemingly incongruously — into the *parashah* dealing with *yovel* (the jubilee year) is because it shares the same underlying message as *yovel*. Hashem commands that real property we have acquired revert to its original owners at *yovel* as a reminder that, in actuality, everything belongs to Him.

If we really believed that Hashem is in control of everything,

Sticks and Stones vs. Words and Tones / 53

explained Rav Weinberg, then there would be no room for the jealousy or intimidation that leads people to engage in *ona'as devarim*. If God is providing everything you need to function, then you have no reason to put down others in order to build yourself up.

❧ Inadvertent Ona'as Devarim

The second form of *ona'as devarim* is the one that is not often noticed by anyone, including the perpetrator, as it occurs when people tend to let their guard down.

When in public, people will go out of their way to be extremely nice and speak with the greatest respect in order to avoid hurting anyone's feelings. When a person crosses the threshold of his home, however, he will often feel that he no longer has to keep up appearances. The words suddenly become harsher and more demanding. And if the words don't change, then often the tone changes. The most polite gentlemen and *eideleh* (gentle, refined) women will unintentionally change into impatient, imperious, and impervious husbands, wives, and parents. In private, we often speak to our spouses and children in a way that we would not dream of speaking in public.

Rav Pam suggested another explanation for the admonishment of *veyareisa mei'Elokecha* in the verse of *lo sonu*: it is there to remind us that even when in the privacy of our own homes, with no outsiders listening to our manner of speech, we must still speak with respect, because Hashem is there, and He is listening just as He does in public.

Imagine how careful we would be if we would know that there is a high-tech system in our homes recording each word we say to our family members. How careful we would be with the words we utter! Surprise! We *do* have such a system in place. When the Vilna Gaon left for Eretz Yisrael, he wrote a letter to his wife, in which he instructed her — among other things — to be careful with her speech, because there are *"baalei gadfin"* (angels) who transcribe every word uttered in our homes. On our judgment day, these angels will play back our words. How will we feel when we hear those words, and those tones?

This point is especially important for men, to whom the Talmud directs its statement of, "*Le'olam yehei adam zahir be'ona'as ishto* — one should exercise extreme caution in regard to aggrieving his wife, *shemitoch shedimasah metzuyah, ona'asah kerovah* — since her tears come readily, she is poised to feeling aggrieved."

Maharal (Ibid.) explains that women naturally look to their husbands for protection, so when the protection is replaced with hurtful attacks on her, it is particularly painful.

It is important for men to remember that they signed a contract requiring them to treat their wives with respect. Among the clauses in the *kesubah* is "*Va'ana okir, va'afarnes, va'eflach, va'eizun yasichi kehilchos guvrin yehudayin* — I will *honor*, support, maintain, and work to sustain you in the manner of Jewish men." Someone told me that he was an *eid* (halachic witness) on a *kesubah* that Rav Pam presided over as *mesader kiddushin*. While preparing the *kesubah*, Rav Pam read it to the *chasan*, explaining it line-by-line. When he reached this line, he said, "And the main thing is: *va'anu okir*. I'll honor you."

Another area in which *ona'as devarim* is frequently overlooked is one in which it may count most. The *Chinuch* alludes to this form in stating that one should even avoid hurting small children with words. I would say that this applies primarily to the children we love most — namely, our own. We must realize that our children look to us for approval, no matter what age they are and at what stage in life they are. A put-down from a parent is extremely painful and can cause lasting damage. I am not suggesting that we should not rebuke our children when necessary, but we must make sure that we are building them with words, not breaking them.

Listen to a *gadol's* approach to rebuking a child.

When Rav Elyah Lopian was in his 90s, a certain young boy would accompany him to and from shul each morning. This boy, who is now a *chinuch* expert in Eretz Yisrael, describes how he was an active, jumpy child, and he would sometimes be bored while escorting the nonagenarian *mashgiach*. To release some of his excess energy, he would kick at stones in the street or pull leaves from shrubs and chew on them.

One day, as they neared Rav Lopian's house, he turned to the boy and asked him if he liked sweets. The boy answered that he did. "Could you come into my house and make a *berachah* on a sweet?" the *mashgiach* asked.

The child enthusiastically accepted the offer. They went up into the apartment, and the *mashgiach* handed him a sugar cube and waited for him to recite a *shehakol*. When he finished the sugar cube, the *mashgiach* began to heap praise upon him. "Do you realize that you are a very *chashuveh* boy?" he asked. "You help an old man get to and from shul each day ..."

Rav Elyah went on and on about how *chashuv* this boy was. When he felt that he had convinced the boy, he said, "Do you want to be even more *chashuv*?"

The *chinuch* expert says he remembers thinking that the *mashgiach* had already done such a great job convincing him of his value that he did not necessarily need to feel any more *chashuv*, but he listened nonetheless.

"Sometimes when boys walk in the street," the *mashgiach* said, "they get a little bit bored and pull leaves from shrubs and put them into their mouths. It is preferable not to do that, because the person who owns the shrubs might not be pleased."

"But we learned in yeshivah," the boy interjected, "that branches of a tree that extend into a *reshus harabim* [public domain] do not belong to the owner."

Someone else might have been tempted to respond by saying, "Listen, kid. I finished *Shas* four times before your grandfather was born. Don't challenge me." But Rav Elyah Lopian said, "You are raising a good point. But I did not say that it is considered theft. I said that it might bother him, and it is not worthwhile to bother someone even if you have a right to do it."

"More importantly," the *mashgiach* continued, "leaves tend to have tiny bugs on them, and each time a person swallows a bug he transgresses five *la'avin* [Torah prohibitions]. A boy who wants to be *extremely chashuv* would not put leaves in his mouth."

R' Elyah then thanked the boy profusely again for accompanying him home, and sent him on his way to yeshivah.

It is astounding to think about the great lengths to which this *gadol* went in order to avoid hurting the feelings of a young boy who warranted a rebuke. Instead of barking an order to him as soon as he saw him yank off a leaf and place it into his mouth, he offered him sweets, convinced him that he was *chashuv*, and then told him how to be even more *chashuv*.

This same *chinuch* expert was once instructed by Rav Chaim Kanievski to teach people that all the mitzvos of *bein adam l'chaveiro* apply when it comes to one's own children.

This may seem obvious, but do we really treat our children as well as we treat our acquaintances from work, shul, *kollel*, or the classes we teach? Or do we tend to let down our guard when dealing with our own family members, and let our rebuke and criticism flow freely?

When children need to be admonished, take care that you are not labeling them or making them feel worthless.

A while back I heard a radio program that consisted of short interviews with ordinary folk who had an interesting incident to relate. One of the people interviewed said that when he was growing up, he was the biggest klutz around. But there was one thing he could do better than anyone: he was a good eater. One day he saw an advertisement in the newspaper for a matzah-ball eating contest. He entered the contest and won by eating ten matzah balls, which he described as being as big as baseballs, in the span of 2 minutes and 56 seconds.

"At the award presentation," he proudly told the interviewer, "Mayor Rudolph Giuliani presented me the award of 'Best Matzah-ball Eater in the City of New York.'"

"My only regret," he concluded sadly, "is that my father was not alive to see me get the reward. He always told me that I was a loser. But I won the contest, and I got to shake Giuliani's hand. I'm not a loser."

Can you imagine? This person went through life with his father's label of "loser" ringing in his ears, and he could not shake that image until he had the dubious distinction of being named New

York City's best matzah-ball eater.

Be careful regarding how you talk to your children. Your words mean so much to them.

◆§ Mindless Ona'as Devarim

The third form of *ona'as devarim* consists of remarks that are made with malice toward none, but are said either out of lack of sensitivity, or worse — plain stupidity and thoughtlessness.

A few years ago, my wife broke her ankle in three places. Surgery, plates, screws — the whole works. She was laid up for a few months. In the process of recuperating, visitors streamed in to wish her well, some of whom had likewise suffered a broken ankle. She observed that the remarks she heard fell into two general categories. There were those who told her, "I also broke my ankle, and I promise you that you will dance in heels at *chasunahs*. I got better, and so will you."

Then there were the people who said, "You will feel it every time it rains."

Even if that is true, what is the point of saying it?

This is a relatively innocuous example. I have heard stories of people who were hospitalized with serious illnesses, and were visited by a "brilliant" friend who said, "My uncle had what you had. You have *no idea* what he went through before he died."

But the prize for insensitivity and stupidity belongs to those who go to be *menachem avel* (console the mourning) parents who are sitting *shivah* for a child, and say, "It must be an *onesh* [punishment] for something."

I wish that I was making up these examples. I'm not. These things happen. And when they happen, everyone present wonders, "What was that person thinking?" The answer is, of course, that they weren't. People blurt out whatever comes to their mind.

I once read a pithy saying that sums up our feelings when we hear people engaging in mindless *ona'as devarim*: "It is a shame that more people are thoughtless than are speechless."

Rav Chaim Ozer Grodzenski was known for his sharp mind. It

was said that he could write two responsa simultaneously with each hand. I cannot do justice to his greatness in less than a few volumes, but suffice it to say that he was called *"rabban shel kol benei hagolah* — the leader of all of the Diaspora," and that his influence spread forth from Vilna to every Jewish community in the world. Quick-wittedness notwithstanding, Rav Chaim Ozer once made a *kabbalah* before Yom Kippur: *"Lachshov kodem kol dibbur* — to think before speaking."

If Rav Chaim Ozer had to think before speaking, it should take us approximately a week to get one word out.

❧ Telegram Speak

Speech is one of the greatest gifts that Hashem has granted us. We should start to treat words like money. Before we spend money, we think twice whether an expenditure is justified or not. Words should be just as precious.

Those of you old enough to remember telegrams know that when sending a telegram, you paid per word. No one approached the telegram operator and began to ramble, because they did not want to overpay. Before sending a telegram, one would sit down with pen and paper and compose the message as briefly and efficiently as possible.

The Chofetz Chaim would say that we should speak as though we were composing a telegram.

We must become more sensitive, and consider the implications and ramifications of our words. Don't go over to a caterer and say, "You know, I once ate at such-and-such hall, and that caterer's food is *terrific*. I never tasted such delicious food." How is the caterer you are speaking to going to feel?

If you go to a *vort* and see an older single, don't say, *"Nuuuu?!"* Do you think that he or she is not trying?

In fact, once a boy or girl gets to a certain age, I have made a strict policy of not even saying, *"Im yirtzeh Hashem* by you." I think it. I say it to myself. But do you know how heartsick a person can

Sticks and Stones vs. Words and Tones / 59

become from hearing *"Im yirtzeh Hashem* by you" hundreds of times?

Sensitivity and forethought. That is all it takes.

✑ Taking the Next Step

It is not enough, however, to avoid hurting people. We must also learn to use our speech for the positive.

A *metzora* (person stricken with a spiritual form of *tzaraas*, a leprosy-like affliction, usually as a punishment for speaking *lashon hara*) must bring two birds to atone for his sins. The *Zohar* explains that one bird atones for *lishna bisha*, improper speech, and the other atones for *lishna tava*, proper (i.e., good) speech. Why is a *metzora* required to bring a *korban* for speaking good words?

The answer is that when we reach the Heavenly court, aside for being held accountable for all of the nasty things we say, we will also have to give reckoning for not using our mouths to compliment people, encourage them, and make them feel good about themselves.

We all have one thing in common: we are all in the "word business," and we are all in the "people business." We constantly talk to people. In that capacity, we can improve the lives of the people around us: our spouses, our children, our co-workers, our classmates, our employees, our students — and all with minimal effort on our part. Words that don't cost you a dime can make such a difference in someone else's life.

Recently my wife had to have a prescription filled. The pharmacist called to say that he did not have the medication in stock, and that he would order it. He called back to say that he had ordered it, but the company sent the wrong size. He called back a third time to say that this time they sent the correct size, but the wrong strength. "I am going to go to another branch of our chain to see if they have the correct item," he said. Mind you, this pharmacist works for the largest pharmaceutical chain in Maryland, not a local corner drug store. But he did as he said, and they called from the pharmacy to say that my wife could come to pick up her prescription.

My wife wanted to thank the pharmacist, but he was not in. She wrote him a little note thanking him for his efforts. The next time I went to that pharmacy, he said, "I got your wife's note. It's so nice to get a kind word every once in a while."

How did the day go in that pharmacy after the pharmacist received that note? I'm quite certain that the pharmacist's employees noticed a change in their boss's attitude. I'm sure that he was less uptight if something went wrong, because he was in a good mood. And those workers went home in a better mood and were nicer to their families, because their boss was nicer to them. There is a ripple affect to *lishna tava*, good speech.

My point here is not to champion the cause of pharmacists and their workers, but to champion the cause of our own husbands, wives, children, and friends. Our words can make such a marked difference in their lives, if we only make the minimal effort to find something nice to say.

No man is so poor that he cannot afford to give a compliment. And no man is above needing a compliment and words of encouragement. No matter how successful, how prominent or accomplished a person is, he can always use a kind word.

When American citizens in Eretz Yisrael have children, they must go to the American Consulate to receive a Consular Report of Birth Abroad (in place of a birth certificate), and, if they wish to travel with their child, they can also apply for a passport.

A *kollel yungerman* I know once filed all of the necessary paperwork, and then suddenly had to travel to America for a medical emergency. In order to take his child with him, he had to change his application from a regular passport application to an emergency one. He called the consulate in a panic, and the vice-consul actually got onto the telephone and told the *yungerman* that he would see to it that the applications were switched.

When the *yungerman* went to pick up the emergency passport several days later, he wrote a simple thank-you note to the vice-consul and his staff for helping him.

The family went to America, took care of the medical issue, and returned to Eretz Yisrael. A few months later, the *yungerman* went

Sticks and Stones vs. Words and Tones / 61

back to the consulate to apply for a Social Security card for his baby. When the person behind the counter saw the name on the application, he said, "We appreciated your note. It is still hanging on the bulletin board in our office."

Apparently pharmacists are not the only ones who appreciate kind words. Bureaucrats do, too. But let's take it to the next level.

The house of Rav Yosef Chaim Sonnenfeld, the Rav of Yerushalayim, was a veritable *reshus harabim* (public domain). People would come for *berachos* and *eitzos* (advice) day in, day out. That was true all year, but on Chol HaMoed his house would turn into a major thoroughfare. Nearly every Jew in Yerushalayim would come to wish him *Gut Yom Tov* and receive his blessing.

One Chol HaMoed, the Lubliner Rav, Rav Eliyahu Kletzkin, was visiting Rav Yosef Chaim while the parade of people came through his house. Suddenly, Rav Yosef Chaim began to do something he had never done before. He told each person who came, "*Mistameh geit ihr tzum Kosel*" (You are probably on your way to the *Kosel*) or "*Mistameh kumpt ihr tzurik fun Kosel*" (You are probably on your way home from the *Kosel*). For the remainder of that day, he said these words to each person who entered his house.

That night, someone asked Rav Yosef Chaim why he suddenly began to make this strange statement to each person.

"I thought to myself," explained Rav Yosef Chaim, "that when Rav Kletzkin would see so many people coming through my home, he would become upset. He is also a *talmid chacham*, and maybe his house is not as full on Chol HaMoed.

"By suggesting to each person that he was coming to see me only because he was on the way to or from the *Kosel*, I left Rav Kletzkin with the impression that if he, too, resided within minutes of the *Kosel*, he would also have so many visitors."

This is the polar opposite of *ona'as devarim*. This is what Shlomo HaMelech refers to as, "*u'leshon chachamim marpei* — the tongue of the wise heals" (*Mishlei* 12:18).

So pharmacists, bureaucrats, and even great *rabbanim* are in need of thoughtful, kind speech. But even that is not all.

The Talmud (*Shabbos* 89a) states that when Moshe Rabbeinu went up to the Heavens, he saw Hashem tying crowns to the letters of the Torah. Hashem said to Moshe, "Is it not the custom in your city to say 'Shalom' when you meet someone?"

"Does a servant precede his master in wishing 'Shalom'?" Moshe replied. The protocol is that the Master speaks first, not vice versa.

"You should have helped Me," Hashem answered.

What does that mean? Does the Almighty need help from a mortal? Rashi explains that Moshe should have said, "*Titzlach melachtecha* — May You succeed in Your endeavor."

When Moshe heard this, continues the Talmud, he said, "*Ve'ata, yigdal na koach Hashem* — And now, may the strength of my Lord be magnified" (*Bamidbar* 14:17).

How do we understand this passage? Does the *Kol Yachol*, the Omnipotent, need words of encouragement?

The answer, says Rabbi Shlomo Freifeld, is that the *Ribono Shel Olam* wanted to teach *us* a lesson. No matter how great a person is, he can always use *chizuk*. No one is beyond the need for encouragement.

It is not enough for us to put an end to *ona'as devarim*, to avoid the snide remarks and verbal abuse that have become so ingrained in our society nowadays. We must also strive for the next level: to find helpful, healing, kind words — words that promote good feelings between people, and will ultimately bring peace and perfection to our world.

Keeping Faith in Troubled Times

We live in a generation that seems addicted to *segulos*. People latch on to every *segulah* that comes to their attention. They do one thing to merit having sons, another for daughters, a third to find *shidduchim* for their daughters. Whether this seemingly quick-fix approach — to life in general, and to Judaism in particular — is appropriate is a subject that is worthy of a lecture of its own. Rather than focus on that point, however, I would prefer to jump on the bandwagon and offer a *segulah* of my own. But unlike most *segulos*, my *segulah* is not based on esoteric sources, but on a conversation found in the Talmud (*Avodah Zarah* 18a).

This essay is based on a lecture delivered in the aftermath of the financial meltdown of 2008, which wreaked havoc on the world economy and left thousands without homes or jobs. Although the examples chosen pertain to that crisis, the greater message can be extrapolated to other crises that crop up in our lives.

Rabbi Chanina ben Teradyon went to visit Rabbi Yose ben Kismah, who was on his deathbed. Rabbi Chanina asked, "Rebbi, what portion will I merit in *Olam Haba* [the World to Come]?"

"Did any incident occur [from which I can determine what sort of portion you deserve (Rashi)]?" asked Rabbi Yose.

"One time," answered Rabbi Chanina, "I had money set aside for my Purim *seudah* [feast], and I inadvertently switched those funds with *tzedakah* [charity] funds. I decided to give all of the money to the poor."

"In that case," said Rabbi Yose, "then may my lot [in the World to Come] be as great as yours."

This passage is difficult to understand, especially in the context in which it appears.

Prior to this portion of the discussion, Rabbi Yose took issue with Rabbi Chanina for teaching Torah in public in spite of the Roman law forbidding it. "I will be surprised," he said, "if they don't burn you with the *Sefer Torah* from which you teach." Following the discussion regarding the World to Come, the Talmud relates that Rabbi Yose's prediction came true. Rabbi Chanina was burned alive, and is remembered as one of the *Asarah Harugei Malchus*, the Ten Martyrs regarding whom we recite *kinnos* on Tisha B'Av and Yom Kippur.

Rabbi Chanina ben Teradyon, a man who literally gave his life for the Torah, could find no greater merit to vouch for his piety than an episode regarding charitable funds!

I once read an explanation of this perplexing passage. From a purely halachic standpoint, Rabbi Chanina would have been allowed to keep the amount that he was certain belonged to him. Why did he give the entire sum to charity? Because he did not ascribe the mix-up to human error or carelessness. He sensed that Hashem was sending him a message to give all the money to the poor.

Rabbi Yose ben Kismah understood that if Rabbi Chanina could see Hashem's Hand in such an ordinary incident, he must be worthy of a great portion in *Olam Haba*. A person who lives his entire life trying to determine, *"Vos vill der Ribono Shel Olam* — what does God want from me?" is one who is guaranteed a portion in *Olam Haba*.

The basis for this appears in a verse in *Parashas Ki Savo*. "You have distinguished Hashem today to be a God for you, and to walk in His ways, and to observe His decrees, His commandments, and His statutes ... *velishmoa beKolo* — and to listen to His Voice" (*Devarim* 26:17).

Ramban notes that the first half of the verse — "to walk in His ways, and to observe His decrees, His commandments, and His statutes" — seems to include just about everything we must do to serve Hashem. What do the words *"velishmoa beKolo"* add?

We can explain that aside from the decrees, commandments, and statutes that appear in the Torah, Hashem has other ways of speaking to us. In days of old, He spoke to us through prophets. To our great misfortune, we no longer have prophets, but Hashem still "speaks" to us through events that occur in our lives. Being receptive to those messages, constantly asking ourselves, "What is God trying to tell me?" may not be a quick-fix, but as we have seen from Rabbi Yose ben Kismah's reaction, it is a *segulah* for entry into the World to Come.

☙ Sensitive Spiritual Sensors

It seems that great people have fine-tuned, sensitive spiritual sensors that enable them to perceive frequent messages from Hashem in their everyday lives, while others can ignore even the most obvious, conspicuous messages from Above.

It is said that when the Chofetz Chaim would hear a clap of thunder, he would say, *"Vus vill der Tatte* — What does Father want?" Indeed, the Talmud (*Berachos* 59a) teaches that Hashem created thunder to "straighten the crookedness of the heart." When we hear a clap of thunder close by, we flinch. For a second or two, we may experience fear. But it takes no less a personage than the Chofetz Chaim to convert that instinctive fear into a perception of Hashem's voice. Most of us go right on with our lives.

Rabbi Elyah Svei was born in Lithuania in a small town called Poltava, not far from Baranovich. When he was a young boy, he entered shul to *daven* Maariv and found the townspeople reciting *Tehillim* with passion and fervor. Rav Elyah commented that he had yet to witness such an outpouring of emotion in a yeshivah. "Who is sick?" he asked.

"Sick?" someone replied. "No one is sick."

"So why is everyone saying *Tehillim* with such desperation?" he asked.

"Didn't you hear? There was an earthquake, and thousands of people died. Hashem must want us to do *teshuvah* [repent]."

Where was this earthquake? Not in the next town, or even on the same continent. It was in some far-flung corner of the earth. Yet the people of Poltava were frightened, because Hashem had shown His wrath. This was enough of a message to inspire them to recite *Tehillim* as if their lives depended on it.

We are not speaking of Rav Chanina ben Teradyon, or even the Chofetz Chaim. These were ordinary Jews of the last century, who lived with enough sensitivity to hear the voice of Hashem calling to them.

The opposite end of the spectrum is represented by a story that occurred with Rav Yechezkel (Chatzkel) Levenstein, the *mashgiach* of Yeshivas Mir in Europe, and later of Ponevezh in Eretz Yisrael.

An irreligious cab driver who was driving Rav Chatzkel remarked that he had once witnessed an open miracle.

When secular Israelis complete their army service, they typically unwind by touring some exotic location. After his army service, this cab driver decided to tour a mountainous region in Africa with some of his army buddies. One night, they awoke to hear one of their friends screaming in terror. The young man was enveloped by a huge boa constrictor, which was squeezing the life out of him.

They had no idea how to free their friend, and they were afraid to do anything to the snake, lest they antagonize it and make it squeeze even harder. Facing what seemed to be inevitable, one of the group said, "I know that when Jews are about to die, they recite *Shema*. Maybe you should recite it now."

As soon as the ex-soldier screamed, "*Shema Yisrael, Hashem*

Elokeinu, Hashem Echad," the snake unwound itself and slithered away into the darkness of night.

"That miracle changed my friend's life," the cab driver concluded. "He vowed to become a *baal teshuvah*, and he kept his word. He traveled directly back to Israel, and is now a thoroughly religious Jew."

Rav Chatzkel turned to the cab driver and asked, *"U'mah itcha* — and what about you?"

"Me?" the driver responded in a quizzical tone. "The Rav doesn't understand — the snake wasn't wrapped around me, it was wrapped around my friend."

At one end of the spiritual sensor spectrum we have the Chofetz Chaim and the Jews of Poltava, on the other end we have the cab driver who witnesses an open miracle and still does not get the message. Where do *we* stand?

✿ The Great Meltdown: A Message From on High

One does not have to be Rav Chanina ben Teradyon, the Chofetz Chaim, or a Jew of Lithuania to come to the awareness that recent events are a message from the *Ribono Shel Olam*.

Recent statistics show that, unbeknownst to us, we were already in a recession as early as December 2007. We are now in a financial crisis the likes of which we have not seen since the Great Depression. We hope and pray that the situation does not deteriorate further. The challenge here is not in perceiving that there is a message, but in interpreting the message and determining what it is that Hashem wants us to do. *Vus vill der Tatte?* What does our Father, Hashem, want from us?

The secular approach to world events is to examine them in terms of cause and effect, to seek natural or human causes for all the problems in the world. For the next 10 or 15 years, economists, historians, and politicians will debate what precipitated the financial meltdown. It will be studied in business schools worldwide for decades to come. Some will claim that it started with the subprime mortgage collapse; others will blame it on deregulation of the banking and investment sector; still others will feel that the federal government was not alert enough to foresee the oncoming crisis.

The next step will be to scrutinize each action taken by the government in the early days of the crisis to determine whether it should have acted differently. Should it have bailed out Lehman Brothers? Did the failure to contain the damage at that point set off the credit freeze?

That is the secular view. It is not the Torah view.

The *Targum* interprets the verse, "*VehaElokim asa sheyir'u milefanav* — and God has acted so that [man] should stand in awe before Him" (*Koheles* 3:14) — as follows: *ube'idan deyeisei puranusa be'alma* — when tragedy befalls the world, *Hashem hu de'avad* — God is causing it. Why? *Begin deyidchalun benei enasha min kadamohi* — so that people should fear Him.

The *Targum* is telling us that the purpose of calamities, crises, and tragedies is to make us aware — once and for all — that God calls the shots.

We Jews should not look for causes for crises. We know that this happened because the *Ribono Shel Olam* allowed it to happen. At the end of Yom Kippur, when we shout at the top of our lungs, *Hashem, Hu haElokim*, we are saying that everything that happens in this world occurs under the authority of Hashem. Rav Chaim of Volozhin writes that the Divine Name *Elokim* represents the fact that Hashem is the *Baal hayecholos u'Baal hakochos kulam*. He contains all the power in the world. Nothing can occur against His will. There are no coincidences.

This crisis, among others, is not man-made. We have received one of the clearest messages from Hashem in recent history. We know that He wants us to do something, but what is it?

Truth be told, it is not for someone like me to interpret such messages for the general public. That is outside my job description. Permit me, however, to deliver the words of a great *gadol*, Rav Elchonon Wasserman, which appear in his classic *Kovetz*

Ma'amarim. In an essay entitled *"Ikvesa D'Meshicha"* ("The Footsteps of Mashiach"), he elucidates a portion of the Torah that predicts what the world will look like in the times immediately preceding the arrival of Mashiach.

In *Parashas Haazinu*, the Torah warns that dreadful circumstances will befall us if we stray from the path of Torah and mitzvos. At some point, however, Hashem will change direction and take pity on us, *"Ki yir'eh ki azlas yad, ve'efes atzur ve'azuv* — when [He] sees that enemy power progresses, and none is saved or assisted" (*Devarim* 32:36).

Rav Elchonon explains this verse to mean that when the rabbinic leaders are no longer able to bring *Klal Yisrael* back onto the Torah path, Hashem Himself will bring about the Ultimate Redemption. In a brief review of Jewish history, he shows that the first time that rabbinic authority was undermined to such an extent occurred during the late 18th century. Certainly, then, we have reached the point of redemption.

Before Hashem redeems us, however, He will make us realize that we are helpless without Him. *"Ve'amar ei eloheimo, tzur chasayu vo* — He will say, 'Where is their god, the rock in whom they sought refuge?'" (Ibid. v. 37). Hashem will bring us to the realization that all the gods in which we place our faith are worthless.

While we no longer serve idols of wood or stone, Rav Elchonon explains that anything that is deified is also considered idolatrous. He enumerates several of the ideological beliefs, such as liberalism, socialism, and communism, that had arisen and collapsed in his times — each with its fair share of *Yidden* who fell prey to its wiles.

Hashem will come to us, says Rav Elchonon, and ask, *"Ei eloheimo* — where are all of your 'isms'? *Yakumu veyaz'ruchem* — let them rise and save you" (Ibid. v. 38).

Then we will come to an inescapable conclusion (v. 39): *"Re'u atah ki Ani Ani Hu* — see now that I, I am He, *ve'ein elohim imadi* — and no god is with Me. *Ani amis va'achayeh* — I am the One Who puts to death and Who gives life, *machatzti vaAni erpah* — I struck down, and I will heal."

And finally: *"Ve'ein miyadi matzil* — there is no rescuer from My Hand."

The times of Mashiach will be characterized by the demise of ideals and ideas in which we place our faith.

The days of philosophical "isms" are indeed gone. Few are consumed with passion for any specific form of government. But Rav Elchonon could not have known that 80 years after his murder by the Nazis, one "ism" would remain in vogue, an ism that we all have worshiped to some extent or another: capitalism, and its loyal counterparts, materialism and consumerism.

Consumerism, as many know, led to the trampling to death of a maintenance worker at a Walmart store in Valley Stream, Long Island. For what? For a limited supply of 50-inch Samsung plasma HDTVs on sale for $798. For Bissel vacuum cleaners for $28. People lined up for hours in the cold and rushed the doors as soon as they opened, as if they had not eaten in days, knocking over this worker along with several shoppers — among them a woman who was obviously expecting a child. In a separate incident in Farmingdale, N.Y., a woman was knocked over by a crowd pushing and shoving to enter another Walmart store. What did she do? She got up and finished shopping before filing a police report. After all, she hadn't waited on that line for nothing! And consumerism almost led to a riot when police ordered the people out of the Valley Stream store to conduct a crime-scene investigation. "We waited for four hours," the masses protested. "We're not leaving."

What has happened to us? We live in a society that lives — if you'll forgive me — from one holiday gift season to the next. A society whose sole mission is buy, buy, buy. People put themselves in debt to buy gifts for people who don't need or even enjoy what they receive.

I am not predicting that we have seen the fall of capitalism, or that the economy as we have known it will never recover. But I *will* say that the faith that people had in the American economy — "the markets will always recover" — and the belief that we can just buy, buy, buy, consume, consume, consume, charge, charge, charge — has been shaken.

Another belief that has been shaken is our faith in the United

States government. Does anyone believe that the current administration knows what it is doing? Does it seem to you that anyone there believes that the astronomical bailout packages will help? Congress has changed course dozens of times, to no avail.

One bitter irony that did not escape me was that on Erev Rosh Hashanah 5769, I had one ear glued to the radio to hear whether Congress would pass the first $750 billion bailout package, hoping desperately it would pass. Brainwashed by a biased media, in my own mind I was thinking, "What is going to happen if they don't pass it?"

At 2 p.m., House Speaker Pelosi announced that the bill was dead. The House Republicans were not willing to be bamboozled into passing a bill that was overloaded with last minute pork-barrel measures, without even the time to read it. Within hours, the stock market dropped 1,000 points. Until then I had never witnessed a day in which the market dropped so precipitously in one day.

I went into Rosh Hashanah with a keener appreciation for the words, "*Hashem Elokei Yisrael Melech, u'Malchuso bakol mashalah* — Hashem the God of Israel is King, and His Kingdom reigns over all." It was clearer than ever that *der Ribono Shel Olam fiert der velt* — God runs the world.

Who can be a greater spokesperson for the general change in attitude than Alan Greenspan? Glorified during his long tenure as chairman of the Federal Reserve, Greenspan had to suffer the humiliation of sitting through a congressional committee trying to determine the cause of the crisis. The man who was affectionately referred to as "the maestro" for his ability to navigate the economy of the United States through many difficult times was forced to admit that the situation has left him, "in a state of shocked disbelief."

I found great *mussar* in the words of George Soros, whose politics I do not share, but who made an observation worthy of far wiser minds than his: "All our ideas, *all human constructs*, have flaws in them. As a child I experienced fascism in the Nazi occupation, and then communism. I learned that both of those ideologies were false. Now I was shocked that even in a democracy, people can be misled to the extent that we have been misled in the last few years."

Do you know what this says? If people the likes of Alan Greenspan and George Soros, who invested their entire lives into building the great deity of capitalism, admit that their faith in the economy and the government has been shaken, then Hashem has shown us Who is in charge.

It is sad to have to draw inspiration from such sources. *Ehrliche Yidden* have always lived with trust in Hashem only. In the words of King David (*Tehillim* 22:5-6), "*Becha batchu avoseinu* — in You our fathers trusted. *Eilecha za'aku venimlatu* — To You they cried and were rescued. *Becha batchu velo voshu* — In You they trusted, and were not shamed." We should not need to see someone humbled before a congressional committee. Our faith should always have been in the Almighty, not in our own fiscal prowess.

⇜§ Change and Hope: A Jewish Perspective

It is ironic that while the economy was beginning to tumble, we had a presidential candidate — who then became president-elect and President of the United States — infusing the nation with a dual message of change and hope. While President Obama's vision for change and hope have proved to be smoke and mirrors and not much different from what we had seen before he entered the White House, it is the duty of every Jew to find the Torah's message of change and hope. We have discussed change and the need to cast away the gods of capitalism and consumerism. Now let's examine the Jewish outlook on hope.

We find clear proof from a blessing that we recite three times daily that the worst thing that a person can do is lose hope.

One of the *berachos* (blessings) in *Shemoneh Esrei* stands apart in that it is the only one that is worded as a curse: *Velamalshinim*.

There was an era in Jewish history when Jews would spread slanderous stories that caused fellow Jews to be incarcerated by the government. *Chazal* decided to "throw the book at them," and composed an entire *berachah* (blessing) to bring the wrath of God upon them. The very first curse leveled at them is "*Velamalshinim al tehi sikvah* — and for the slanderers let there be no hope." The most destructive curse is to lose all hope.

We find equal proof in the opposite extreme. Several blessings after *Velamalshinim*, we recite *Modim*, a *berachah* of thanks. We list all the great things that Hashem does for us, and we conclude with, "*mei'olam kivinu Lach* — we have always placed our hope in You."

In all times, especially in trying times like these, we must be thankful that we have a *Ribono Shel Olam* in Whom to place our hope.

The story is told of a man who came home one day and found his house in flames. As he stood outside watching the flames lick through the windows, his neighbors were astounded to hear him recite the *berachah*, "*Shelo asani goy* — Who has not made me a gentile."

"Why now?" asked his neighbors, fearing that he had lost his mind from the anguish of watching all of his family's possessions being turned into ash.

"Now more than ever," he responded, "I am happy that I am a Jew. When a godless gentile sees his home being destroyed, he can lose hope. A *Yid* has the *Ribono Shel Olam*. He has faith, and as such, he has hope."

A longtime friend from Seattle — a 54-year-old who had never smoked a single cigarette in his life — was recently diagnosed with lung cancer. I was scheduled to be out west, so I decided to make a side trip to spend a few hours with him. Between treatments, we took a walk along the shores of Lake Washington, and we discussed topics that people ponder when faced with such challenges. When I arrived back home, I called and asked him to write down some of the thoughts he had shared with me. Bear in mind that this man is a *baal teshuvah*, and his wife is a *giyores* (convert). Here is his letter.

> While I would not have chosen this test, I continue to look for the *berachos* in it, not the *kelalos* [curses]. I remember asking my wife, "Can you imagine going through this without a solid belief in Hashem and without a supportive community?"

Now more than ever we appreciate the extraordinary foundation that *Yiddishkeit* provides for us. I shudder at the thought of how I would have dealt with my condition without it. The secular world focuses on anger, blame, and bitterness, instead of accepting a challenge for what it is. In the meantime, we have the power of *teshuvah*, *tefillah*, and *tzedakah*.

My friend's message shouts, "*Baruch Hu Elokeinu she'bra'anu lichvodo, vehivdilanu min hato'im* — Blessed are You, Hashem, Who created us for His glory, and separated us from those who stray." As long as we have faith, we have hope.

These are challenging, trying times. Many of our brethren have lost their jobs and are suffering the indignity of having to grovel for work. People are losing their homes. Others have had their utilities shut off. Now more than ever, we must realize that we are in the *Ikvesa D'Meshicha*. In line with the verses at the end of *Haazinu*, the last Mishnah of *Maseches Sotah* predicts that in the *Ikvesa D'Meshicha*, we will be forced to realize that *ein lanu al mi l'hi'sha'ein ela al Avinu sheba'shamayim* — we have no one on whom to rely other than our Father in heaven. We have indeed come to realize that we cannot rely on the Treasury, or on the government, or on our 401(k)s, which have now been reduced to 200½(k)s. We can rely only on Hashem.

Someone recently visited Rabbi Gamliel Rabinovitch, an *adam gadol* in Eretz Yisrael, and asked him why we are going through this crisis. Rav Rabinovitch, who is of the caliber of individuals who can say such things, responded that everything that was pre-destined to have occurred before Mashiach could come has already occurred. Now we are just waiting. Perhaps the primary purpose of this crisis is to get us to want him to come.

One final thought. We have seen that the purpose of thunder is, literally, to "put the fear of God into us." Why, then, is thunder always followed by rain? Rain is such a wonderful thing. We cannot exist without water to drink, and crops would not grow without rain. Isn't it incongruous that thunder, which is meant to frighten us, is associated with life-giving rain?

Rav Elyah Lopian once expressed a simple, but beautiful thought: When thunder accomplishes what it is supposed to accomplish, and it does put the fear of God in us, then we can merit to see the blessings that follow.

We occasionally need thunder to set us straight. Once that has been accomplished, the *Ribono Shel Olam* says, "Here are your *gishmei berachah*, your much needed rains that bring blessing."

We have heard the thunder all too often in recent times. We heard it in *Mercaz Harav*, and then in Mumbai. When it accomplishes what it is meant to accomplish, it forces us to the inescapable conclusion of, "*Re'u atah ki Ani Ani Hu* — see now that I, I am He, *machatzti vaAni erpah* — I struck down, and I will heal." Only then will we merit the *gishmei berachah* of abundant *parnassah* and to see *Mashiach Tzidkeinu,* may he come speedily, in our times.

My Son, Your Son ... the *Eibishter's* Son

A memory from kindergarten, which I attended more than 50 years ago, was recently stirred. I was in the car with several family members, and Rabbi Akiva's statement (*Talmud Yerushalmi, Nedarim* 9:4), "*Ve'ahavta lerei'acha kamocha; zeh klal gadol baTorah* — love your neighbor as you love yourself; this is a great principle of the Torah," came up in conversation. My 3-year-old grandson sitting in the back seat suddenly perked up and said, "I know that song," and proceeded to serenade us with the familiar song that was part of my kindergarten education. I suppose that if I learned that song and my grandson learned that song, then every child attending a Jewish preschool in the past five decades likewise learned that song. And if the song is so timeless, it is because the message is one that resonates with every one of us. We all realize how important it is to foster love and unity between Jews.

Since we have all been infused with the importance of this mitzvah from such a tender age, I suppose it should not be too difficult for us to answer a few questions about it.

1) Think of the last Jew, who was not a member of your family, to whom you spoke. Do you love him or her? If you answer *no*, are you violating the mitzvah of *ve'ahavta lerei'acha kamocha* — Love your neighbor as [you love] yourself?

2) Imagine that you purchased a new car, and your neighbor came over to admire it. Upon examining the car he says, "This is a beautiful car. I would like one, too. Can you please buy that exact model for me?"

   When you respond with a quizzical look, he continues, "Well, if you would love me as you love yourself, you would want me to enjoy life as much as you do, so you would buy me the car."

   Is he correct? Does *ve'ahavta lerei'acha kamocha* require you to buy him a car?

3) Due to construction in the left lane, you are caught in heavy traffic. Most drivers merge into the right lane upon seeing the first sign indicating that the left lane is closed farther along, leaving the right lane at a standstill, and the left lane wide open. If you cruise down the left lane and squeeze into the right lane just at the point when the left lane ends, cutting off dozens of cars in the process, have you violated *ve'ahavta lerei'acha kamocha*?

If your response to the above questions was, "I don't know," don't feel bad. Although most of us know the literal translation of *ve'ahavta lerei'acha kamocha* — love your neighbor as yourself — we are about to learn that neither *"ve'ahavta* — love," nor *"kamocha* — as yourself" are used in their conventional sense in this verse.

☙ Level #1: Do No Harm

As is the case with many mitzvos, the *Rishonim* debate the halachic parameters of *ve'ahavta lerei'acha kamocha*. Our discussion will focus on the opinion of the Ramban, as expressed in *Parashas Kedoshim*.

The Ramban writes that the Torah "exaggerates" (Ramban's word: *haflagah*) in stating that we must love our neighbors as ourselves. He offers two logical proofs to back his opinion:

(a) It is impossible that the Torah demands that every Jew must love *all* others *as much* as he loves himself, because most people are incapable of fulfilling this mitzvah. *Chizkuni* is even more emphatic, stating that it is *impossible* to love others as much as we love ourselves.

(b) The same Rabbi Akiva who states that *ve'ahavta lerei'acha kamocha* is a great principle of the Torah also deduces from the Torah that one's own life takes precedence over the lives of others. If two people are traveling through a desert, for instance, and one has enough water for one person to survive, and the other doesn't have any water, the one with the water should drink it himself and not give any to his friend. If *kamocha* means that we must love our neighbors as much as ourselves, how can the person with the water leave his friend to perish while he travels on?

The Ramban concludes, therefore, that both *ve'ahavta* (love) and *kamocha* (as yourself) are not to be taken literally.

The Ramban's explanation of this mitzvah provides the answers to the first two questions on our quiz.

If you don't love the last Jew you spoke to as much as you love yourself, it is fine, because *ve'ahavta* does not mean love. And if you would not be willing to present your neighbor with a brand-new car, it is also fine, because *kamocha* does not mean that you must give him everything that you want for yourself.

We have determined what *ve'ahavta lerei'acha kamocha* does *not* mean. But what *does* it mean? The definition of this mitzvah appears in a well-known story from the Talmud (*Shabbos* 31a).

A non-Jew approached Shammai and told him that he would convert to Judaism on the condition that Shammai would teach him the Torah while he stood on one foot. Shammai felt that he was insincere, and sent him away. The man came to Hillel and repeated his request, and Hillel responded, "*Da'alach sani lechavrach lo saavid* — What you dislike, do not do unto your friend.

"*Zu hi kol haTorah*," Hillel concluded. "This is *the entire Torah. Idach* — the rest, *peirusha hu* — expounds on this rule. *Zil gemor* — go and study."

Hillel's rule is reminiscent of what — I am told — is considered the first rule of medicine: do no harm. Before a doctor sets out to heal a person, he should first ascertain that the steps he is about to take will not make the patient worse. Similarly, Hillel taught this convert that the foundation of the entire Torah rests on the simple rule of "Do No Harm." Don't do anything that bothers, disturbs, or annoys someone else. And you are the yardstick of what is considered bothersome, annoying, or obnoxious. If you find something disturbing, make sure not to do it to others.

I find this teaching encouraging. Most of us are incapable of attaining the level of *ahavas Yisrael* that we have seen among our *gedolim*, who would do anything and everything for a fellow Jew. But we can aspire to the first ground rule set forth by the Talmud. We can avoid annoying or hurting others.

Perhaps Rabbi Akiva and Hillel's delineation of this mitzvah as a fundamental principle of the Torah explains the seemingly harsh terminology found in *Bava Kamma* (50a).

The Talmud states that if one removes rocks from his field, he should not throw them into the public domain, lest his discarded rocks injure others. The Talmud relates that one individual was throwing rocks from his field into the public domain, and a pious Jew said in passing, "*Reika* [empty one], why are you throwing rocks from a domain that does not belong to you to one that does belong to you?"

The rock-thrower mocked the pious Jew. *This is my field*, he must have thought to himself. *Why did he say that it is not mine?*

He did not realize that the pious Jew was conveying a basic rule in life: we have no way of knowing how long our possessions will remain ours. A while later, the rock-thrower became destitute and had to sell his field. One day he was walking past the field that had once belonged to him, and he tripped and hurt himself on one of the rocks that he had thrown into the public domain.

The lesson from this story is clear, but why did the pious Jew address this man with the harsh adjective, "*reika* — empty one"?

The commentators (*Ein Yaakov*) explain that the mitzvah of *ve'ahavta lerei'acha kamocha* is fundamental; someone who does not fulfill it is regarded as empty, because it is considered to be the *entire* Torah.

"Do No Harm" is a level toward which we can strive. We can avoid hurting and annoying others, and the mitzvos will pile up.

But there is a potential downside to this seeming windfall of mitzvos. Any time we do engage in hurtful or rude behavior, we violate this mitzvah.

This brings us back to the third question on our quiz. If you cut off a long line of cars in traffic, then you violate the mitzvah of *ve'ahavta lerei'acha kamocha*. We all become annoyed and even angry when we are waiting patiently on line and some wise guy cuts us off — so we should not cut off others.

Rabbi Eliyahu Meir Klugman told me that he was once waiting with several others in an anteroom of Rav Elyashiv's house. Rebbetzin Elyashiv wanted to ask her husband a question, but before she walked into his room she asked all those assembled in the anteroom whether she could go before them. She practiced *ve'ahavta lerei'acha kamocha*, and *da'alach sani lechavrach lo saavid*.

An alert Jew will find many situations in which he can fulfill *ve'ahavta lerei'acha kamocha*, or alternatively, fail miserably and violate the mitzvah.

What happens when a person is late for Maariv and can't find a convenient parking spot? Some people will double-park, reasoning that the owner of the car they are blocking is probably *davening* in the same *minyan*, and that if they leave a bit early when Maariv is over, the person whom they are blocking will be none the wiser. But what if that person happened to have *davened* in the previous *minyan*, and is impatiently waiting for 15 minutes? The double-parker has violated a Torah-level mitzvah of *ve'ahavta lerei'acha kamocha*.

It's a warm summer night and the neighbors' windows are open. You are standing in front of your home conversing with a friend as if it is 11 in the morning instead of 11 at night. If your loud voice prevents someone from falling asleep, you have violated the mitzvah of *ve'ahavta lerei'acha kamocha*.

The Chasam Sofer concludes one of his responsa (Vol. I, 180) with the disclaimer that he wrote it without looking into any *sefarim*, since his wife, who had recently given birth to a premature baby, was resting in the room where his *sefarim* were kept. If the Chasam Sofer preferred to write an intricate *teshuvah* without *sefarim* rather than disturb his wife, how can we blatantly violate *ve'ahavta lerei'acha kamocha* by carrying on a disturbingly loud conversation outdoors?

If you are at a *kiddush* where there is inadequate seating, how can you allow your three children to sit comfortably while adults stand? Aside from the negative *chinuch* message this sends to your child, it is extremely annoying to the adults who are standing and watching your child lick the chocolate off his cookie. And anything that is annoying is in violation of *ve'ahavta lerei'acha kamocha*.

Would we even for a second consider not putting on *tefillin* one morning? Would we even contemplate not hearing *tekias shofar* on Rosh Hashanah or not eating matzah on Pesach? Certainly not! We would not allow a Torah-level mitzvah to slip through our fingers. Yet somehow, *ve'ahavta lerei'acha kamocha*, which is of equal import as these mitzvos, can slip through our fingers several times a day.

Our first lesson in *ahavas Yisrael* must be to stop doing things that antagonize or annoy our fellow Jews.

ᱣᱷ Level #2: "Fargin"

But the mitzvah of *ve'ahavta lerei'acha kamocha* is not limited to doing no harm. There is some level of emotional feeling that we must have toward our fellow Jews. Let us return to the Ramban and see how he defines this portion of the mitzvah.

"There are times that a person loves his friend enough to wish that he has wealth, but does not want him to have wisdom as well," writes Ramban. "And when he loves a friend even more, he wishes that his friend could have everything — wealth, possessions, honor, understanding, and wisdom — *but not as much as he himself has*. He will always want more for himself than for his friend."

The Ramban is noting an interesting character trait. We are willing to allow others to have everything — but not as much as we have.

Let me give you an example. The Schwartz's daughter gets engaged, and their future son-in-law has all the qualities one can seek in a *shidduch*. He's a *talmid chacham*, has sterling character traits, he's tall and handsome, and he comes from a wonderful family. In short — a real prince. Now let's say that the Schwartz's next-door neighbors, the Weinfelds, are also looking for a *shidduch* for their daughter. Of course Mrs. Schwartz is a *mentsch*, and she wants the Weinfelds to find a wonderful son-in-law. Wonderful, indeed — but not as good as hers.

You think that people are not like that? The Ramban says that people can be that way, and that it is this jealous attitude that the Torah seeks to eradicate in commanding us to love our fellow Jews.

There is a Yiddish word that does not seem to have an accurate English translation: *fargin*. Perhaps the reason why it exists only in the Yiddish language is because it is such a uniquely Jewish concept. Even the creator of modern Hebrew, who drew almost no words from Yiddish, could find no word to replace it. Someone told me that in the midst of a conversation with an Israeli, his counterpart said, "*Hu lo yodei'ah lefargin* — he doesn't know how to *fargin*."

To *fargin* means to be willing that someone else should have just as much — or even more — than you do. That is a very difficult level to attain, but we should all strive for it.

When your son or daughter becomes engaged, you have a golden opportunity.

There was a woman who had three children on the *shidduchim* "market" at the same time, all of whom were over 23 years of age. As you can imagine, the situation dominated her life.

At the time, a spate of *kiddushim* was being given for older single girls. It seems that someone had approached a certain *gadol* to ask for a *berachah* for a *shidduch* for their not-so-young daughter, and the *gadol* asked, "Did you make a *kiddush* when she was born?"

When the parents answered in the negative, the *gadol* said, "That is the problem. One of the standard blessings that people wish the parents at a *kiddush* is that they should raise their daughter *l'chuppah*. Since she is lacking all those *berachos*, she is unable to get married."

Rumor had it that those parents made a *kiddush*, and shortly thereafter their daughter got engaged. Rumors spreading as they tend to do, before long there were dozens of *kiddushim* held for older girls.

This woman was so distraught over her situation, that she began to wonder whether she had made a *kiddush* when her 25-year-old daughter was born. Try as she might, she could not recall any details of her daughter's *kiddush*. She went to Rav Dovid Feinstein to inquire whether she should make a *kiddush* at this juncture.

Rav Dovid Feinstein told her that in her situation she had no reason to do so. This woman worked in a New York clothing store that catered to a *frum* clientele, and all she heard, day in, day out, was, "The *kallah* needs ...," "I need a dress for my son's *aufruf* ..." As much as this woman is the type who does *fargin* others, the constant reminders of her plight were a lot to bear. R' Dovid Feinstein offered her a new perspective on her job.

"You're a very fortunate woman," Rabbi Feinstein said. "When people's children become engaged, it means that their *mazel* is shining on them. They then have the *koach haberachah*, the power to bless others. Rather than make a *kiddush* to receive *berachos* for your daughter, each time someone comes in to shop in preparation for a *chasunah*, ask for a *berachah*."

The woman followed Rabbi Feinstein's advice, and — lo and behold — within a year, all three of her older singles were engaged or married.

If you are in a situation in which your *mazel* is shining upon you, you should wish the same upon others. And according to the Ramban, the mitzvah of *ve'ahavta lerei'acha kamocha* dictates that you should wish wholeheartedly that their *chasan* or *kallah* should be just as good as yours.

◆§ Level # 3: The Ultimate Level

I think that there is a loftier goal that we can strive for in fulfilling the mitzvah of *ve'ahavta lerei'acha kamocha*. Let me begin with a question. We have seen the Ramban's teaching that the words *ve'ahavta lerei'acha kamocha* should not be taken literally, because most people are incapable of loving others as much as they love themselves. If so, why did the Torah use those words? Why not write the mitzvah as the Talmud defines it — "don't do unto others that which you would not want done unto you"?

The Torah imparts more than just rules that we *must* live by. It also teaches us what the ideal *ratzon* (will) of Hashem is. The Torah chose to state the mitzvah in the words *ve'ahavta lerei'acha kamocha* to teach that while it is beyond the scope of ordinary humans to love their friends as much as they love themselves, Hashem wants us to work toward that goal.

When we read about *gedolei Yisrael*, we find that many of them did reach that level of love for their fellow Jews. How did they manage to attain that level? I think that they developed their love for everyone through a concept mentioned by the *Tomer Devorah*. He writes that all members of *Klal Yisrael* are *she'eir basar*, flesh and blood, to one another. While this sounds like a beautiful concept in theory, most of us do not feel that bond. But *gedolei Yisrael* do. They live with a constant awareness that the *neshamah* of every Jew comes from the same place — a very holy place, under the Heavenly Throne — and that, metaphysically and spiritually, we are all one body. When a person bites his tongue, he does not become angry at his teeth. An elbow is not jealous of a knee, because they are part of the same body. Similarly, *gedolei Yisrael* are able to feel the bond between them and their fellow Jews so strongly that they find no room for anger, jealousy, or hatred toward others.

This idea was articulated beautifully by Rabbi Shimshon Pincus. He was once counseling a couple experiencing trouble with *shalom bayis* (marital harmony). The wife told Rabbi Pincus that one of the issues that bothered her the most was that her husband refused to eat the food she prepared for him. When Rabbi Pincus asked the husband why he refused, he sheepishly explained that he had not taken care of his teeth when he was younger, and he was not able to chew the food. Rabbi Pincus — who was not a man of means by any stretch of the imagination — gave the man money to purchase dentures.

A *talmid* who heard about his rebbi's generosity said, "Rebbi, you barely have enough money for your own family's expenses. How can you pay for someone else's dental work?"

"Let me ask you a question," responded Rabbi Pincus. "If this was my own son, would you wonder why I am paying for his dental work?"

"No," answered the *talmid*.

"What is the difference?" said Rabbi Pincus. "My son, your son, the *Eibishter's* son — it's all the same."

Rabbi Pincus felt that bond of *she'eir basar* with every Jew, and he saw no difference between paying for his own son's dental work or someone else's son's dental work, because we are all sons of the *Ribono shel Olam*.

Occasionally, even we ordinary folk can attain this level. R' Hirsch Pruzansky was a beloved member of the Lakewood community who passed away in an untimely fashion. When R' Hirsch's son was studying at an out-of-town yeshivah, R' Hirsch decided to surprise him with a cheesecake for Shavuos. He told his neighbors whose sons were also studying at that yeshivah that he was intending to make the trip, and that he would be happy to take cheesecakes to their sons as well. Many parents brought packages for their sons, but some, for whatever reason, did not.

On the way to the yeshivah, Mr. Pruzansky stopped at a bakery and purchased cheesecakes for the rest of the boys, so that they too would feel the spirit of Yom Tov. To Mr. Pruzansky, it did not make a difference whether it was his son or someone else's son. All the *bachurim* at the yeshivah were sons of the *Ribono Shel Olam* and deserved care packages.

This concept explains the incredible patience that *gedolim* have for all members of *Klal Yisrael*. A woman once came to Rav Schach and asked him to explain the basic tenets of *emunah* to her. Rav Schach could easily have told her to visit one of hundreds of Bais Yaakov teachers in Bnei Brak, all of whom are capable of teaching *emunah*. But he didn't. He spent 15 minutes explaining *emunah* to her.

The woman left happily, but was back just 15 minutes later with a request. "I am afraid that I will forget what you told me," she said. "Can you please write it down?"

Rav Schach took the pad that she proffered and wrote down all that he had told her.

A few minutes later she knocked on his door yet again. "I can't read the Rosh Yeshivah's handwriting," she complained. Rav Schach took the notebook back and rewrote the illegible sections.

How did Rav Schach have the patience?

Most people would have the patience if it were their own child struggling with this issue. Rav Schach considered all members of *Klal Yisrael* his children, because they are all children of the *Ribono Shel Olam*.

It also explains how *gedolim* were able to dismiss political differences they had with other factions and treat as their own dissenters who were in need of assistance. Rav Yoel Teitelbaum, the Satmar Rebbe, was known for his firm stance regarding Zionism. Yet, when an Israeli sporting a *kippah serugah* — a type of yarmulke worn by religious Zionists — visited him, the Rav graciously welcomed the man into his study. The man explained that his wife was in dire need of surgery, and that he did not have money to cover the operation.

"How much do you need?" asked the Rebbe.

"One thousand dollars," the man answered. This story took place many years ago, and $1,000 was considered a lot of money.

My Son, Your Son ... the Eibishter's Son / 89

The Rebbe reached into his drawer, withdrew $930, and handed it to the man. The Rebbe's *shamash* (attendant) could not contain his curiosity. "If the Rebbe was ready to give the man $930," he asked, "couldn't he give the entire thousand?"

"Had I given the full sum," the Rebbe explained, "the man would have kicked himself, thinking that he should have asked for $2,000. Now he probably thinks that all I had was $930, and that he received all that I could give."

Not only did the Rebbe put the differences between his own beliefs and this man's politics aside and give him the money he needed — he put enough thought into the matter to assist him in a manner that would not leave the man upset at himself. Why? Because this man, along with the rest of *Klal Yisrael*, was a child of Hashem.

The Apter Rav's undying love for his fellow Jews was so exemplary that he became known by the name of his *sefer, Oheiv Yisrael*. Once, when on a train in Europe, he was harassed by members of the *haskalah* (enlightenment). They quickly engaged him in a heated debate, and spoke to him in an extremely derogatory fashion. His adversaries were becoming extremely upset, and even seemed to be on the verge of attacking him physically. One of them reached into his pocket for a cigarette, and the Rebbe immediately offered him a match. "Can I give you a light?" he asked politely.

That simple gesture defused the entire argument. It is hard to attack someone who loves others — who had heaped verbal abuse upon him — so much, that he is still able to offer a light.

This is the same Apter Rav who was famous for his teaching that each *parashah* in the Torah contains a *remez* (allusion) to the mitzvah of *ahavas Yisrael*. "Rebbe," a Chassid once asked, "where is the *remez* in *Parashas Balak*?"

"*Balak*?" the Rebbe responded. "The very name of the *parashah* alludes to *Ahavas Yisrael*! The letters *veiz, lamed,* and *kuf* that make up the name of the *parashah* are an acronym for *ve'ahavta lerei'achah kamocha*."

"But Rebbe," a Chassid protested, "*ve'ahavta* begins with a *vov*, not a *veiz*, and *kamocha* starts with a *kof*, not a *kuf*."

"*Oy*, if you are so punctilious with the letters," replied the Rebbe, "then you will never be an *oheiv Yisrael*."

This sounds like a cute story, but the deeper message that the Rebbe was trying to convey is a very pertinent one. If we want to learn to love our neighbors, and aspire to reach the level of *ahavas Yisrael* that the *gedolim* attained, then we must learn to move beyond the pettiness that makes us pursue issues to the letter of the law. We must learn to overlook small differences between us, and love all Jews just for being themselves, despite all their failings.

Rabbi Aharon Shechter, rosh yeshivah of Yeshivas Rabbeinu Chaim Berlin, was once walking home from shul after Minchah on Shabbos, when he chanced upon a sad scene. Three formerly *frum* boys who had left the fold were loafing on a street corner, smoking. So as not to embarrass them, he walked past them with the group of people who were escorting him. He then detached himself from his entourage half a block later, walked back to the boys, and said, "*Kinderlach! Ich hub eich lieb.* Children, I love you. If you ever want to speak to me about anything, please come to my house. My doors are open for you 24 hours a day."

We can be sure that it pained the venerable rosh yeshivah to see *Yiddishe kinder* desecrating Shabbos, but he realized that what they needed most at that point was not rebuke. They needed to hear that they were loved by someone who knew that they were still children of the *Ribono Shel Olam*, and as such, deserving of his love. Sure enough, within the week one of the boys knocked on his door, and the rosh yeshivah set aside hours upon hours for a son of the *Ribono Shel Olam*.

✌ Sinas Chinam — Is It Really for Nothing?

Our discussion on *ahavas Yisrael* would be incomplete if we did not examine the flipside of the coin: *sinas chinam* (baseless hatred). Each year as Tishah B'Av approaches, we are reminded that the second *Beis HaMikdash* was destroyed because of *sinas chinam*, and that only when we have removed that hatred from our midst will we be redeemed from this *galus*.

I have always been bothered by a question. Does "baseless hatred" really exist? *Baseless*? Have you ever met someone for the first time and decided that you don't like the way he parts his hair, so you are going to hate him? There is always *some* reason for hatred. Why is it called *sinas "chinam"*?

Rav Elyah Lopian was bothered by this question, and found the answer in a minor divergence between a passage that appears in *Talmud Bavli* and a similar one that appears in *Yerushalmi*.

In *Bavli*, the Talmud (*Yoma* 9b) states that the first *Beis HaMikdash* was destroyed because of the sins of adultery, murder, and idolatry, and the second *Beis HaMikdash* was destroyed because of *sinas chinam*. *Yerushalmi* inserts several words. It states that the second *Beis HaMikdash* was destroyed *because the people loved money*, and hated one another with baseless hatred.

The reason why the hatred was considered baseless, deduces Rav Elyah Lopian, is because its roots lay in nothing more than jealousy of one another's money. When hatred is not the result of a person's actions, but due to the fact that he has a nicer house or car, a better job, or more *nachas* from his children, then it is baseless.

It would seem that since the underlying problem of *sinas chinam* was the rampant jealousy that existed among people, we must rectify that trait in order to bring about the Final Redemption. But jealousy is so ingrained in human nature — existing ever since Kayin killed Hevel — that it seems almost impossible to eradicate. How can we become less jealous of others?

Let us examine the roots of jealousy.

Are we jealous of things that we do not need? Is anyone jealous of someone else's eyeglass prescription? Certainly not! We understand that the lenses in our glasses are custom-made for us and our neighbor's lenses for them.

Part of the solution to jealousy, then, is to become greater *ma'aminim* (believers) in Hashem, and specifically, in *hashgachah pratis*, Hashem's personal supervision and intervention in the lives of each and every Jew. We must begin to believe — really believe, not just pay lip service to the concept — that Hashem provides each one of us with exactly what we need in order to complete our mission here on earth. If there are things that we do not have, it is because we do not need them.

Once we come to the realization that Hashem is intimately involved in our lives, and has put us onto earth with as much or as little as we require to accomplish our specific life's mission, there is no longer a need to feel jealous. Just as we are not jealous of our neighbor's lenses, we would not be jealous of his Lexus. If he has a Lexus, it is because he needs it. If you don't have one, it is because you don't need it — much as you don't need his lenses.

If my hypothesis is correct, it may provide the answer to a difficult question about the *gemara* we mentioned earlier, regarding the convert who came to Hillel and asked to be taught the entire Torah, and was told that the entire Torah was an elucidation of the mitzvah of *ve'ahavta lerei'acha kamocha*. It would seem that that maxim might apply to the entire realm of mitzvos *bein adam l'chaveiro* — the mitzvos that pertain to interpersonal relationships. What happened to the mitzvos of *bein adam laMakom* — the mitzvos that pertain to man's relationship with God? What does *ahavas Yisrael* have to do with the mitzvos of *succah*, matzah, *shaatnez*, and all others that do not seem to affect our friends and neighbors? Didn't Hillel overlook half the Torah?

The Talmud states that various leaders of *Klal Yisrael* found their generations incapable of focusing on all the mitzvos in the Torah at once, and they sought to narrow our focus to a number of mitzvos that would keep us on the proper path. The last one to limit the list was the prophet Chabakkuk, who states that we can focus on but one mitzvah: "*Tzaddik be'emunaso yichyeh* — the righteous person shall live through his faith" (*Chabakkuk* 2:4). This teaches that *emunah* is the key to all mitzvos of the Torah.

According to our hypothesis that *ahavas Yisrael* and *emunah* in Hashem are intertwined, the mitzvah of *ahavas Yisrael* is indeed a key to the entire Torah. You can love your fellow Jew only if you believe that Hashem has given you all that you need, and you feel no jealousy toward your neighbor. Since Chabakkuk states that *emunah* is the key to the entire Torah, the *emunah* you develop in your effort to come to love your fellow Jews will result in your excelling in all other mitzvos as well.

"Nothing" — A Matter of Relativity

Rabbi Mattisyahu Salomon once offered a parable explaining why *sinas chinam*, no matter how well-founded it seems, is still considered baseless.

I must stress that this is just a parable — it never happened and, I hope, it never will.

The parable is that an elementary-school student was once playing with a pencil in class, flipping it from side to side and twirling it around his finger. Every few seconds the pencil dropped to the floor, and the child picked it up and continued to play with it. The constant motion and the noise made when the pencil fell were extremely disconcerting, and after a few minutes the teacher instructed the boy to stop.

The boy didn't listen. He just kept on twirling and dropping, twirling and dropping. A few minutes later the teacher repeated — this time more emphatically — *"Stop playing with the pencil."*

The boy ignored his teacher once again and continued to twirl and drop, twirl and drop. Finally, acting out of frustration, the teacher picked up an object that was on his desk, strode over to the child, and hit him sharply on the hand. Either the object was too sharp, or the blow was too strong — the result was that the child's finger was severed from his hand. The boy was rushed to the hospital, but nothing could be done to repair the damage.

The next day the parents came to the school to speak to the teacher. "How could you do such a thing?" they asked. "You injured our child for absolutely no reason."

"It was not for no reason," the teacher responded. "He was playing with a pencil!"

"Are you insane?" the parents asked incredulously. "Do you really think that playing with a pencil is a reason to maim a child for life?"

Who is right? Technically, the teacher is correct. It wasn't for *nothing*. But we all know that he is definitely wrong. Playing with a pencil is not enough of a reason to disfigure a child for life. And when the reason is inadequate, it is not a reason at all. It is *chinam*.

When *Chazal* teach that the *Beis HaMikdash* was destroyed because of *sinas chinam*, they do not mean to say that there was *no* reason for the hatred. There is always *some* reason. But in relation to the damage that *sinah* causes, all reasons fall by the wayside and become meaningless.

◆§ The Panacea

At Minchah on Shabbos we pray "*Atah echad, veShimcha echad* — You, Hashem, are One, and Your Name is One. *Umi ke'amcha Yisrael goy echad ba'aretz* — And who is like Your nation, Yisrael, one [unified] nation on earth."

Klal Yisrael is built on unity. We do not have a *Beis HaMikdash* because we can have one only when all systems are running properly; when we are divided, the system is down.

Knowing that the price of our hatred — while we may think that we have justifiable reasons to hate — is that we cannot have a *Beis HaMikdash*, then we must ask: Is it really worthwhile? Is anything worth the price of not having a *Beis HaMikdash*, not having Mashiach? Remember, if it is not worth the price, then it is like a child losing a finger for twirling a pencil.

The next time you find yourself upset over something, and you want to begin to hate, ask yourself whether it is worthwhile. Are you willing to postpone the arrival of Mashiach and the ingathering of the exiles because you didn't get *maftir*? Are you willing to live with all the problems that beset *Klal Yisrael* — the dreadful illnesses, the heartrending accidents, the children leaving the fold, the terrorist attacks in Eretz Yisrael, problems with *parnassah* and *shidduchim* — are you willing to continue living with all of these problems because you were invited only to the *chuppah*?

We all know that it is not worthwhile. We may have seemingly valid reasons for disliking others, but in the final analysis, the reasons are as valid as severing a finger of a child who was twirling a pencil. *Klal Yisrael* is suffering too much. We need the cure to all of our troubles, and we can attain it only through unity.

Let's put our pettiness aside, put our ill feelings aside, and bury our jealousy, so that we can come together as a *goy echad*, one nation, and merit to greet Mashiach Tzidkeinu.

When Winning Isn't Everything

Several years ago, Orthodox Jewry worldwide, and one community in particular, was sent reeling by a shocking revelation. Without dwelling on the specifics, thousands upon thousands of Jews found that they had unknowingly been eating *neveilos* and *treifos* (nonkosher poultry) for quite a while.

A close friend of mine, Rabbi Moshe Brown, asked me a question about that incident, based on a story that is told regarding the Beis HaLevi, the patriarch of the Soloveitchik/Brisk dynasty.

Once, shortly before Yom Kippur, the Beis HaLevi had to be on the road, and he paid a brief visit to Rav Yehoshua Leib Diskin. Cognizant of the fact that the Beis HaLevi would be traveling on Erev Yom Kippur when it is a mitzvah to eat, Rav Yehoshua Leib prepared a parcel of food for the rest of the Beis HaLevi's trip. A portion of chicken was one of the foods placed in the parcel.

When the Beis HaLevi was en-route, he opened the package and was disconcerted to discover that a putrid odor was emanating from the piece of chicken. The smell was so intense that the Beis HaLevi couldn't bring himself to taste the chicken. Surmising that the smell might be a result of the chicken having been tightly wrapped for some time, he set it aside to see if the smell would dissipate. A while later, he once again tried to eat the chicken, but the stench was still overwhelming.

A non-Jewish passenger who was traveling with the Beis HaLevi beheld a peculiar scene: the rabbi picked up the chicken, and then put it down — once, twice, three times; finally, after the third time, the man's curiosity got the better of him and he asked, "What's the problem?"

"This chicken smells bad," the Beis HaLevi explained.

"Let me smell it," said the non-Jew. He took a good whiff and said, "There's nothing wrong with this chicken. You can eat it."

The Beis HaLevi picked it up once more and tried to put it in his mouth, but he just couldn't.

"If you don't want to eat the chicken," said the non-Jew, "can I have it?"

The Beis HaLevi gladly parted with the offensive item and the non-Jew devoured it with gusto and experienced no ill effects.

When the Beis HaLevi arrived at his destination, a telegram from Rav Yehoshua Leib Diskin was waiting for him. He wrote that a *she'eilah* (halachic query) had been found in another part of the chicken and had rendered the entire fowl *tereifah*.

Rav Yehoshua Leib had commented to his students that in truth there was no need to send the telegram, because he was certain that the Beis HaLevi could not have eaten a *tereifah* piece of chicken. The Talmud comments in several places (*Yevamos* 99b et al.) that Hashem does not allow even the animals of righteous people to err inadvertently, let alone the righteous people themselves. Rav Yehoshua Leib concluded, therefore, that sending the telegram was *lifnim mishuras hadin* — going beyond the requirement of the law — since there was no way that Hashem would have allowed the Beis HaLevi to eat *tereifah*.

Obviously, noted Rabbi Brown, we are no longer on the level

of *tzidkus* (piety) or Torah knowledge of the Beis HaLevi. It is still shocking, however, that the cumulative *zechusim* (merits) of the thousands of members of that community and the tens of thousands of others who partook of this supplier's poultry at *simchos* should not have equaled the merits of the Beis HaLevi. How could it be that all of the Torah study, *chesed*, and mitzvos of that community did not protect it from inadvertently partaking of *tereifah* food?

A similar question was posed by one *adam gadol* to another. He wondered what had happened to the *zechus hatzibbur*, the merit of the community. Why hadn't the *zechus hatzibbur* prevented this debacle?

This second *adam gadol* — who, I should say, is universally accepted — responded with an acerbic comment, which I will preface by noting that he was not referring to the specific community primarily affected by this story, but to the entire Jewish community at large. "The *zechus hatzibbur* did not help in this case," he said, "because we are not a *tzibbur*."

A *tzibbur* is a group of individuals who *join together* for the common good. Nowadays, with *machlokes* (disputes), divisiveness, and contention in *Klal Yisrael*, a community is nothing other than a mélange of myriads of individuals. The hundreds of thousands of hours of Torah study and mitzvos produced by a community may add up in volume to those of the Beis HaLevi, but the lack of unity results in their forfeiting the cumulative effect, and there is no *zechus hatzibbur*.

What this *adam gadol* conveyed may be implicit in *Talmud Yerushalmi* (*Pe'ah* 1:1). The *Yerushalmi* states that the people in the days of Dovid HaMelech were all righteous, but when they went out to battle they were defeated because there were gossipers among them who caused divisiveness. In contrast, the generation of the exceedingly wicked King Achav consisted primarily of idol worshipers, but they succeeded in battle because there was peace among them. That is the power of a *tzibbur*, a community united.

In *Meshech Chochmah* (*Shemos* 14:29), Rav Meir Simchah of Dvinsk explains that Hashem can dwell in a community of idol worshipers, as the verse states in reference to the *Ohel Moed*, "*Hashochein itam besoch tum'osam* — that dwells with them amid their contamination" (*Vayikra* 16:16).

But when *Klal Yisrael* is beset by divisiveness and infighting, Hashem lets things take their course, and the outcome is disastrous.

≈§ The Dangers of Machlokes

In recent years, it seems that we hear of more and more tragedies. Be they fatal car accidents, young people stricken with cancer, or a host of other misfortunes, we are left shaking our heads and wondering why there is so much pain in the world. Why do children go to bed at night without being able to say good-night to a parent who is in the hospital? Why must young women cry themselves to sleep after being widowed? We must ask ourselves what Hashem wants from us.

It is not for us ordinary folk to attribute certain tragic circumstances to specific *aveiros* (sins). It can be extremely detrimental for us to attempt to determine this on our own. But it is the purview and job of an *adam gadol* to guide *Klal Yisrael* as to where their focus should be in order to extricate themselves from this tragic cycle. I want to share a portion of a letter from Rav Aharon Leib Shteinman, one of the great Torah leaders of our generation:

> To our great sorrow, we have seen a marked increase in the number of widows and orphans. Who knows if this is not because of *machlokes*? Although it is possible that the one who suffers the punishment was not involved personally in the *machlokes*, we know that all Jews are *areivim* [guarantors] one for another.

Rav Shteinman is suggesting that the lack of harmony among us is the cause of tragedy upon tragedy. The *Shechinah* is not protecting us, and we are subject to the vagaries of nature and statistics.

Rav Shteinman is not the first to make this connection. There is a frightening *Arizal* on the verse, "*Ki yipalei mimcha davar lamishpat, bein dam ledam, bein din ledin, u'vein nega lanega, divrei rivos bish'arecha* — If a matter of judgment is hidden from you, between blood and blood, between law and law, between plague and plague — matters of dispute in your cities" (*Devarim* 17:8).

The *Arizal* (*Likkutei Torah, Parashas Shoftim*) writes that while the *Beis HaMikdash* was being destroyed and Jerusalem was being pillaged, the angels in heaven asked Hashem, "You wrote in Your Torah that the blood of an animal or bird that is slaughtered must be covered. How is it that human blood now flows freely in Jerusalem? You wrote in Your Torah that one may not slaughter a cow and its calf on the same day, yet now parents are being murdered along with their children. You wrote in Your Torah that one must remove the possessions from his house prior to the Kohen proclaiming that the house is impure [so as not to render those possessions valueless]. How is it that the *Beis HaMikdash* is being burned with all of its precious vessels inside?"

Hashem answered, "Is there peace in the world? Where there is no peace, nothing can exist."

The *Arizal* suggests that this is alluded to in the aforementioned verse. *Ki yipalei mimchah davar lamishpat* — when you cannot understand the judgment, *bein dam ledam* — what is the difference between the blood of an animal, which must be covered, and the human blood that is allowed to run freely in the streets; *bein din ledin* — between the halachah that precludes us from slaughtering a cow and its offspring on the same day, and the reality of parents and children being murdered at the same time; *u'vein nega lanega* — between the laws of *negaim*, in which possessions are removed from a house to forestall rendering them tainted, and the destruction of the *Beis HaMikdash* with all its vessels in it, without regard for their value.

The answer is right there in the verse, concludes the *Arizal*: *Divrei rivos bish'arecha* — it is because there are disputes in your cities.

In our times, too, we ask these painful questions. There are tragedies that are incomprehensible. How is it that terrorist attacks leave blood dripping on the walls and streets of Yerushalayim? How is it that car accidents take parents and their children on the same day? How is it that shuls worldwide are being firebombed and the beautiful shuls of Gush Katif were razed to the ground with everything in them?

Divrei rivos bish'arecha.

Machlokes is extremely dangerous.

Rav Shteinman made another point in that letter. He writes that *machlokes* is more severe than most people are aware of. There is a *lav* (prohibition) of *velo yihiyeh cheKorach vecha'adaso* — not to be like Korach and his assembly (*Bamidbar* 17:5). According to several *Rishonim*, this verse contains a Torah-level prohibition not to engage in *machlokes*.

Yet somehow, notes Rav Shteinman, we have developed tolerance toward this transgression.

Imagine if I would tell you that there is a rav, rosh yeshivah, or rebbi who is a great *tzaddik*. He is extremely righteous in all areas, I say, except one: he doesn't keep *Yom Tov Sheni shel Galuyos* (the Second Day of Tom Tov in the Diaspora).

"*Tzaddik*?" you will undoubtedly exclaim. "How can you call him a *tzaddik*? If he doesn't keep *Yom Tov Sheni*, he's not even *frum*!"

You would react similarly if I told you that he has but one idiosyncrasy: he likes eating *neveilos*.

And if I mentioned that his vice is an occasional break-in to his neighbor's house to help himself to some cash, you would be *appalled*.

Yet if I tell you that a person is extremely righteous, except that he is embroiled in *machlokes*, you may have no problem with it. It seems unimportant in the grand scheme of things. Why is that so?

The answer, I think, is that there are no exceptions to the halachos of *Yom Tov Sheni*, *neveilah*, or stealing. But there are certain circumstances in which *machlokes* is not only permissible, but it is a mitzvah. A *machlokes* undertaken *l'sheim Shamayim* (for the sake of Heaven) is one that you *must* wage.

And herein lies the rub. Every single person who becomes embroiled in a *machlokes* is somehow convinced that his *machlokes* is *l'sheim Shamayim*. If you pay attention to the claims of the two parties in any *machlokes*, you will hear that no one ever has an ulterior motive. Whether it is an intra-family *machlokes*, with each side claiming that they are fulfilling their father's true will; a *machlokes* in the direction a yeshivah should take, in which the Torah's honor is at stake; or even a *machlokes* in a business, with each partner claiming that the other party is a swindler who should be exposed before he can rip off others — in the minds of those involved, it is invariably a *machlokes l'sheim Shamayim*. They are either standing up for their father's honor, the Torah's honor, or the honor of upright businessmen who are in danger of being swindled. Never for themselves.

And when you fight God's war, you never give up.

The Mishnah in *Avos* (5:17) states, "Any dispute that is *l'sheim Shamayim* will endure." The simple understanding of these words is that a dispute that is undertaken with proper intentions will have lasting results.

Rabbi Yisrael Salanter offers an additional elucidation of these words: When a person thinks he is waging war for the sake of Heaven, you can be sure that *the battle* will last forever, because he *knows* he is doing God's work. He has been Heaven-sent to rid the community of the rav against whom he has initiated a war, because the rav is bad for the community. *It's a mitzvah* to get rid of his son's rebbi, because he is turning kids off. He *must* expose the organization that is defrauding people of their *tzedakah* funds. And in a holy war, all weapons can — even *must* — be used. *Lashon hara* (slander) becomes permissible. *Malbin pnei chaveiro* (embarrassing another person) is permissible. We're dealing with a holy cause!

Let me break the news: The overwhelming majority of people in our generation are not equipped to fight a battle *l'sheim Shamayim*. As noble as a *machlokes* is when it begins, most humans are not capable of sticking to the issue. A *machlokes* will inevitably become personal, and once it is personal, the *l'sheim Shamayim* aspect falls by the wayside.

◈§ The Need to Win

Perhaps the reason why a *machlokes* will usually become personal is because buried deep in our hearts, there is a burning desire to "win."

Evidence of this burning desire struck me while pondering a strange phenomenon. Why is it, I wondered, that spectator sports have become a universal obsession? People all over the world — Asians, Americans, Europeans, Africans — have become obsessed with sports. It bridges not only cultural gaps, but societal gaps as well. A wealthy entrepreneur will root for his team as fanatically as the struggling day-worker he employs.

I once spent several days in Europe while the World Cup was in contention. You would have thought that you were in a ghost town. You could walk through the streets for hours without seeing a soul.

Why are people so crazy about sports? Why are people in one city in a good mood on a Monday because their football team won the day before? Why do New York City residents across the board go into mourning when the Giants lose four football games in a row?

What is behind this obsession?

It seems to stem from the desire to win. In the words of Vince Lombardi, "Winning is not everything, it is the *only* thing." And if we can't win ourselves, then we will do so by living our lives vicariously through the players on the football field or the basketball court.

When it comes to *machlokes*, the desire to win is so overwhelming that it trumps everything else. Nothing else matters. The true will of a parent, the proper path in Torah, the need for unity — will all fade, and all that will remain will be the need to win, win, win.

It is said that a butcher in Brisk once slaughtered a cow and found something wrong with one of its organs. He took it to Rav Simchah Zelig Rieger, the *Av Beis Din* (head of the rabbinical court) of Brisk, who ruled that the animal was *tereifah*. Despite the significant financial loss he had just incurred, the butcher walked out of *beis din* without uttering a word of complaint.

Several weeks later, the butcher was involved in a *din Torah* with another Jew. Rav Simchah Zelig ruled against the butcher, and this necessitated his paying an inconsequential sum of money to his adversary. When the rav issued his ruling, the butcher went ballistic. He lost his temper and began to denigrate Rav Simchah Zelig, to the stunned silence of all present.

Rav Simchah Zelig was dumbfounded. The cow that he had ruled to be *tereifah* was probably worth ten times the amount he required the butcher to pay in this *din Torah*, and the butcher had had no problem accepting that ruling. Why did he react so outrageously in this instance? The question bothered him so much that he decided to present it to Rav Chaim Soloveitchik.

"In the case of the cow," explained Rav Chaim, "it is not as though the butcher 'lost' and the cow 'won.' The cow did not win. But in this case, the money is not the issue — the issue is that he lost, and his adversary won. That is why he exploded."

The Chofetz Chaim told of someone involved in a dispute with the mayor of his town. One thing led to another, and before long the argument had escalated into a full-blown battle, and this person swore that he would do everything he could to get rid of the mayor.

One day, he came up with a plan. "I will go to the secular government," he told his wife, "and tell them that the mayor manipulated the draft and exempted from service the children of parents who could afford to bribe him."

"*Na'ar vus du bist*," his wife cried. "You fool! Our son was one of those whom the mayor exempted from the draft. If you inform on the mayor, the government will launch an investigation, our son might be sent to the army, and we might even end up in jail on bribery charges!"

"*I DON'T CARE!*" the man retorted. "Let our son go to the army and we'll go to jail, *but he has to lose.*"

Sound ridiculous — perhaps even impossible — but that is the nature of *machlokes*. It makes people irrational.

The Chasam Sofer, who fought many a battle in his day, had a pithy, profound saying that he would tell his students: "*Miyamai lo nitzachti adam, ve'al yedei zeh lo nitzchuni adam* — In my life, I never defeated anyone, and because of that, no one ever defeated me."

The Chasam Sofer fought his battles, but he never left the other party feeling that he had been defeated. That is why no one ever felt that he had to defeat the Chasam Sofer.

✌︎ Anticipating Machlokes

All this talk about *machlokes* may seem superfluous to you. You may have never been involved in a *machlokes*, and you don't foresee any reason why that should change.

You must realize, however, that there will possibly come a day when you, too, could find yourself in a situation that might lead to *machlokes*. It might be with members of your family, with your neighbors, or with congregants in your shul, but that day may come.

In fact, as if a Messenger on High wanted to demonstrate to me how prevalent *machlokes* is, on the very day that I was preparing this *derashah* regarding *machlokes*, a letter arrived in the mail from someone in Brooklyn who recently had a dispute with his landlord.

It seems that the landlord had given the tenant permission to leave his *succah* standing at the side of the house. One fine day the tenant noticed that his *succah* was missing. The landlord, annoyed at the sight of the *succah* protruding from the side of his house, had thrown it out.

Now what would you do if you were that tenant?

The nature of the world is that opportunities for *machlokes* spring up, seemingly out of nowhere, and it is up to us to decide how to react. And if we leave the decision for the moment when we are already emotionally involved, we will invariably end up becoming embroiled in the *machlokes*.

Therefore, strange as this may sound, I suggest that we should take the time to prepare for the eventuality of *machlokes*. We already prepare for every other eventuality. When the Powerball lottery reaches $300 million, and you buy a ticket, you start planning what you are going to do with the money, right? You wonder whether you should take the winnings in one lump sum or as an annuity. Then you start to wonder whether you should run the *tzedakah* foundation on your own or hire a professional to run it for you. A few days later, the lottery is drawn, not one of your numbers matches, and you revert to regular life. But you prepared yourself … just in case.

There are people who cannot carry a tune in a bucket, and yet they prepare for the occasion when they will be asked to *daven Ne'ilah* for the *amud*. They will rarely be asked to *daven* a weekday Minchah, but they prepare for *Ne'ilah*. Is it so strange, then, that I say that we should be prepared for *machlokes*, which is so prevalent?

We must take time to decide *now*, before we begin to get hot under the collar, what we will do when the opportunity for *machlokes* arises.

I have a few suggestions for possible courses of action:

❧ #1: Be Mevateir

Everyone should resolve to be *mevateir*, to forgo and to forgive. *Even if you are right*, it is worthwhile to forgo in order to avoid the terrible fate that *machlokes* brings in its wake.

Each morning in *Pesukei D'Zimrah*, we say the verse, "*Hasam gevuleich shalom, cheilev chittim yasbi'eich*" (*Tehillim* 147:14). The simple translation of these words is, "It is He Who makes your borders peaceful, and with the cream of the wheat He sates you."

The Chasam Sofer (*Bereishis* 44:28) offers a homiletic interpretation. He writes that in the mind of each and every person, there are certain red lines that he will never cross. A wise person decides that his red line is *shalom*, peace. He decides that no matter what, he will never cross the line and become mired in a *machlokes*. The reward for someone who is *sam gevuleich shalom*, who makes peace the border over which he will never step foot, says the Chasam Sofer, is *cheilev chittim yasbi'eich* — Hashem provides him with the "cream of the crop."

It is important to bear in mind this lesson from the Chasam Sofer, especially when a *machlokes* arises over money. In order to avoid the *machlokes*, you may have to forgo, or even pay, tens of thousands of dollars. But in the long run, the cream of Hashem's crop is worth far more.

A wealthy Jew once told me that a battle had erupted in a family in his community. Before long, it had spread to the shuls in which they *davened*, and then to the entire community. It was an ugly situation. This Jew found out that a check for $25,000 to one of the parties could lay the issue to rest. Able to part with that kind of money without risking his financial standing, he wrote out a check and the issue was resolved.

One day later, this man received a call from his lawyer. In an unrelated incident, he had been involved in a lawsuit; the lawyer had called to inform him that the judge had thrown the case out of court. Had the case been accepted, the potential loss would have been much more than $25,000. *Cheilev chittim yasbi'eich*.

Now, I am not suggesting that you will always see results as quickly as this man did, but you can be sure that you will not lose for avoiding *machlokes*.

So my first piece of advice is to walk away. You're right, you're wrong, it doesn't matter. Walk away.

There was a fellow who for many years would *daven* Shacharis for the *amud* in Ponevezh on the *Yamim Nora'im*. As he aged, his voice became weaker, and he could no longer be heard over the din of the air-conditioners. So the air-conditioning was shut off during Shacharis. I don't know whether you have ever been in Bnei Brak in September, but it is very difficult to be without air-conditioning even if you are not packed into a *beis midrash* with 1300 other people. After a year or two, several *mispallelim* came to the *gabbaim* and complained that they simply could not hold out. The heat was unbearable. The *gabbaim* approached the *baal tefillah*, but he was not prepared to give up his *chazakah*. They went to Rav Shach and asked him what should be done.

Rav Shach listened to both sides, and then he said, "*Ihr zent beider gerecht* — You are both in the right. The *baal tefillah* should be able to keep his *chazakah*, and the *tzibbur* should not have to suffer from the heat."

Then the elderly rosh yeshivah turned to the *baal tefillah* and said, "In my entire life, I have never seen a person who was *mevateir* and lost out."

I heard this story from a reliable source, who reported that this *baal tefillah* had five children, each of whom had a difficult problem. Within one year of heeding Rav Shach's advice, all five difficulties were resolved. You don't lose from being *mevateir*.

~§ #2: Settle It the Proper Way

If, for some reason, you cannot be *mevateir*, make sure to resolve your *machlokes* in the proper manner. Take your case through the channels meant for Torah Jews — whether by going to *beis din* or through arbitration by a rav who is trusted by both sides.

Beis din was created for the purpose of settling such disputes, and that is where Jews who believe they have been wronged should turn to reconcile their differences. Simmering in hatred of your adversary and refusing to speak to him will not accomplish anything positive for you. It destroys not only you, but the entire *tzibbur*.

~§ #3: Just STOP!!!

Finally, if you haven't been *mevateir*, and you haven't gone to *beis din* or to a rav, and you opted not to speak to your neighbor for 10 years or to your sister in 15 years, or you haven't been attending family *simchos* because you hate your brother-in-law, then I have three words for you. *Just stop it*. That's it. Bury the hatchet. *Machlokes must* be eradicated before it eats us up.

If you think the scenarios I just portrayed are fictional, it is my sad duty to inform you that they are true. Any rav can tell you about families that have been destroyed because of *machlokes*. They can relate stories of siblings who haven't spoken for years, of parents who haven't been in contact with their children in decades, mostly due to some obscure disagreement that no one remembers. Admittedly, it is hard to put aside your differences when you don't even know how they began. But do it anyway.

#4: Don't Let It Happen

If the maxim "An ounce of prevention is worth a pound of cure" is true for all other areas in life, it is all the more so for *machlokes*. When you are thrust into a situation in which someone says or does something to you, and every fiber of your existence wants to react, the most difficult — but also the best — advice I can offer is: don't say *anything*.

The Talmud (*Chullin* 89a) states, "*Ein ha'olam miskayeim elah bishvil mi sheboleim es atzmo bish'as merivah* — the world exists only in the merit of one who controls himself during a dispute." The Talmud is not engaging in hyperbole. *The world exists* in the merit of those who can shut their mouths and thereby prevent *machlokes* from festering. If it is difficult to grasp how powerful this merit is, let me illustrate with the following story.

A childless couple had spent 20 years exploring every fertility treatment known to medical science, as well as traveling from *gadol* to *gadol*, from Rebbe to Rebbe, and from *mekubal* to *mekubal*, for *berachos*, advice, and *segulos* — but to no avail.

After all those years, they poured out their sad saga before Rav Chaim Kanievski. He listened intently, and then said, "*Nu, efsher dus iz der gezeirah* — maybe this is the decree."

Upon hearing these words, the couple began to cry bitterly. Rav Chaim saw how devastated they were, and then said, "Perhaps there is one thing that will work. Get a *berachah* from someone who is *boleim es atzmo bish'as merivah* — a person who remains silent during times of dispute."

The couple left his house, bewildered. What do you do with such an *eitzah*? Where do you find a person who has kept quiet when challenged? In the Yellow Pages under *boleim*? It seemed hopeless.

Fast-forward four years. An unrelated family wanted to buy a *dirah* in Bnei Brak. After searching for quite some time, they finally found an apartment that met all of their criteria. One day, as they were in the *dirah* finalizing the arrangement with the seller, a woman with a wild look in her eyes walked in and said, "Don't you *dare* buy this apartment. I live nearby, and the seller built an addition to his apartment without my permission, and it damaged my apartment. I have a halachic claim against him, and I will continue to pursue that claim against anyone who buys the apartment. *Keep your hands off!*"

The potential buyers were in a quandary. On the one hand, the apartment was perfect, and the seller insisted that the woman had no valid claim. On the other hand, the woman's ominous threat rang in their ears.

They sought the advice of Rav Nissim Karelitz, perhaps the greatest halachic authority in Bnei Brak. They told him the story, and he immediately responded, "I know this woman. I presided over this *din Torah*, and this woman does not have a halachic leg to stand on. The seller did not do anything wrong. Buy the apartment and don't give it a second thought."

The couple bought the apartment and moved in several months later. As the new people on the block, they wanted to meet their neighbors and make friends. They were very pleased, therefore, when, several days later, they received an invitation to a neighbor's bar mitzvah.

They arrived at the bar mitzvah and the wife began to socialize and introduce herself to her new neighbors. Suddenly, who should walk into the women's section but the woman who had warned them not to buy the apartment! She made a beeline for the table where the wife was trying to make a good impression on her new neighbors. "I told you not to buy that apartment," she shouted. "You are the same sort of *ganev* [thief] as the seller ...."

She continued to rant and rave for a few minutes, and the woman under attack was aghast. She was about to shout back that Rav Nissim Karelitz had told her that this disturbed person was wrong, when she suddenly felt a hand on her shoulder. She looked up and saw a middle-aged woman with a pleading look in her eyes. "*Don't say anything,*" the woman begged. "*Please! Just keep quiet.*"

Hard as it was, the woman kept quiet. Then this middle-aged woman asked her, "Now, right now, please give me a *berachah* that I should have a child."

This is not a fairy tale. The woman who was *boleim es atzmah bish'as merivah* gave her a *berachah*, and one year later, after 25 years of marriage, that childless couple was blessed with a baby.

Such is the power of a person who is prepared to avoid *machlokes* at all costs.

It's Never Too Late
for Teshuvah

Paint Your Masterpiece

In many communities, it is customary to auction off the *aliyos* for the *Yamim Noraim* (High Holy Days). It is considered a great merit to receive an *aliyah* during the *Yamim Noraim,* and people vie for the privilege. The third *aliyah* at Minchah of Yom Kippur, which is also the last *aliyah* of the *Yamim Noraim,* is called *Maftir Yonah,* and often carries the highest price tag. There is a belief that purchasing *Maftir Yonah* is a *segulah* for wealth.

I researched the source of this *segulah,* and it may disappoint some people to know that the source seems spurious. But while a financial windfall from *Maftir Yonah* is doubtful, the spiritual windfall that we can reap is a certainty. Even a simple understanding of *Yonah* provides us with powerful lessons, but the Gaon of Vilna's elucidation is particularly compelling. Drawing from Midrashim and *Zohar,* the Vilna Gaon asserts that when *Yonah* is understood allegorically, it contains a message that can change our outlook on life.

✍ The Second Calling

The first verse of *Yonah* reads as follows: *"Vayehi devar Hashem el Yonah ben Amittai leimor* — And the word of Hashem came to Yonah, the son of Amittai, saying."

The Vilna Gaon begins his elucidation by stating that the story of Yonah is a metaphor for the sojourn of the human soul on earth. The word *Yonah* is a metaphor for the *neshamah* (soul). *Amittai*, which comprises the same letters as *Amiti* (the True One), is a reference to Hashem, Who is the essence of Truth. The soul of every single person on earth is the offspring of Hashem. Thus, the first verse is read as follows: "The word of Hashem came to the soul, offspring of the True One."

What does Hashem tell the soul? *"Kum lech el Nineveh, ha'ir hagedolah* — Arise, go to Nineveh, the great city," which represents the vast and beautiful universe we inhabit. *"Ukrah alehah* — and call out to it." Hashem sends our souls down with a *keriah*, a calling. We were sent to make an impact on this world.

Upon its descent, however, the soul finds a beautiful and alluring world waiting for it: *"Vayeired Yaffo* — he went down to Yaffo." *Yaffo* comes from the word *yafeh*, beautiful. *"Vayimtzah aniyah* — he found a ship," a reference to the physical body. *"Ba'ah Tarshish* — bound for Tarshish." Throughout *Tanach*, Tarshish is a city noted for its abundance of gold, silver, and great riches.

Yonah, the soul, comes into a human body, which carries the soul as cargo, into an alluring world replete with temptation. And the soul is distracted. Before long, it becomes so engrossed in the allurements of the mundane world that it forgets its mission here on earth. Then there comes a fateful moment toward the end of life, when a great storm lashes the "ship." The human body becomes sick and frail. The soul suddenly realizes that it has ignored its mission, and that it must now suffer the physical pains of illness. Finally, the soul, Yonah, finds itself inside a great whale — the grave — and it is filled with overwhelming anguish for having failed to fulfill its mission in life. But Yonah is given a second chance. The soul is sent down again, and it is told, *"Kum lech el Nineveh, ha'ir hagedolah* — go back to the world, *ukrah eilehah es hakriah asher anochi doveir eilecha* — and this time I expect you to deliver the message and fulfill the mission on which I sent you."

The Vilna Gaon is referring to a concept called *gilgul neshamos* (reincarnation of souls). It is a mystical concept, and I must admit that I am somewhat out of my element when it comes to Kabbalah. On a basic level, however, it means that most — if not *all* — of us have been to this world at least once before. One of the primary lessons we can draw from *Sefer Yonah* is that we are each sent on a mission, and if we fail to complete it, we will be forced to return to this world a second, third, or fourth time, until we get it right.

Let us look at a poignant example of how *gilgulim* complete the mission they were sent to fulfill.

The Talmud (*Gittin* 58a) records a story that is so painful that we read it on Tishah B'Av as a reminder of the bitter fate that befell our nation in the era of the destruction of the *Beis HaMikdash*.

A son and a daughter of Rabbi Yishmael ben Elisha, the Kohen Gadol, were sold as slaves to two different masters. The two masters met, and each bragged about the slaves he had purchased. "I bought a slave whose beauty is beyond compare," said one.

"And I bought a maidservant whose beauty is beyond compare," said the other.

The two came up with a great idea. "Let's marry them to each other, and split the children between us."

They acted on their plan without hesitation. They placed the slaves into a pitch-black room, figuring that the results would be inevitable. They were wrong. The son sat in one corner of the room crying all night. "How can I, a Kohen, son of Kohanim Gedolim, marry a maidservant?" he thought.

His sister placed herself in the opposite corner and began to weep. "How can I, a Kohenes, daughter of Kohanim Gedolim, be married to a slave?" she reflected.

When the first rays of dawn peeked through the windows in the room, they recognized each other and began to weep. They cried with such fervor that their souls departed.

What a horrible fate. How could such a terrible thing have happened to Rabbi Yishmael ben Elisha and his pure children?

We have no way of explaining such tragic events. But Rav Menachem Azaryah (Rama) of Pano reveals an astounding fact. The souls of those two children were the souls of Amnon and Tamar, the children of King David. When they were in the world the first time, they were left in a room by themselves and Amnon violated Tamar. They had been returned to this world to repair the harm that was done to their souls. Returning as brother and sister, being placed into a similar scenario — and remaining pure — effected this rectification. As soon as they completed that mission, their souls departed for a better place.

Upon hearing *Maftir Yonah* on previous Yom Kippurs, we have thought about *teshuvah* and about the futility of evading Hashem's command. The Vilna Gaon teaches us that Yonah is about us. It is a reminder that we have a calling, and if we fail to fulfill it, we will have to repeat the journey.

৺৵ The Mission: Your Achilles' Heel

The Talmud (*Eruvin* 13b) records a fundamental debate that raged for 2½ years between the academies of Hillel and of Shammai. One academy felt that humans would have been better off had they never been born, and the other felt that humans are better off having been born. They finally arrived at the conclusion that we would have been better off *not* being born, but now that we are here we should "examine our ways."

This passage is extremely difficult to understand. Hashem is the essence of good, and He created humans with the express intention of benefiting them. Could the Talmud be suggesting that Hashem was actually doing a disservice to the billions of people born since Creation? And why did the academies conclude that now that we were born we should "examine our ways"? They should have said that now that we were born we should do mitzvos and fulfill Hashem's will.

The Vilna Gaon suggests that the academies agreed that it is to one's benefit to be born once. Hashem has certainly provided us with a great opportunity by placing us into this world. The point of their dispute was whether it is worthwhile to keep returning to the world as reincarnated souls. One academy felt that it is worthwhile for a soul to keep coming back, because on each trip to the world it has additional opportunities to serve Hashem. The other academy felt that it is best for the soul to fulfill its mission on its first sojourn and not come back as a *gilgul*.

They came to the conclusion that the soul is better off completing its mission the first time, but in a case when it did not, it had better "examine its ways." The choice of words here answers a fundamental question regarding *gilgulim*: how is one supposed to know what it is that his soul failed to accomplish in its previous trip to earth, so that he can repair that failing?

God does not leave us in a quandary, says the Vilna Gaon. We can determine what it is that we were sent to repair by *examining our ways*. By discovering our weaknesses, the issues that keep cropping up in our lives, we determine what flaws we must correct.

If it seems that Hashem is constantly sending you a specific *nisayon* (challenge) or you have a proclivity toward one particular sin over all others, it is clear that your soul was exposed to that sin in its previous *gilgul*. If you have an issue with money, for instance — you can't seem to get enough of it, or you simply cannot give it away — then money may be the reason for your reincarnation. You are here to learn to curb your obsession with money.

Interestingly, we typically overlook the main purpose of our mission. What is the usual attitude of a person who excels in most areas of life, but fails in one? Sometime we see a wonderful person who gives *tzedakah*, does *chesed*, and studies Torah, but he has one Achilles' heel: his temper. Generally, such an individual will "write off" the trait in which he fails. "No one is perfect," he reasons. "I'm good enough as is."

The Vilna Gaon teaches us that this is a fatal error. That write-off may very well be the precise area that the soul was sent to repair, and it can spend 70 or 80 years on earth without making any progress.

We each have our "write-offs." We have issues that seem impossible to deal with, and we simply record them as losses on our personal balance sheets. In-laws, for instance. Most people can deal with everything and everyone, other than their mother-in-law. Maybe the reason you are here is because you failed in your relationship with your mother-in-law — or brother- or sister-in-law — in your previous *gilgul*. Don't dismiss anything as unimportant or resign yourself to a certain situation as being irreparable, or you may be slated for a return visit yet again.

≈§ What Is Your Mission Statement?

Corporate America has coined the term, "mission statement." Every self-respecting company — from Fortune 500 firms to organizations that consist of a boss, a secretary, and a one-line telephone — has a mission statement. On Yom Kippur, as we read the story of *Yonah*, we should remember that we, too, must have mission statements. We were sent to the *ir hagedolah* on a mission, and if we don't fulfill that mission, we will repeatedly suffer the anguish that a *neshamah* feels when it must descend to earth yet again.

I once received a letter from a woman, a stranger. She wrote that she had always been in the best of health, when suddenly she began to suffer with cardiac problems. She was hospitalized for a week — a week that she now considers a watershed event in her life.

"When a heart goes on the blink and all cardiac activity is thrown out of whack," she wrote, "it makes you realize how tenuous one's grip on life really is. The weirdest thing was that I was not afraid to die, but I had this terrible feeling of, 'not *yet*. I'm not ready — *yet*. I didn't do enough — *yet*.'"

The feeling this woman experienced was her soul communing with her. Her soul realized that it was still far from fulfilling its mission in life. It was not ready to go back to the world of *neshamos* — yet.

At one point during President George W. Bush's second term in office, he named Joshua Bolton as White House Chief of Staff. On his first day on the job, Mr. Bolton distributed "countdown clocks" to the staff. These clocks were set to keep track of how many days, hours, and minutes remained to President Bush's term in office. One day, for instance, the clock showed that there were 873 days, 23 hours, and 21 minutes left to the Bush presidency. His message to the staff was that they still had enough time to achieve their goals, but not enough time that they could afford to waste any of their precious minutes.

Imagine if we were to have countdown clocks that would show how much time we have left on earth. How different our lives would be! How careful we would be to uncover the issues that plague us, and repair them without delay.

But *avodas Hashem* is typically divided between *sur mei'ra* (turning away from evil), and *asei tov* (doing good), and our mission in life cannot be limited to repairing blemishes from previous *gilgulim*. The verse in *Yonah* refers to the soul's descent to earth as a *keriah*, a calling. A calling is generally understood as a positive aspect of *avodah*. In order to fulfill our mission, we must determine what our calling in life is, and work on actualizing our potential as well. How does one determine his calling?

When it was time to construct the *Mishkan* (Tabernacle), Hashem told Moshe, "*Re'eh karasi besheim Betzalel ben Uri ben Chur* — See, I *have called* by name: Betzalel, son of Uri, son of Chur" (*Shemos* 31:2). This connotes that Hashem had already called Betzalel by name. When we read the *parshiyos* leading to this verse, however, we do not find any reference to this calling. To what is Hashem referring?

Betzalel's calling was inborn, explains Rav Moshe Feinstein. The next verse reads, "*Va'amalei oso ruach Elokim, bechachmah, u'visvunah, u'vedaas, u'vechol melachah* — And I have filled him with a Godly spirit, with wisdom, insight, and knowledge, and with every craft." Hashem does not fill a person with such talents for naught. Being provided with talents of this magnitude is the most clear-cut calling of all.

Just as the Vilna Gaon taught us that we must examine our weaknesses to determine the negative trait that we must focus on repairing, so too must we find the specific strengths and talents that Hashem has granted us, for they are the keys to determining, and fulfilling, our calling.

The idea of a calling generally resonates with the young and idealistic, who actively seek to make their mark on the world, if not to leave it a changed place. As we grow older, however, we settle into the quotidian routine of paying the mortgage, raising the kids, and making a living, and we lose sight of our mission. We become drugged by the narcotic called complacency. We make a decision — consciously or subconsciously — to become what the Chazon Ish dubs, *"beinonim beshitah."* We make it our policy to be mediocre.

Human nature idealizes the status quo. Our worldview falls in line with the folk-saying, "The worm that infests the horseradish thinks that it is the sweetest place in the world." We say, "This is who I am. I'm 40 years old, this is the way I have always been, and this is the way I will always be. Let me be."

We adore complacency. The Torah abhors complacency.

In *Parashas Mishpatim*, we read about an *eved Ivri* (Jewish slave) who chooses to stay with his master beyond the six-year limit set by the Torah. The procedure in such instances is to have the master bring the slave to *beis din*, stand him at the doorpost, and pierce a hole in his ear. He then becomes an indentured slave, and may remain in his master's service until *Yovel* (the Jubilee year). *Rashi* explains that an ear that heard Hashem say, "*Ki Li Yisrael avadim* — for the Children of Israel are servants to Me," and chooses to remain a servant to one of Hashem's servants, deserves to be pierced.

Admittedly, it is not particularly pleasant to be the one whose ear is pierced. But what did the master do wrong? Why does he have to go through the gruesome experience of placing a person against the doorpost and pounding an awl through his ear? Why is he at fault for being such a great guy that the slave doesn't want to leave?

Rav Yisrael Salanter explains that the master has sinned by fostering an atmosphere of complacency. The atmosphere in his home must be one that can lead a person to say, "I like being a servant. I don't mind my lowly status. I don't have to strive for better."

There is an illness called "early retirement" that infects the mind-set of many Americans. Western society has created a goal of retiring by age 55, or, in the worst-case scenario, age 65. Everyone looks forward to the day that he will be able to retire.

Retire, and do *what*? What are you going to do with your 20 or 30 remaining years — drive your wife crazy? Read the newspaper four times a day? Play golf over and over and over again? You are never going to be declared the world's best golfer!

Early retirement is not a Torah *hashkafah*. If the *Ribono Shel Olam* granted us 70 or 80 years, we are supposed to use them productively.

Rav Samson Raphael Hirsch points out that the very first rite performed by Kohanim in the *Beis HaMikdash* each morning was *terumas hadeshen* — taking of the ashes. A Kohen would remove a portion of the ashes generated by the offerings that had been burnt on the Altar during the previous day and night, and place these ashes next to the Altar. The purpose of this rite, says Rav Hirsch, is to remind the Kohanim not to fall into the trap of smug self-satisfaction. Yesterday may have been a very successful day in the *Beis HaMikdash*. But that was yesterday. Now it is time to start anew. As his melodious words intone: "The thought of what has already been accomplished can be the death of that which still must be accomplished. Woe unto him who, in smug self-complacency, thinks that he can rest on his laurels."

If we are to complete our mission in this trip to the physical world, we must avoid being lulled into the complacency of daily routine. We must discern our calling and actively strive to fulfill it.

❧ Painting a Masterpiece

There is a famous American fictional short story about a girl who contracts pneumonia during the winter in the pre-antibiotic era, when the body's immune system was the only way to fight illnesses. This girl, bedridden for day after day, loses her will to live. When the ivy vine outside the girl's window begins to shed its leaves, she resolves that when the last leaf falls, she too will die.

The doctor tells her roommate that without the will to live, the girl will certainly die.

Try as she might, the roommate could not shake her friend from the notion she had concocted. The roommate unburdens herself to an old curmudgeon, a failed artist who lives in the building's basement and dreams of one day creating a masterpiece. When she mentions her friend's belief that her life will slip away with the last leaf, the man becomes angry at the thought of a life wasted because of fevered imaginings.

That night, there is a terrible storm. As they listen to the wind howling outside, the roommate worries that when the sun rises the next morning, no leaves will remain on that vine.

Her prediction almost comes true. When she lifts the shade the next morning, only one leaf remains clinging to the vine. To the patient's surprise, however, that leaf holds onto the vine no matter how fiercely the wind blows. The girl decides that if that last leaf could survive all the wind and rain, then she could also hold onto life. She begins to eat again, and she makes a complete recovery.

The doctor tells the roommate that the grumpy old artist has contracted pneumonia and has been taken to the hospital, but there is little hope that he will survive. After his death, the roommate tells her friend the secret. On that fateful, stormy night, that old man had climbed up to the girl's window and painted his best work ever. He painted an ivy vine with one leaf — one last leaf that never fell.

In the process, he contracted the illness that would take his life, but not before he had managed to paint his masterpiece.

We must all do the same. We must find the talents that the *Ribono Shel Olam* has given us and paint a masterpiece. We must do something memorable, something of which we can be proud. If you'll pardon the morbid tone, we must do something that I call, "*Matzeivah* material" — something significant enough to have engraved on our tombstones after 120 years.

~§ Matzeivah Material

It is interesting to hear what great people considered meaningful enough to engrave on their tombstones. If I were to ask people what they consider Rabbi Akiva Eiger's greatest achievement, some would point to his *teshuvos* (responsa), and others would argue that his novellae are more important. Both of these works are analyzed and scrutinized by those engaged in intense Torah study until this very day. But Rabbi Akiva Eiger had his own opinion of what his masterpiece was. He left a will stating that he wanted the following words etched on his tombstone: "*Saval yissurim kol yamav* — He suffered all of his days." Rabbi Akiva Eiger considered his illness, with which he had been afflicted from the age of 16, to be his masterpiece.

No one in our day and age will ever write anything that will come close to the Talmudic works of Rabbi Akiva Eiger. But many of us suffer from pain and illness. The way we handle that test can be our masterpiece.

The intense need to paint a masterpiece may be what motivates ordinary individuals to do extraordinary things. It might explain the life's work of one Rabbi Yosef Eckstein. Born in Budapest in 1944, Reb Yosef was one of few Jewish infants to survive the Holocaust. His father would often tell him, "You survived for a purpose." Rabbi Eckstein could not have known what that purpose was until he married and fathered four children, all of whom died at a young age of Tay-Sachs disease. His plight inspired him to create an organization called *Dor Yesharim*. Using genetic testing, *Dor Yesharim* discreetly informs people who are considering marrying each other whether they are at risk of bearing children with Tay-Sachs. Rabbi Eckstein's mission statement is, "I will do everything in my power — *al pi Torah* (according to Torah Law) — to make sure that there never again will be such a grieving father and mother."

Not many of us are inspired or tragically compelled to create such masterpieces. But we don't have to. Our daily lives can become masterpieces.

When my father died several decades ago, I was wisely advised to write an elaborate text for his tombstone. My children hardly knew my father, and my grandchildren were born after his passing. One day, however, they will visit his grave, and they will learn from the inscription on his tombstone who he was and what he stood for.

One of the lines I wrote was, "*Asah kibbud eim atarah l'rosho* — he made honoring his mother his crowning glory." My father brought his mother over to the United States from Germany in 1940, and my grandmother lived with us for nearly 20 years. She never learned English, and she never adapted to this country. At times, this presented a great challenge — for my father, and especially for my mother.

When my grandmother became too ill to be cared for at home, my parents had little choice but to put her into a nursing home. My father went to visit her *every night*, except Friday night. He took me with him many times. It got to a stage where she did not know who he was, and she certainly had no idea who I was. But he nevertheless continued to visit her every night.

Many of us are privileged to have aging parents. It's not easy to have them in our homes. It is arguably the most difficult mitzvah. But it can be your masterpiece.

Your masterpiece can be raising your children. It won't be a headline-grabbing masterpiece. It will require painstaking work that will take decades to complete. But we all know families that motivate us to say, "Boy, those parents did some job raising their children." That is a masterpiece.

A while back, my grandchildren attended a Jewish carnival. One of the entertainers was the "Ballooner Rebbe." At the carnival, he handed out balloons he had twisted into magnificent shapes. He could not accommodate all the children present, but my granddaughters happened to receive balloons. As they were leaving the carnival, they saw a woman standing near the door with her very young son. The woman was severely handicapped. With her crutches, she had been unable to navigate the crowd and reach the Ballooner Rebbe. My granddaughters whispered something to my daughter, who answered, "Of course." They then approached the woman and asked whether they could give their balloons to her son.

"Thank you very much," the woman answered, "but I want my little boy to learn that you cannot get everything in life." That woman is painting a masterpiece. Rather than succumbing to the temptation of bringing her son temporary happiness, she set a broader, tougher goal of helping him to succeed in life.

A masterpiece can be a specific mitzvah that you perform to perfection. The Rambam writes (*Peirush HaMishnayos, Makkos* 3:16) that if you perform one mitzvah without ulterior motives and out of love, you merit a portion in the World to Come.

Make a mitzvah your masterpiece. Imagine how wonderful it would be to be remembered for *bikur cholim* (visiting the sick), for knowing Mishnayos by heart, or for your devotion to your *kevias itim laTorah* (consistently setting aside time for Torah study).

A fellow who recently began to paint a masterpiece wrote to me for advice. His friend had fallen ill, and as a merit for his friend's recovery, he asked a group of friends to accept upon themselves not to talk during *davening* (prayer). He printed up contracts as follows:

> I, _____, accept, *bli neder*, not to talk during *davening* from date X to date Y. In this *zechus*, may *ploni* have a complete recovery, among all other sick members of *Klal Yisrael*.

"I have been doing this for nearly two months now," the fellow writes. "When I *daven* in shul and I hear people talking — and I was one of them a short time ago — it sounds so strange. How can anyone talk while *davening* to Hashem?

"What would be the best way to get *Klal Yisrael* to stop talking in shul?" he asks.

He undertook a monumental project, but it could be his masterpiece. He began with his shul, and could then move on to his neighborhood, and then his city, and so on. He could paint one of the most beautiful masterpieces of all time.

Paint Your Masterpiece / 127

I know a woman who tries to prepare almost everything for Shabbos by Thursday night, thus easing the tension that is prevalent in many Jewish homes on Friday afternoon. One custom she began years ago was to set the Shabbos table on Thursday night, so that the spirit of Shabbos begins to permeate her home from then. What a beautiful impression it makes to enter her home on Thursday night and find the table set for Shabbos! This is a masterpiece that many of us can paint, if we only take the time and make the effort to plan and prioritize.

✑ Don't Rob Your Soul

Have you ever noticed how the atmosphere in shul seems to change when we are about to begin *Ne'ilah*? From my vantage point in the *beis hamidrash* in Yeshivas Ner Yisrael, I see many signs that the end is near. The sun turns orange and begins to set, bathing the entire area in a golden glow. If I turn to the side of the *beis midrash*, I see the once sun-bathed lawn engulfed in shade. Somehow, the temperature seems to rise before *Ne'ilah*. I look at the *bachurim*, and I note the intensity on their faces, the recognition that this is the last chance for this Yom Kippur.

Sadly, our minds sometimes wander to what we are going to eat. We forget that *Ne'ilah*, which lasts — at most — two hours, is the most precious time of the year. If we were controlled by our *sechel* (intellect), we would want *Ne'ilah* to go on forever. We are so elevated, so pure, so close to Hashem at that point, that it is truly a shame to let it go.

As we *daven* the final *Shemoneh Esrei*, we can hear the heartrending sobs of people begging Hashem for mercy one last time. Suddenly, as the whole *tefillah* — and with it the whole Yom Kippur, and perhaps the entire Elul and *Aseres Yemei Teshuvah* — comes to a head, we utter words that just don't seem appropriate to the moment.

"*Vatiten lanu Hashem Elokeinu es Yom HaKippurim hazeh* — Hashem, You gave us *Yom Kippur*. *Keitz u'selichah lechol chatoseinu* — as an end to all of our sins." We are at the apex of *teshuvah*, of *mechilah, selichah,* and *kapparah*.

For what? *"Lemaan nechdal mei'oshek yadeinu* — So that we should refrain from stealing."

So that we should refrani from WHAT? Stealing? That is our problem? For 23 hours we have been *davening* and reciting *al cheit* after *al cheit*, *ashamnu* after *ashamnu*. And when we finally reach the crescendo, we say that it all comes down to theft? When is the last time you stole or shoplifted? Is Yom Kippur really all about, *"Lemaan nechdal mei'oshek yadeinu?"* Are we no more than petty thieves?

Yes, answers the Gerrer Rebbe. If we don't use the talents, the strength, and the gifts that Hashem grants us for the correct purposes, then we are thieves. If we don't complete our mission on earth, we are guilty of theft. We are robbing our souls.

On Yom Kippur, we must remember why we are here. We must learn to envision our souls hearing the call that we read in the *haftarah* just before *Ne'ilah*: *Vayehi devar Hashem el Yonah ben Amittai leimor*. These are the words of the *Ribono Shel Olam* — not only to Yonah who lived thousands of years ago — but as the Vilna Gaon explains, to the soul of each one of us, offspring of Hashem. *Kum, lech el Nineveh, ha'ir hagedolah* — go down to the world, the vast universe. *Ukrah eilehah es hakriah asher anochi doveir eilecha*. We have a mission. We may have failed before in that mission. And if we fail again, our souls will have to suffer the anguish of coming down again and again.

At *Ne'ilah*, we beg Hashem to help us avoid robbing our souls. In the aftermath of Yom Kippur, we must work on achieving that goal. We must make sure to rectify all that we damaged during our previous incarnations. We must complete our mission so that our *neshamos* can go back to their rightful place, under the *Kisei HaKavod* (Throne of Glory), where they can bask in the ultimate warmth of Hashem's Presence, and enjoy the greatest of all pleasures.

Baby Steps Toward Hashem

One of the greatest *baalei teshuvah* of all time — although most people don't know him in this capacity — was King Menasheh ben Chizkiyahu, one of the Judean kings. In case the details of the *Tanach* you studied in high school have faded, let me refresh your memory: Menasheh spent the first 22 years of his reign attempting to eradicate any vestiges of Torah study or observance from *Klal Yisrael*. Rather than compose my own list of his atrocities, I'll quote directly from *Divrei HaYamim*:

> Menasheh was 12 years old when he became king, and he reigned for 55 years in Jerusalem. He did what was evil in the eyes of Hashem, like the abominations of the nations that Hashem had driven out before the Children of Israel. He rebuilt the high places that his father Chizkiyahu had broken down. He erected altars to Baal. He made *asheirah*-trees, and he bowed down to the entire host of the heaven and worshiped them. He built altars in the Temple of Hashem — about

which Hashem had said, "My Name shall be in Jerusalem forever." He built altars to the entire host of the heaven in the two Courtyards of the Temple of Hashem. He passed his sons through the fire in the valley of Ben-Hinnom, practiced astrology, read omens, did sorcery, performed necromancy and conjured up spirits; *he was profuse in doing what was evil in the eyes of Hashem, to anger Him.* He placed the graven image that he had made in the Temple of God ...

(*II Divrei HaYamim* 33:1-7)

Menasheh led Judah and the inhabitants of Jerusalem astray to do more evil than the nations that Hashem had destroyed from before the Children of Israel.

(Ibid. 33:9)

Obviously, we are not talking about a run-of-the-mill evildoer. We are talking about one of the worst *reshaim* in history. Aside from the "impressive" list of sins listed in *Divrei HaYamim, Chazal* teach that when Menasheh had completed his monstrous rampage, all Torah knowledge had been eradicated from *Klal Yisrael.*

Considering Menasheh's resume, it is not surprising that one opinion in the Mishnah (*Sanhedrin* 90a) lists Menasheh as one of the kings who, along with the incredibly wicked kings Yeravam ben Nevat and Achav, will not merit a portion in the World to Come.

There is another opinion in that Mishnah, however. Rabbi Yehudah says that Menashe *does* have a portion in the World to Come. The Talmud (Ibid. 103a) explains that one who says that Menasheh does not have a portion in the World to Come discourages future sinners from attempting to do *teshuvah.*

Since Rabbi Yehudah maintains that Menasheh's *teshuvah* was accepted, I think that we can use his repentance as a prototype to study, especially since many of the lessons we can reap from it will be highly encouraging to those of us who feel that *teshuvah* is beyond us.

৩ A Dubious Repentance

Let us continue to read from *Divrei HaYamim* to ascertain how Menasheh did *teshuvah*.

> Hashem spoke to Menasheh and his people, but they did not listen. So Hashem brought against them the officers of the king of Assyria's army, and they captured Menasheh with hunting hooks, bound him in chains, and led him off to Babylonia. *But in his distress*, he beseeched Hashem, His God, and he humbled himself greatly before the God of his fathers. He prayed to Him, and He was entreated by him and heard his supplication, and He returned him to Jerusalem, to his kingship. Then Menasheh realizes that Hashem is God.
>
> (II Divrei HaYamim 33:10-13)

We see that Menasheh did *teshuvah* under duress, but we cannot conceive of how desperate he was at the time.

A Midrash (*Pirkei D'Rabbi Eliezer* 42) fills in some details. It relates that when they brought Menasheh to Babylonia, they placed him into a large vessel and lit a fire under it. Being cooked alive sounds pretty bad, but apparently it was not enough to get Menasheh to do *teshuvah* just yet. The Midrash states that Menasheh began to cry out to each and every one of the idols and false gods that he had worshiped until then. Only after he had exhausted every single name in his "god rolodex" did he finally turn to Hashem and begin to pray. Even then, however, he did not do so in the most respectful manner.

"I'll give God a chance," he said. "Let's see whether He'll create one of His great miracles as He did for my fathers." Another Midrash (*Rus Rabbah* 5:6) contains an even more negative narrative; it states that Menasheh said, "I will cry out. If God answers me, fine, if not, then I'll know that they are all the same."

It is obvious that Menasheh's *teshuvah* was no more than an act of desperation. He was "giving God a shot." It reminds me of a story that a chaplain in Baltimore told me. A woman once called to him and said that her husband was terminally ill, and the doctors did not expect him to survive for more than a few more days, which, indeed turned out to be the case. She wanted a rabbi to come to the hospital and speak to her husband at his bedside. The chaplain drove to the hospital, and the woman met him outside her husband's room and said, "Rabbi, I am just warning you that my husband is an atheist. It is best to avoid any mention of God."

The chaplain went in and spoke to the man for a few minutes without any mention of God. Just as he was about to leave, the man said, "Rabbi, aren't you going to say some kind of prayer with me?"

"Your wife told me that you don't believe in God," the chaplain reminded him.

"Yes," concurred the man, "but *just in case* ..."

This man hedged his ultimate bet, just as Menasheh did.

If you and I were judges in the Heavenly Court, we probably would have denied Menasheh the right to repent. Indeed, the Midrash (Ibid.) states that when Menasheh called out to Hashem so insincerely, the *malachei hashareis* (ministering angels) "closed the windows of heaven" and attempted to block his *teshuvah* from rising to the heavens. "Master of the World," they pleaded, "this person placed a graven image in the Temple — how can You accept his repentance?"

Not only did Hashem accept Menasheh's *teshuvah*, but He dug a tunnel under the Heavenly Throne, a place where no angel has jurisdiction, in order to enable Menasheh's *teshuvah* to reach Him.

Hashem is the Final Judge, and He chose to overrule the objections of the Heavenly Court, thereby turning Menasheh into a role model of *teshuvah* for those who would otherwise lose hope.

There are several important lessons that we can extract from Menasheh's repentance:

Lesson #1: Teshuvah under duress is accepted

Teshuvah under pain, or with a gun to one's head, or in a vessel of boiling water, or lying in a hospital bed hooked up to machinery — are all acceptable forms of *teshuvah*.

In the courtroom of the human mind, this is surprising. Imagine someone coming to apologize for offending you, and then you notice that there is a person behind him holding a gun to his back, forcing him to apologize. You would conclude that in no way is this a real apology.

The concept of *teshuvah* under duress being accepted is so novel, in fact, that no less a personage than Adam HaRishon was certain that it was invalid.

After Kayin murdered his brother Hevel, Hashem reprimanded him, and he confessed his guilt and begged for forgiveness. The Midrash (*Bereishis Rabbah* 22:13) relates that Adam HaRishon asked Kayin what happened while he was being judged, and Kayin answered, "I did *teshuvah*, and Hashem accepted it."

Adam HaRishon clapped his hands to his face in shock and said, "Such is the power of *teshuvah*? I did not know!"

Rav Tzadok HaKohen of Lublin (*Pri Tzaddik, Vayeilech/Shuvah* 13) notes that it is clear that Adam HaRishon knew that *teshuvah* existed, but that he was surprised by how powerful *teshuvah* is. Why?

Adam knew that there was *teshuvah mei'ahavah* — repentance that one undertakes out of love of Hashem. When a person feels that he has hurt someone whom he loves, his *teshuvah* is sincere. Adam also knew that there was such a thing as *teshuvah mei'yirah* — repentance undertaken out of fear of Hashem. Although less sincere, it still causes the wrongdoer to humble himself before Hashem. But *teshuvah* under *duress*? Why should that work?

Indeed, it is a great *chiddush* (a novel concept). But if Menasheh's inferior, flawed *teshuvah* was accepted after all the damage he had done, then we can be *sure* that our *teshuvah* will be accepted no matter the circumstances that force us to repent.

Why, indeed, did Hashem accept such a flawed repentance? Perhaps in order to teach us another lesson in *teshuvah*.

⋲§ Lesson #2: Hashem eagerly awaits your teshuvah

The Talmud tells us that Hashem chose to accept Menasheh's *teshuvah* in order to leave the door open for future *baalei teshuvah*. There would come a time when people would feel so far gone, so distant, that they would assume that there would be no hope for them to return to Hashem. Menasheh set a precedent for all future generations. Menasheh's story teaches us that even the worst of the worst can repent. If one who served every single idol available and attempted to eradicate all vestiges of Torah from *Klal Yisrael* could repent, then I'm sure that we can too, no matter how bad we consider ourselves. Why? Because Hashem really and truly wants us to return.

Have you ever noticed that all of the *berachos* in *Shemoneh Esrei* end by defining Hashem as One Who can provide the specific form of salvation that we seek: He is the *Chonein Hada'as* — the Gracious Giver of knowledge; the *Rofeh Cholei Amo Yisrael* — the Healer of the sick of His nation, Israel; *Bonei Yerushalayim* — the Builder of Jerusalem. Only one *berachah* stands out. We ask Hashem, "*Hashiveinu Avinu l'Sorasecha* — Bring us back, our Father, to Your Torah, and bring us near, our King, to Your service, and influence us to return in perfect repentance before You. Blessed are You, Hashem, *Who desires repentance*."

Why is this *berachah* different from all the rest?

The answer is simple. Hashem can do everything for you. He can give you knowledge, He can heal you, He can build Jerusalem — all without your input. *But He cannot do teshuvah for you.*

There is one thing He does do, however. He profoundly *desires* your *teshuvah*, and eagerly awaits the day when we will choose to return to Him.

This is true for every day of the year. We recite the *berachah* referring to Hashem as a *Rotzeh B'teshuvah* three times each weekday. But this is especially true for *Aseres Yemei Teshuvah*, during which Hashem is particularly close to us, and waits at the proverbial telephone for our call.

The closest example I can give to describe our situation during *Aseres Yemei Teshuvah* is one that is poignant, but apt. Many of us know at least one set of parents who have suffered the horrible fate of having a child leave the fold. This is by far one of the most painful experiences a parent can have. Many of these children have severed all ties with their families, but the parents never give up hope. They wait and wait, certain that one day that child will come back. "*He's turned the corner,*" they think to themselves. "*He's coming home.*" They sit at that phone hoping that it will ring.

If that is true for a set of parents who have human emotions and will still remember their anguish even when the child returns, how much more is it true for Hashem, Who simply wants us to come back to Him, and Who can erase the past. As Rambam puts it, "Yesterday [i.e., prior to doing *teshuvah*], the sinner was hated before Hashem, disgusting, cast away — an abomination. Today, he is beloved, pleasing, held close — a "friend."

Contrast this with human relationships. Let's view a hypothetical case in which there is a business partnership between two people. One of them suddenly loses a bundle of money on the stock market and begins to embezzle cash from the business to cover his losses. The other partner cannot figure out why the business seems to be losing money, until one day the embezzler breaks down and admits that he has been pilfering money from the business. "I was afraid I would lose my house, my family, and my community standing," he says. "I promise you that if it takes me until the day I die, I will pay back every penny I stole."

Even if his partner agrees to stay in business with him, a certain measure of distrust will remain between them. The honest partner will always be looking over the embezzler's shoulder to make sure that he is not filching money from the business.

Let's take the most horrific scenario — may we never know of such a story — of a husband who betrays his wife. Even if his wife takes him back — for the children, for their *shidduchim*, or for whatever other reason — it is extremely difficult to repair the damage.

We human beings do not easily forget being wronged. Hashem is different. "Yesterday [i.e., prior to doing *teshuvah*], the sinner was hated before Hashem, disgusting, cast away — an abomination. Today, he is beloved, pleasing, held close — *a "friend."* A friend, with absolutely no residual negative feelings.

By accepting Menasheh's *teshuvah*, Hashem sent us a message: I am a *Rotzeh B'teshuvah* — I can't do *teshuvah* for you, but do I ever want you back! And when you come back, I will accept you with open arms, and the iniquities of the past will no longer exist.

৺ઙ Lesson #3: Keeping it up

The first two lessons from Menasheh make it easier for us to repent, but the third is a challenge.

Menasheh's *teshuvah* may have started off insincerely, but once it was accepted, he spent the next 33 years — *thirty three years!* — following up on that *teshuvah*. In the words of *Divrei HaYamim*:

> [Menasheh] removed the strange gods and the image from the Temple of Hashem and all the altars he had built on the Mountain of the Temple of Hashem and in Jerusalem, discarding them from outside the city. He rebuilt the Altar of Hashem and slaughtered peace-offerings and thanksgiving-offerings on it, and he commanded Judah to worship Hashem, the God of Israel.
>
> (*II Divrei HaYamim* 33:15-16)

This begs the question: what is the difference between Menasheh and us? If the *teshuvah* of so treacherous a man could last for 33 years, why does it often seem that our *teshuvah* lasts no more than approximately 33 hours? Why do we often find ourselves engaging in the same forms of behavior that we repented for on Yom Kippur, just a few days later? What is Menasheh's secret?

Rav Dessler (*Michtav MeiEliyahu* Vol. IV, p. 79) explains the vast difference between Menasheh and us as being due to "*retzinus —* seriousness."

The Midrash (*Pirkei D'Rabbi Eliezer* 42) states that when Menasheh was in that heated vessel, he said, "*Ekrah l'Elokei avosei* **bechol libi** — I will call to God of my fathers *with all my heart.*" Menasheh's *teshuvah* was not lip-service. It may have been accepted by default, but he promised Hashem that once he would be saved, he would turn his life around, and he meant that sincerely. By doing so, he brought to bear one of the most powerful forces that exist on earth: the irresistible force of the human will. Menasheh, the passionate, focused, and intransigent *rasha*, took the same willpower he used in pursuing evil, and turned it toward the service of Hashem.

I want to tell you something that may come as a surprise. Every single one of us has that same ability. If we can only harness our own willpower, we can move mountains — or at least boulders, as we are about to see.

Shlomo HaMelech wrote, "*Chazisah ish mahir b'melachto —* have you seen a man with alacrity in his work? *Lifnei melachim yisyatzav —* he will stand before kings" (*Mishlei* 22:29).

The Midrash (*Koheles Rabbah* 1:1) states that "a man with alacrity in his work" refers to Rabbi Chanina ben Dosa.

Rabbi Chanina saw the people of his village bringing offerings to Jerusalem, and he said, "Everyone is bringing offerings to Jerusalem, and I am not?" Immediately, he went into the forest and found an enormous boulder. He sanded it, polished it, engraved it, and then proclaimed, "I will bring this to Jerusalem."

Now, obviously, there is no way that one person can bring a boulder to Jerusalem, so he looked for people to help him. When a group of five people came along, he asked them whether they would be willing to transport his boulder to Jerusalem.

"Pay us 100 gold coins," they said, "and we will take it to Jerusalem." But Rabbi Chanina did not have 100 gold coins. Shortly thereafter, Hashem sent five angels in human form to appear before Rabbi Chanina. Rabbi Chanina asked them to take the boulder to Jerusalem and they agreed to do it for five gold coins, on the condition that Rabbi Chanina would help them carry it.

Rabbi Chanina gladly accepted their offer, and no sooner did they place their hands on that boulder, than they suddenly found themselves in Jerusalem. By the time Rabbi Chanina turned to pay them, they had disappeared. He went to ask the sages in the *Lishkas Hagazis* (a room in the Courtyard of the *Beis HaMikdash* in which the *Sanhedrin* judged the most difficult cases) how to pay the workers who had vanished, and they deduced that the "workers" must have been angels.

What is the significance of this Midrash?

Rabbi Shlomo Freifeld, the legendary rosh yeshivah of Sh'or Yoshuv, explains that this Midrash teaches us the unlimited power of the human will. That boulder was brought to Jerusalem because Rabbi Chanina was so insistent that it get there. Whatever he lacked in brute strength, he made up for with willpower. When one's desire is that strong, Hashem will enable him to move mountains — or, in this case, boulders. If the person can't do it naturally, Hashem may cause a miracle, but where there is absolute will, there will absolutely be a way.

The Talmud (*Temurah* 16a) states that one of the *shoftim* (judges/rulers) of *Klal Yisrael* was named Osniel ben Kenaz; he was also referred to as Yabetz. But, in fact, neither of these is his given name. He was actually named Yehudah achi Shimon. Why, then, is he referred to as Osniel? *She'anao Keil,* because God listened to him. Where do we see that God listened to him? In a verse that states, "Yabetz called out to the God of Israel, saying, 'If You bless me and expand my borders and Your hand is with me, and You keep me from harm, that I not be distressed ...' And God granted him that which he requested" (*I Divrei HaYamim* 4:10).

The Talmud explains Yabetz's words of prayer as follows:

"If you bless me" — in Torah.

"And expand my borders" — that I may have students.

"And Your hand is with me" — may I not forget the Torah that I study.

"And you keep me from harm" — may I have friends like me.

And the clincher: "That I not be distressed" — if You don't grant my request, then I will die of anguish.

What happened? — "And God granted him that which he requested."

Why doesn't this work for the rest of us? We also ask Hashem for help in many areas, even in spiritual matters, and we rarely see our requests being filled to this extent.

The difference between Yabetz and us, says Rav Tzadok HaKohen of Lublin, is that Yabetz said, "If not, I am going to die."

This is what Shlomo HaMelech had in mind when he said "*Chazisa ish mahir b'melachto* — When you see a passionate person, a man on a mission, *lifnei melachim yisyatzav* — you can be sure that he will stand before kings one day."

When I was growing up, I had friends who were not just baseball fans in the colloquial sense, but the sort of baseball *fanatics* for whom the shortened form *fan* was invented. These kids could tell you the batting average of every second baseman in the American league in the month of May. A person who saw them memorizing such a trivial, nonsensical statistic would have thought, "Who cares? Will it make a difference in a year or five years what Nelly Fox batted in 1959? What a waste of time! Nothing will become of a child who spends his time memorizing statistics."

I'll tell you what may become of such children. *Lifnei melachim yisyatzav*. One day, some of them may harness that passion and diligence and use it to memorize *Shas*.

That was Menasheh. He was a *mahir b'melachto* when he was a *rasha*. His wickedness was virtually unmatched. But then he turned around, and *lifnei melachim yisyatzav*. He stood before the King of kings in *teshuvah* for 33 years.

The primary difference between Menasheh and us is that he managed to fire up the power of human will and desire, and ours lies dormant within us.

Baby Steps Toward Hashem

⤳ Make a Down Payment

So how do we awaken the willpower that lies dormant within us? I know of only one method: making *one kabbalah* (resolution) — something taxing, but not overwhelming — and telling yourself, "I will do this, no matter what."

Kabbalos are like exercise. When a person feels that he is starting to develop a midriff bulge and he must exercise to get rid of it, how does he start? He wakes up in the morning and does five sit-ups. You and I know that five sit-ups are not going to get rid of that flab. But a determined person will continue to do five sit-ups for a week or two, then move up to ten, and then to twenty-five, and before long, he or she is back in shape.

Similarly, when you begin to make *kabbalos*, start off small, and build slowly until you become great. Don't try 100 sit-ups the first week. Don't accept upon yourself something that you cannot handle. It may seem noble, but when you drop it a week later, you'll have squandered your impetus to do *teshuvah*. Realize that no matter how miniscule a *kabbalah* seems, it is still effective — as long as you stick to it. *Teshuvah* is not a matter of becoming a *tzaddik* overnight, but of taking baby steps back to Hashem.

But aren't we supposed to be convinced on Yom Kippur that we are going to be perfect from now on? No. Rabbi Yisroel Reisman quotes his rebbi, Rabbi Avrohom Pam, as saying that a *kabbalah* is like a down-payment.

When someone wants to purchase a used car from a private seller, and requests permission to show the car to his mechanic and to his wife — make that, to his wife and to his mechanic — the seller will often agree, but only if the buyer leaves a deposit of, say, $500. If the car is worth $12,000, why does the seller accept a down payment of only $500, a mere pittance when compared to the sale price?

The seller accepts it because that pittance shows that the buyer's intentions are serious.

Until recently, one could purchase a house by putting down 10 percent of the sale price, and taking a mortgage for the remaining balance. Why did the bank accept those terms? Because that 10 percent indicated that the customer was serious.

That is what we show Hashem with our *kabbalos*. We realize that it might take 30 years to complete our *teshuvah*, much as it will to pay off our mortgage, but we tell Hashem, "I know that I owe You a lot more than this, but look, I am serious this time. I am already starting to do *teshuvah*."

A *kabbalah* may seem pitiful when compared to the "outstanding balance," but this system really works.

Several years ago I spent a Shabbos in Omaha, Nebraska. A fellow came over to me and said, "Rabbi, I want to tell you that I keep kosher."

"That's very commendable," I said, unsure of why he was sharing that piece of information with me.

"Do you want to know how I started keeping kosher?" he continued.

In my line of work you're always interested in a good story, so I gladly lent him my ear.

"One Saturday afternoon in September, I drove from Omaha to Lincoln, Nebraska, to pick up my brand-new Cadillac from the dealer. While driving on the highway on the way home, I got hungry, so I stopped at a McDonalds to pick up a cheeseburger. I got back into the car and began to drive again, and I was feeling really great. My son had just graduated from college, here I was in a new Cadillac, and to top it off, the Nebraska Cornhuskers won that day."

(In Nebraska they take their college football very seriously.)

"Then I began to think, 'This isn't right. You are so good to me, God. You gave me all of this. Why do I deserve it?'

"I decided to make a deal with God. It was two weeks to Rosh Hashanah. I decided that for those two weeks — but *only* for those two weeks — I would keep kosher.

"Two weeks later I thought to myself, 'Okay, I kept my end of the deal. Now I can eat nonkosher again.' But then I reconsidered. 'It's not right to eat nonkosher before Yom Kippur,' I decided. 'I'll continue to eat kosher until after Yom Kippur.'"

Mind you, this fellow had no idea that the *Rama* writes that one should eat only *pas Yisrael* during *Aseres Yemei Teshuvah*. But he kept kosher until Yom Kippur. After Yom Kippur he thought about it again, and said, "It's only about ten weeks till Chanukah. But *that's it*."

I'm sure you can fill in the rest of the story.

This man made a *kabbalah*. It was only short term. Then he added a little more time to his initial *kabbalah*, and then a little more, and now he keeps kosher all the time.

Nowadays, Atlanta, Georgia has a Jewish community that boasts all the amenities of a regular *frum* community — a *cheder*, Bais Yaakov, a *kollel*, a *mikveh* — you name it, they have it. But when Rabbi Emanuel Feldman became the rav there in the late 1950s, there was not even one *minyan* of Shabbos-observant Jews. Someone told me that he was in Atlanta for the first Yom Kippur after Rabbi Feldman became the rav. "On that Yom Kippur," he recalled, "Rabbi Feldman got up and said, 'I want everyone in this room to keep *one* thing, for *one* year.'"

If the entire *frum* community in Atlanta was built on baby steps toward Hashem, then we can certainly build our *teshuvah* in that manner.

✺ You Can Do It

Aside from demonstrating to Hashem that you are serious about doing *teshuvah*, a *kabbalah* is a way to prove to yourself that when you set your mind to something, you can do it. The knowledge that you have control over your life is one of the most empowering and exhilarating feelings a person can possess.

Let me share another story about Rabbi Shlomo Freifeld. Approximately four decades ago, a fellow who was virtually uninitiated to the world of the Talmud walked into Sh'or Yoshuv and asked to join the yeshivah. As fate would have it, the yeshivah was studying *Bava Basra*, which happens to be the biggest *mesechta* (tractate) in all of *Shas*. The tome is so large that you can probably get carpal-tunnel syndrome if you hold it for too long. This newcomer came to his room on his very first night there, and told his roommate, "I'm out of here tomorrow. Have you seen the size of that book? There's no way I can learn the whole thing."

The roommate hurried to inform Rabbi Freifeld of the newcomer's decision. Drawing on his wisdom and understanding of the human psyche, Rabbi Freifeld summoned the yeshivah's bookbinder and instructed him to take the very first *daf* of *Bava Basra* and bind it between two covers. "I know that you won't be able to write *Bava Basra* on the spine because it will be so thin, but at least write the letters *beis beis* as an acronym," he concluded.

When the bookbinder came back with his craft project, Rabbi Freifeld summoned the newcomer and said, "This is *your Bava Basra*. You are going to study it with me until you know the *shakla vetarya* [dialogue] of the Gemara backward and forward. When you finish it, I will make a *fleishige siyum* for the entire yeshivah, because you finished *Bava Basra*."

Four decades later, that fellow is still sitting and learning. Rabbi Freifeld showed him that he could do it, if he broke it down into baby steps.

Our *teshuvah* may not be as much of a watershed event as Menasheh's was, but then again, we haven't been attempting to eradicate Torah from *Klal Yisrael*, and we haven't placed idols into the *Beis HaMikdash*. For us, it is not a matter of returning in one fell swoop. It is a matter of taking small, deliberate steps back to Hashem.

Getting Our Priorities Straight

Some years, *rabbanim* have an easy time choosing a topic for a *teshuvah derashah*. There are years in which events that occur right around the *Yamim Noraim* (High Holidays) provide ample material for a *derashah*. A year that comes to mind is 2001, when the 9/11 attacks on the World Trade Center and the Pentagon several days before Rosh Hashanah shocked America and the world into a new reality. My *derashah* that year focused on that event and I'm sure that many other *rabbanim* around the country also took the opportunity to reflect on what the attacks meant to us as *frum* Jews.

If there is one event that dominated the news in 2008, it was the collapse of the sub-prime mortgage sector, and the havoc that it

---

This Teshuvah Derashah was delivered in the year 2008 (5769).

has wreaked on the economy. Even people whose jobs were not directly impacted by the downturn were certainly affected to some degree by the powerful reverberations.

When I first chose this topic when I wrote my *derashah* in August of that year, the next sentence was to have read, "Perhaps no single event symbolizes this cataclysmic event as does the collapse of Bear Stearns."

Just a few weeks later, when I was ready to deliver the *derashah*, that sentence was rendered obsolete by scores of other events that eclipsed the Bear Stearns collapse. I found myself revising my *teshuvah derashah* each time I delivered it. In fact, in the course of just one week, I had to update my list to include the following: the collapse of Lehman Brothers, the buyout of Merrill Lynch in what we would have to describe as a "fire sale," the rescue of AIG, the collapse of Washington Mutual Savings Bank, and several other shocking news items. In a matter of a few weeks, the economic foundation of the United States –- and by default, of the world-at-large — was shaken, and it left the entire nation in a state of uncertainty.

Nevertheless, I would like to return to the collapse of Bear Stearns, because shortly thereafter, one of their *frum* employees delivered a speech entitled, *"From Bear Stearns to Bava Metzia,"* and I would like to discuss some of the thoughts he expressed. As background, it is important to know that Bear Stearns was no run-of-the-mill investment firm, nor was this particular employee a run-of-the-mill broker. Bear Stearns had not suffered a single losing quarter in its 86-year history. Not one. Yet Bear Stearns was in existance one Friday, and by Monday it was gone, bought out by J.P. Morgan for a laughable price. I'll let the employee's resume speak for itself: "I was on Wall Street for 25 years, including 20 years at Bear Stearns. I had some great calls, and made people a lot of money. I was on the institutional investor all-star team for 16 years, and on the Wall Street Journal All-Star team for 9 years."

Upon the failure of Bear Stearns, this man was offered a position at J.P. Morgan, but he decided to take some time off to reassess his life goals. In the speech that he delivered shortly thereafter, he outlined five lessons that he learned from his years on Wall Street and from the demise of his firm. I would like to discuss two of them.

Losing Track of Priorities

In a lesson that he titles, "Every cost has a benefit, and every benefit has a cost," this man says, "Wall Street is a great place to have a career — especially from a financial standpoint. Moreover, there is prestige and power associated with Wall Street. But there is a cost to being on Wall Street, and it probably exists in other high-power positions as well: you lose track of your priorities.

"The Talmud (*Pesachim* 50a; *Bava Basra* 10b) states, '*Olam hafuch ra'isi.*' We will find the next world to be the reverse of this one. This was a difficult passage for me to understand until I left the high-powered world. What we think is important loses its importance. The things I feared losing the most were the small things: the loss of a secretary, the car services waiting at my beck and call. The thing that I gave up most easily was time: time with my family, both quality and quantity time, which I now realize are most valuable."

You are probably wondering what this man's thought has to do with *Yamim Noraim*. The answer lies in the words, "*But there is a cost to being on Wall Street, and it probably exists in other high-power positions as well: you lose track of your priorities.*"

Let me explain.

One of the most unique rites performed on Yom Kippur in the times of the *Beis HaMikdash* was that of the *sa'ir hamishtalei'ach*. In this rite, a he-goat would symbolically bear the sins of all of *Klal Yisrael*, and would be sent to the Judean desert and pushed from a cliff to its death. In fact, the English term *scapegoat* is derived from this rite.

This offering is different from all other *karbanos* brought during the year. There was no *shechitah* (slaughter) and no blood sprinkled on the Altar.

Even stranger, many commentators associate this offering with Eisav. They point out that it is no coincidence that the Torah uses the word *sa'ir* to describe Eisav (*ish sa'ir* — a hairy man).

The *Kli Yakar* (*Vayikra* 16:22) writes that the correlation between Eisav and the *sa'ir* that bears our sins is rooted in the fact that Eisav and his descendants are partially responsible for our sins. In his words, "*Kol mezimasam hu lehachti es Yisrael* — their entire purpose in life is to entice *Klal Yisrael* to sin." Therefore, says the *Kli Yakar*, it is only right that the *sa'ir*, a representation of Eisav, should bear the sins of *Klal Yisrael* that he caused.

I'll deepen the mystery behind the rite of the *sa'ir hamishtalei'ach* a bit further by quoting a statement from *Chazal*. The Torah states that the *sa'ir* is to be sent out to the desert with an *ish iti* — a designated man. *Chazal* state that the *ish iti* was a man who was destined to die within the year.

Why was it important that the man who went with the *sa'ir hamishtalei'ach* be a man who was going to die during that year?

To explain this esoteric concept, I will share some thoughts I heard from Rabbi Mattisyahu Salomon, *mashgiach* of Beth Midrash Govoha in Lakewood.

✑ Judaism: It's Not About Asceticism

In order to understand this subject, we must return to the earliest known conversation between the twin brothers, Yaakov and Eisav. *Tanna D'Vei Eliyahu* (19) relates that while they were in their mother's womb, Yaakov said to Eisav, "There are two worlds, *Olam Hazeh* and *Olam Haba*. *Olam Hazeh* consists of eating, drinking, business dealings, marrying, and having children. *Olam Haba* contains none of these physical pursuits. It is entirely spiritual. Let's make a deal. You take *Olam Hazeh*, and I'll take *Olam Haba*."

Tanna D'Vei Eliyahu states that Eisav accepted the offer, as we can infer from his decision 15 years later to sell his *bechorah* (primogeniture), which was a spiritual entity, for the grand price of a bowl of lentils.

Some 70 or 80 years after the sale of the *bechorah*, Yaakov began his journey back to Eretz Yisrael. He had spent 20 years hiding from his brother Eisav, who wanted to murder Yaakov after he received their father Yitzchak's blessings as part of the *bechorah* package. During his last few years in hiding, Yaakov had become extremely wealthy, and he was traveling with an impressive entourage: four wives, eleven children, servants, camels, donkeys, cattle, and many flocks of sheep and goats.

At the showdown, Eisav, who had not forgiven or forgotten the insult of losing the *berachos,* came to meet Yaakov with intention to murder him. Beholding this spectacular scene, Eisav wondered, "*Mi eileh lach* — who are these to you?" (*Bereishis* 33:5).

Tanna D'Vei Eliyahu explains that Eisav was asking, "Didn't we agree that you would take *Olam Haba,* and *Olam Hazeh* would be mine? What happened to our deal? You are using *Olam Hazeh* as much as I am!"

"These possessions," answered Yaakov, "are not considered use of *Olam Hazeh*. I did not acquire possessions for the sake of having them. They are merely the means with which I will perform my mission here in *Olam Hazeh,* so that I can receive my reward in *Olam Haba*."

In this Midrash, Yaakov Avinu sets forth the Jewish outlook on *Olam Hazeh.* Judaism is not a religion of asceticism. We are not meant to be hermits or to live in monasteries isolated from the world like monks and nuns who are expected to spurn the physical aspects of life. We are to take an active role in perfecting this world, and we are meant to utilize many of the possessions and pleasures that *Olam Hazeh* proffers in order to fulfill our mission. As long as possessions and pleasure do not become ends in and of themselves, but we treat them as the means with which to complete our mission on earth, we are welcome to partake of whatever this world has to offer.

Eisav, on the other hand, espoused the life of Epicureanism, in which money and pleasure are ends in themselves. You pursue pleasure and money to have and enjoy them, and you strive to acquire more and more.

If possessions and pleasure become our life's goal, then we no longer lead the life of Yaakov. We begin to follow in the footsteps of Eisav. Unfortunately, in the course of a lifetime, we occasionally become enthralled with the world of Eisav. We get caught up in the pursuit of pleasure and possessions, and we lose sight of what is *ikkar* (primary), and what is *tafeil* (secondary). The *Kli Yakar* teaches us, on a metaphysical level, that that is exactly Eisav's goal: to lure us into his world of materialism, so that we lose our focus on our mission here on earth.

Let me give you some examples of losing focus.

When our oldest son, Yaakov, experienced his second Chanukah at the ripe old age of 1½, we bought him his first Chanukah present: a truck. As a *kollel* couple, we did not have much money to spend, but we spent 20 hard-earned dollars on that truck. It came in a nice box, which had been gift-wrapped.

On the first night of Chanukah, after lighting the menorah, we gave our Yaakov the box. Yaakov ripped open the wrapping paper, and we opened the box for him and took out the truck. Yaakov excitedly began to play. With the box.

That is what happens to us. We make an *ikkar* into a *tafeil*, and a *tafeil* into an *ikkar*. The issues in life that should become major focal points become minor ones, and vice-versa.

I have a friend in the rabbinate who was counseling a high-powered couple who would remain at work until late at night. Each night, their children, who were cared for by a nanny, would stand at the window and wait for their parents to come home.

The rabbi asked, "Why are you doing this?"

"We are doing it for the good of the children," they responded. "We want to provide them with everything they need in life."

Everything, that is, except for one vital thing: a set of parents.

This couple fell into the trap of making the means into an end.

~§ Mai Ba'is T'fei?

The Torah requires us to redeem firstborn male children in a ceremony called *Pidyon Haben* (redemption of the son). The father of the child hands five silver coins to the Kohen, who then relinquishes his rights to the firstborn child. As part of the ceremony, the Kohen asks the father a question that must be the most rhetorical question ever asked: "*Mai ba'is t'fei* — What do you want more, *liten li bincha bechorcha* — to give me your firstborn son, *oh ba'is lifdoso be'ad chamesh selaim* — or to redeem him for five coins?"

I don't think that in the recorded history of mankind, any father ever answered, "Keep the kid, I'll take the five coins." At least not with a firstborn.

When my rosh yeshivah, Rav Yaakov Yitzchok Ruderman, would be asked to speak at a *Pidyon Haben*, he would say that the question of *mai ba'is t'fei* is not asked of a person only once in his lifetime. Rather, life is a series of questions of *mai ba'is t'fei*. Do you want the life of Yaakov or of Eisav? Are your sights set on a totally physical existence, or do you think about spirituality? It is a question of, "Do you live for *Olam Hazeh* or for *Olam Haba*?"

I know someone who was told that his son was struggling in yeshivah, and needed tutoring. The man said that he could not afford to pay for the tutoring because he had just renovated his house. I also know a successful attorney who took out a second mortgage on his house to pay for tutors for his children. *Mai ba'is t'fei*. Which one is more important?

The city or neighborhood that a person chooses to live in, the shuls in which he *davens*, are also part of the question of *mai ba'is t'fei*.

Following a speech in Great Neck, New York, in which I mentioned this concept, a young Iranian fellow who was completing a residency in internal medicine came over and told me that several days earlier he had been forced to make an important decision. He wanted to do another residency in gastroenterology, but he decided that he would consider working only in a hospital that was in the vicinity of an established Jewish community. If he could not find a hospital that met that requirement, he would remain an internist. His advisor told him, "You cannot limit yourself to a few select cities on the East and West coasts of the United States. Can't you put your religion on hold for three years?"

That was a *mai ba'is t'fei* question, and it is one that is worth not hundreds or thousands of dollars, but potentially millions of dollars that he could make in the course of a career as a gastroenterologist rather than as an internist.

Another example: People add extensions onto their homes.

There is nothing wrong with that. When your family grows, you need more space. The problem is that people generally get caught up in the construction craze, and begin to "upgrade" their plans. Thus you hear the famous words, "Well, once we're doing it, we might as well …" The plans become more and more elaborate, as suddenly someone realizes that, "Granite is so pedestrian. It is so prosaic. Can't we put in something else?"

You see women, accompanied by their mothers, husbands, and decorators, hovering over samples of mosaic bathroom tiles, and notice the anguished looks on their faces. After all, what will happen if they choose a tile that is one shade off?

I'm never sure whether the urgency with which people discuss "window treatments" should evoke laughter or sadness. When I was growing up, we had either curtains, window shades, or Venetian blinds. Window *treatments*? Are the windows sick? Why do they need "treatments"?

I know of a woman who went to an upholsterer to have her dining-room chairs reupholstered. In the process of choosing her fabric, she told the upholsterer that she wasn't sure whether to take a certain fabric; she was nervous that she did not love it. "Lady," the upholsterer responded, *"it's just fabric*. You don't need to love fabric. And material should not make you nervous."

We live in a world of Must Haves. The *Must Have* pocketbook. The *Must Have* pair of shoes. The *Must Have* knapsack — as if it will hold your children's school supplies any better than a different knapsack.

The most egregious example in recent memory of misplaced priorities was a statement a woman made about a Bugaboo. Some of us hicks never even heard of a Bugaboo, but apparently the type of baby carriage called a Bugaboo has become the latest Must Have. I heard a woman say — and I am not making this up — "I think I am going to have another baby, so I can buy a Bugaboo."

We have become such a trivial society. We place so much value on the external trappings — such as the ridiculous requirements people now have when seeking *shidduchim* for their children (See "*Shidduchim*: Ending the Crisis" for a more complete listing.) One woman remarked, for instance, that she would not take another daughter-in-law who was a scraper. "What is a scraper?" you ask. A scraper is a person who scrapes leftover food from the plates while at the dining-room table. No more scrapers in my family. Isn't that trivial? Isn't it silly?

One summer, I traveled to South Africa. On one leg of the trip, I went to Victoria Falls in Zimbabwe. I spent two days in Zimbabwe, and one day in Botswana. In Africa, and especially in Zimbabwe, which is a poverty-stricken country, it is quite common to see women walking for miles while balancing objects on their heads. I saw a woman carrying what must have been a 20-pound bag of oranges on her head.

"That's an amazing feat," I commented to my guide.

"It is a very important skill," he replied. "In fact, there are families that won't take a daughter-in-law into their family unless she can carry something on her head."

I thought, "Wait until this gets back to New York!"

The truth is, however, that Africans have it right. Balancing objects on one's head is a valuable skill in their part of the world — while we are focusing on trivialities such as scrapers vs. non-scrapers.

~§ Eisav's Role; Our Response

The cause of these misplaced priorities is Eisav. As the years go by, we are drawn more and more into Eisav's world, and we lose the battle that began between Yaakov and Eisav. We forget that there is a fundamental difference between Eisav's outlook on this world and ours.

That battle, which began in the womb, came to a head on the fateful night when Yaakov battled Eisav's angel until dawn. Eisav's angel sought to vanquish Yaakov, once and for all, but the Torah states, "*Vayar ki lo yachol lo* — [the angel] perceived that he could not overcome [Yaakov]." What did he do? "*Veyiga bechaf yereicho* — he struck the *yerech* [hip socket] of Yaakov" (*Bereishis* 32:26).

The term *yerech* is used in the Torah to symbolize one's ability to produce offspring. When the angel saw that he did not stand a chance against Yaakov himself, he salvaged whatever he could — he struck at Yaakov's descendants and corrupted them with the notion that pleasure-seeking is an end in itself.

It is the result of that resounding blow from Eisav's angel, and the ever-present snare set by Eisav's descendants, to which *Kli Yakar* refers when he says that Eisav is responsible for many of our sins.

Eisav's role in our downfall notwithstanding, it is we who are guilty for taking the bait. When the *Beis HaMikdash* stood, each Yom Kippur we would take a *sa'ir*, send it away, and pledge, "Never again. I will not fall prey to the enticement of the *Ish Sa'ir*."

But merely sending away the *sa'ir* is not enough. *Teshuvah* (repentance) is not that simple. Hashem gave us Yom Kippur as an opportunity to examine our lives, discover where we have strayed in the previous year, and rededicate ourselves to our true mission in this world.

๑ Jolting Us Awake

The call of the *shofar* during Elul and Rosh Hashanah is meant to awaken us from our slumber, to remind us that we must jolt ourselves out of our slothful existence of following our baser instincts and instead inject meaning into our lives. Sometimes Hashem decides that it will take more than just the call of the *shofar* to awaken us, and He sends cataclysmic events to startle us. To our friend from Bear Stearns, it took the collapse of his company to awaken him from his slumber. But the lesson he learned from that event is one of the main messages of Yom Kippur, and it should not take the collapse of one's company to remind a person not to lose track of priorities and turn trivial things into major issues.

It took a fatal disease to make another man understand this lesson. The name Randy Pausch may be familiar to some of you. He was a professor of computer science at Carnegie-Mellon University who died of cancer at the age of 47.

In many universities, it is customary to ask professors to deliver a "Last Lecture," in which the professor is asked to imagine that he is delivering the final lecture of his career. The idea is for the professor to impart some memorable words of wisdom to his students and colleagues. When Randy Pausch was asked to do this, he had no need to pretend that it was his last lecture, because it actually was. Unbeknownst to his colleagues, Randy had been diagnosed with pancreatic cancer, and, at the time he delivered his lecture, his doctors had told him that there was nothing more that medical science could do for him.

In his remaining time, Randy co-authored *The Last Lecture*. More telling than the book itself is the dilemma that he describes in the introduction. He wonders whether he should take out the time to prepare the lecture, or whether he should spend the limited time he had left with his wife and children.

If there is one sentence in the book that makes the entire book worth reading, it is the sentence in which he states that he wrote the book to stress, "the importance of overcoming obstacles, of enabling the dreams of others, of seizing every moment, because time is all you have, and you may find out one day that you have less of it than you think."

At his death, his wife said, "Randy was so proud that the book inspired parents to revisit their priorities, particularly their relationship with their children."

A Jew should not need a last lecture from Randy Pausch to crystallize in his mind what is important and what is trivial. A Jew has a Yom Kippur to remind him.

Perhaps this explains why the *ish iti*, the man who takes the *sa'ir hamishtalei'ach* out to the Judean desert, must be someone who is going to die during the coming year. A person who is facing death represents the main message of the *sa'ir hamishtalei'ach*. He realizes what is important and what is trivial, because he knows that his clock is running down, and he had better focus on his true priorities while he still has the time. A person who can see his priorities so clearly is one who will definitively dismiss Eisav's overtures to sin and focus on his true mission in life.

◈§ An End to "Shtick"

This idea also explains an enigmatic comment from the *Zohar* on the verse, "*Vayashav bayom hahu Eisav ledarko Sei'irah* — So Eisav started back that day on his way toward Se'ir" (*Bereishis* 33:16). Following the encounter in which Yaakov explained that using possessions properly in order to fulfill one's purpose on earth is not considered utilization of *Olam Hazeh*, Eisav went back home. Asks the Zohar, "*Eimasai*" — When does Eisav leave us? *Bish'as Ne'ilah* — when we beseech the *Ribono Shel Olam* during *Ne'ilah* on Yom Kippur."

What does the *Zohar* mean? Where does Eisav go, and why at *Ne'ilah*?

Of the five *tefillos* that we *daven* on Yom Kippur, only during *Ne'ilah* do we utter the words, "*Lema'an nechdal mei'oshek yadeinu*" — Hashem gave us Yom Kippur, "so that we should refrain from stealing." As we have noted elsewhere ("Paint Your Masterpiece"), this line of the liturgy seems peculiar. Theft is not the sin that any of us would list first on our repentance list. We are not shoplifters or petty thieves. Why are we taking the last few minutes of Yom Kippur to focus on something that seems so alien to us?

I think that the *Zohar* alludes to a possible explanation. People do not descend to the level at which they are ready to steal from others in one fell swoop. First we begin to look at Eisav's world and we become entranced by the beauty and sophistication of what he has to offer. Suddenly, money and the possessions that money can buy become infused with significance. Before long, almost nothing will stand between us and the possessions that we crave. Granted, we may never actually walk into a store and leave with an item for which we have not paid, but shy of that, we will use "inventive thinking" to minimize the amount we pay.

Whose fault is it? Were this a world that belonged exclusively to Yaakov, our priorities would remain before our eyes on a constant basis, and we would not be tempted into indulging in *Olam Hazeh* for its own sake. It is Eisav who entices us to indulge, and he may seduce us into doing so in a less-than-legal manner.

At the moment of *Ne'ilah* when we say, "*Lema'an nechdal mei'oshek yadeinu*," and commit ourselves to avoiding any sort of "shtick," we send Eisav away and commit to a life of Yaakov.

~§ Building a Legacy

All of these ideas dovetail with another nugget of wisdom that our friend at Bear Stearns garnered from the collapse of his firm. He said that a person must think about his legacy.

When this man began working at Bear Stearns, there was a daily *minyan* for Minchah in a stairwell of the office building, an outcome of the fact that the building had once belonged to Olympia and York, a strongly Jewish firm. When Bear Stearns moved two blocks away and there was no longer an option of *davening* in a stairwell, our friend from Bear Stearns was influential in moving the *minyan* into a conference room in the new location. The *minyan*, which had originally been comprised of ten men, gradually grew to a daily attendance of close to thirty people, and nearly 100 people on fast days, when they would read from a *Sefer Torah*.

The irony is that Bear Stearns is gone, but the Minchah *minyan* lives on, housed now by J.P. Morgan rather than by Bear Stearns. That is part of this man's legacy.

What is your legacy going to be?

Rav Chatzkel Levenstein was one of the greatest *mussar* personalities of the 20th century. He was *mashgiach* in Mir in Poland, and he journeyed with the yeshivah to Shanghai and held the yeshivah together through World War II. He eventually became *mashgiach* in the Mir in Yerushalayim and ultimately in Ponevezh Yeshivah in Bnei Brak. The man was actually an angel in the form of a man.

In an interim between Shanghai and Yerushalayim, Rav Chatzkel spent several years in the Mir in Brooklyn. At one point during his tenure there, he gave a *mussar* discourse to the *bachurim*, in which he said as follows:

I have heard that there is a place in America where there are actors and actresses who are the richest and most self-indulgent people in America.

But those people die just as everyone else does. At the funeral of such an actor or actress, a person of their own ilk stands at the grave and delivers a eulogy. What does he say about the deceased? Does he talk about how handsome and rich the deceased was, or how beautiful and brilliant she was? Does he talk about how many houses, cars, and boats he or she owned? No. In the history of the world, no one ever stood at an open grave and described the dead person as a beautiful or wealthy person. They comment on the fact that no matter how glamorous and busy a life he led, he would always take the time to visit his parents, or that despite her fabulous wealth and fame, she still kept up with her childhood friends. They remember the deceased for helping the poor, the homeless, and the unfortunate.

Before an open grave, *sheker*, falsehood, closes its mouth. For a few minutes, *emes*, the truth, reigns. And everyone realizes that the only acts of true value that a person performs in this world are his acts of kindness.

Think about your legacy.

Consider the things that you focus on most often in terms of your legacy. Will your focal points today be part of your legacy? Will they matter next week, next month, next year, or next decade?

Do you want to be remembered for the model of the car that you drove, or for the type of parent you were to your child? Do you want to be remembered for the square footage of your home, or the kind of son or daughter you were to your parents? Will you be remembered for major business deals you made, or for the type of neighbor you were, the friendships you made and kept, the Torah you learned, and the Torah you taught?

When you think of life in terms of your legacy, you realize what truly matters, and that the rest is trivial. You realize that the other pursuits are from the world of Eisav, and that you, as a descendant of Yaakov, must strive for more.

The *Yamim Noraim* in general and the *se'ir hamishtalei'ach* in particular are about focusing properly and rededicating ourselves to our mission in life. As *Yidden*, we should not need a world event like the Financial Meltdown of 2008 or a fatal illness, *chas ve'shalom*, to compel us to focus on what really matters. *Ashreinu mah tov chelkeinu* — how fortunate we are to have a Yom Kippur, an opportunity to reexamine the purpose of our existence, and distance ourselves from the lure of Eisav's world.

Let's make sure to capitalize on it.

The Blame Game

The Rambam (*Hilchos Teshuvah* 2:2) writes that there are three parts to proper *teshuvah* (repentance): (1) *kabbalah al he'asid* — the sinner must make a wholehearted commitment not to repeat his sin in the future; (2) *charatah al he'avar* — he must regret having committed the sin in the past; (3) *vidui* — verbal confession of the sins.

If I were to take a poll asking people to rank these three steps in order of difficulty, I would venture to say that most people would rank *vidui* as the easiest of the three, *charatah* on the next level, and most difficult in people's minds would be *kabbalah al he'asid*.

Vidui, the verbal articulation of our sins, is something that we do ten times each Yom Kippur, and it does not seem particularly difficult. *Kabbalah al he'asid*, on the other hand, seems extremely difficult — especially since the Rambam sets the bar very high by stating that Hashem Himself must be willing to bear witness that the person is sincere in making this commitment.

I think that this perception is mistaken. I think that *vidui* requires much more than allowing the words *Ashamnu, bagadnu, gazalnu* and the list of *Al Cheits* to roll off our tongues. Furthermore, the step of *kabbalah al he'asid*, which seems particularly difficult, is actually much easier than we imagine it to be.

We can glean some important lessons from a chapter in *Tanach*, but I must preface this section with a disclaimer. We are going to discuss the "sins" and "mistakes" of one of the greatest men in the history of *Klal Yisrael*, Shaul HaMelech. *Chazal* (*Yevamos* 121b) tell us that many of the "sins" that were attributed to great people in *Tanach* were considered sinful only because Hashem expected more from them. If we were to commit some of the "sins" of our forefathers, they might even be considered mitzvos for us. Since the *Navi* and *Chazal* recorded these events, we may draw certain conclusions and apply them to our lives, but it is imperative that we remember that even after the incident we are about to discuss, Shaul was described by Dovid HaMelech as a perfect *tzaddik* (see *Mo'ed Katan* 16b).

As we read in the *haftarah* of *Parashas Zachor* (*I Shmuel* 15:1-34), Hashem sent the prophet Shmuel to command King Shaul to wage war with, and to obliterate, the monstrously evil nation of Amalek. He is instructed to wipe out all members of the nation and destroy all their possessions, even their livestock. The wording of the prophecy is explicit, and cannot lend itself to misinterpretation.

That is not what happens. Shaul and the people take pity on the choicest animals and bring them back with them. Even more calamitous, Shaul does not kill Agag, the king of Amalek.

Hashem tells Shmuel HaNavi, "I have reconsidered My having made Shaul king, for he has turned away from Me and has not fulfilled My word." Shmuel is so disturbed that he spends the entire night grieving. Shockingly, when Shmuel goes to meet Shaul the next morning, the latter greets him with the following words: "*Baruch atah laHashem* — blessed are you to Hashem! *Hakimosi es devar Hashem* — I have fulfilled the word of Hashem."

That statement is mind-boggling. Shaul has been commanded to kill all the Amalekites, including their livestock, and he has not done so. We would have expected the conversation to go as follows:

"Shmuel, there's something I have to tell you."

"Yes, King Shaul?"

"We didn't actually wipe out all of Amalek's animals. We took the best ones to slaughter as offerings."

But Shaul simply says, "*Hakimosi es devar Hashem.*"

"And what," asks Shmuel, "is this sound of the sheep in my ears and the sound of the cattle that I hear?"

"I have brought them from the Amalekite," Shaul responds, "for the people took pity on the best of the sheep and cattle in order to bring them as offerings to Hashem, your God ..."

Shmuel sharply reminds Shaul that Hashem had commanded him to wipe out *all* the animals, and then confronts him once more, asking, "*Velamah lo shamata bekol Hashem* — why did you not obey the voice of Hashem?"

Once again, Shaul sticks to his story. "*Asher shamati bekol Hashem* — But I *did* heed the voice of Hashem ... I brought Agag, king of Amalek, and I destroyed Amalek. The people took sheep and cattle — the best of that which was to be destroyed — in order to bring offerings to Hashem, your God, in Gilgal."

"Does Hashem delight in offerings," Shmuel responds, "as [He does] in obedience to the voice of Hashem ... Because you have rejected the word of God, He has rejected you as king!"

Shocked, Shaul finally confesses his guilt, but not without excusing himself. "I have sinned," he says, "... for I feared the people and I hearkened to their voice."

Shmuel rejects Shaul's argument and turns to leave, but Shaul grasps the hem of his tunic and tears it.

"Hashem has torn the kingship of Israel from upon you this day, and has given it to your fellow who is better than you," Shmuel says.

Finally, after this entire dialogue, Shaul repeats, "*Chatasi* — I have sinned."

This chapter in *Tanach* demonstrates an important insight into the human psyche. We don't have an easy time admitting guilt. It is so difficult for us to say, "I'm wrong" or "I'm sorry."

Rav Leib Chasman, one of the *mussar* greats of the previous generation, once chastised a person for doing something wrong. The person insisted that his action was justified. They argued the point, and finally the person said to Rav Leib, "You're right."

"That's not enough," Rav Leib replied. "You need to say, 'I'm wrong.'"

Before Yom Kippur, we are to ask for forgiveness from those whom we hurt during the year. The execution of this halachah leaves something to be desired. I have often heard people, who, *knowing* that they did something wrong to their fellow man, approach him and say, "*If* I did anything wrong to you this year, please forgive me" or "*If* I offended you in some way ..." Few people will actually go over to someone and say, "I was wrong for hurting you."

It is hard to fault people for this failing. It took the great King Shaul four rebukes to finally admit, "I have sinned" — without giving an excuse. It is therefore understandable that we would have a difficult time saying it.

The utter uniqueness of the ability to say, "*Chatasi* — I have sinned," may explain an unusual verbal construction in a chapter in *Tanach* dealing with the story of Dovid HaMelech and Bas-sheva.

When Nosson HaNavi came to chastise David for his actions, David's response was, "*Chatasi.*" If you look at a *Navi* scroll, you'll find a break (indicated by the appearance of the letter *samech* in printed editions of *Tanach*) directly following this word. King David's immediate confession of his guilt is so unusual that the *Navi* makes a point of indicating that he said *only* the word *chatasi*, and did not attempt to justify his behavior.

The inability to say, "I was wrong," poses a great problem when it comes to the *teshuvah* process. Admitting that we were wrong is the essence of *teshuvah*. It behooves us to try to understand the psychological battle that Shaul had to fight within himself before he admitted his guilt, so that we can try to succeed in our own *teshuvah* process.

❧ Disconnecting the Ego

The first question we must ask is: Why do we have such difficulty admitting our guilt?

It seems that the primary difficulty in admitting guilt is that it causes a tremendous blow to our egos.

The Talmud (*Yoma* 22b) relates that Shaul had a halachic rationale for not fulfilling Hashem's command to the last letter, which he derived via a *kal vachomer* (an a fortiori argument) from the law of *eglah arufah*. He had developed a *"shtikel Torah"* (novel approach to a Torah subject), and had invested too much into his thesis to say, "I made a mistake. I was wrong."

It is interesting to note that in the one instance in the Talmud in which a person willingly backed down and acknowledged his culpability, he is referred to in glowing terms.

A *Tanna*, Shimon (some say his name was Nechemiah) HaAmsuni, was renowned for his hypothesis that the word *"es"* in the Torah is inherently extraneous, and in every instance where it is found it teaches something that we would not have known otherwise. In most cases, the word *"es"* teaches that something analogous to the subject of the verse is likewise included in the halachah mentioned. For instance, there is a verse that instructs us not to derive any benefit (physical or financial) from a certain type of meat. Because the verse states, *es besaro* — its meat — rather than merely *besaro*, Shimon HaAmsuni taught that it is also forbidden to derive benefit from the hide of the animal.

Thus, in the first verse in the Torah alone, Shimon HaAmsuni found some sort of teaching alluded to in each of two appearances of *es*: *es hashamayim v'es ha'aretz*. To give you an appreciation of how much time and effort he invested in developing his thesis, the word *es* appears more than 4,000 times in the Torah.

Then came the day that he reached the verse, "*Es Hashem Elokecha tirah* — Hashem, your God, shall you fear" (*Devarim* 10:20). He stopped short and said, "There is no one in the world who can be compared to Hashem and who deserves to be feared on that level. My supposition must have been wrong."

The Blame Game

"Rebbi," his students asked. "What will happen to all of the *derashos* (homiletic teachings) you developed based on the word *es* until this point?"

Now, if King Shaul found it difficult to step away from a *shtikel Torah* that he had developed on the spur of the moment during the battle against Amalek, how much more difficult should it have been for Shimon HaAmsuni to step away from his life's work, which had taken decades to develop? His response, therefore, is all the more astounding:

"*Kesheim shekibalti schar al hadrishah* — just as I earned reward for formulating the *derashos*," he replied, "*kach akabeil schar al heprishah* — so will I earn reward for abandoning [my thesis]."

Shimon HaAmsuni — whose readiness to admit that he had been wrong is so exemplary that the incident is quoted no less than four times in the Talmud — teaches us that Hashem is well aware of how difficult it is to step back and to admit that we were mistaken. He therefore gives us as much credit for the minute that it takes to retract a thesis as we received for all the years of toil invested in developing it.

We can now understand the true difficulty in the step of *vidui*, confession. *Vidui* is not about beating your chest and rattling off *al cheit* after *al cheit*. *Vidui* is about looking at your life and asking yourself, "Am I doing things right? Is my entire life going to waste because of some basic flaw in my *weltanschauung*?"

That is difficult. Looking at yourself in the mirror and saying, "Maybe I'm wrong," seems like a painful — perhaps an almost *impossible* — step. But that is what *vidui* is truly about.

I want to share a letter that a woman from Philadelphia sent me. From what I can gather, she is a middle-aged woman who started to become a *baalas teshuvah* approximately six years before she wrote this letter. A fully observant woman today, she struggled mightily during the process of becoming *frum*. She had been dressing *tzanua* (in a modest fashion) for three years at this point, but there was one thing she couldn't bring herself to do: she could not throw away her pants. To explain her struggle, she wrote an essay titled, "Saying Goodbye to My Pants."

"Each time I had tried," she wrote, "I just couldn't do it. I felt that I would end up missing my pants — especially my jeans. I would put them away and resolve to do it at another time — a time when I would have the strength to confront my pants, to show them who is *really* 'wearing the pants.'

"If my pants could talk, they would tell the story of a woman who is beginning to realize that in her struggle to say goodbye to her pants, she was truly struggling with something much greater."

The greater struggle she describes is that of transforming her concept of what being a woman is all about. She had to make the radical shift from how Western civilization regards women to how Judaism regards them, and it was extremely difficult to change her outlook at her stage in life. This woman concluded with the following summation: "I had been defining myself more by my outer image than by my inner soul and true essence. I did not realize that my [style of] dress reflected my commitment to my soul and my unique calling as a Jewish woman. I had been seeing modest dress more as a restriction than as a way to transcend and become so much more."

That is *vidui*. That is *teshuvah*. Looking at yourself and saying, "Has my outlook on life been correct, or have I been wrong?"

Unfortunately, we all have our "pants." We all have something that we consider an integral part of us — something that we know we should part with, but find it extremely difficult — because we know that it will require us to rethink everything that we hold dear. Part of the *vidui* process is identifying, and coming to grips with, your "pants," and then finding the strength to make the difficult choice of parting with them.

The Defense Mechanisms

We now understand *why* Shaul would not want to admit that he made a mistake, but there is something in the story that still seems impossible to understand. With the cattle and sheep taken from Amalek providing "musical accompaniment," how could Shaul say to Shmuel, "*Hakimosi es devar Hashem*?" Furthermore, why did he stick to his version of the story twice more, despite Shmuel's persistent efforts to get him to admit his guilt?

It seems — and again, we must remember that we are not criticizing King Shaul, but trying to learn lessons for our own struggle — that Shaul employed several classic defense mechanisms used by all humans when faced with a reality that they cannot confront.

◈§ Defense Mechanism #1: Denial

Humans have the ability to deny facts that are obvious to everyone in the world other than the denier. We see this behavior in play when dealing with terminally ill patients and their families. Sometimes the patient himself, sometimes well-meaning family members, will refuse to accept that the disease is incurable.

My daughter was taking a course in order to become an occupational therapist. Another *frum* girl, whose father had a form of cancer that is considered to be incurable, was in her program. During one of their medical classes, the professor — who had no way of knowing that this girl's father was ill — chanced to mention that specific form of cancer and said, "This is a terminal cancer."

The girl walked up to the professor after class and said, "It is *not* terminal. Not everyone dies from this cancer."

"I'm sorry," the professor said, oblivious of the situation, "but these are the facts based on statistical evidence of curability. It is terminal."

"IT IS NOT TERMINAL," the girl insisted.

She simply could not accept the truth. Her professor was correct, but she was in denial.

And once again, if the great King Shaul could be in denial, so can we.

The Rambam, in recording the Torah readings for Yom Kippur, writes: "At Minchah, we read the [portion of] *arayos* (illicit, forbidden relationships) that appears in *Acharei Mos*, so that those who have transgressed any of these sins should remember, be ashamed, and repent" (*Hilchos Tefillah* 13:11).

I have a question on the Rambam. By the time we reach Minchah on Yom Kippur, we have been in shul for approximately 8 to 10 hours, and have said *vidui* no less than six times: twice at Maariv, twice at Shacharis, and twice at Mussaf. Can there really be a person who has committed so grave a sin during the year, and it would simply never dawn upon him to do *teshuvah* unless we jog his memory by reading — at Minchah — the portion of the Torah prohibiting such relationships? Is there a person who suddenly rouses from a reverie and says, "Oh goodness! I just remembered that I committed a gross violation of the Torah!"?

The answer is: *Yes*. There can be a person who spends 8 hours in shul, says *vidui* six times, and is still in denial over matters that occurred in his personal life. It may take until the waning hours of Yom Kippur, when he hears a lengthy list of *arayos* being read from the Torah, to shake him free of his denial and force him to come to grips with what he has done.

✂§ Defense Mechanism #2: Rationalization

In the second part of their conversation, when Shmuel asks Shaul where the animal sounds are coming from, Shaul responds, "We took some of the animals to slaughter as offerings to Hashem."

Shaul rationalizes his behavior. Wasn't it only right to bring offerings as a sign of gratitude to Hashem for helping them win the battle?

The rationalization that you must be most wary of is the one in which you are convinced that you are doing a mitzvah. There is no stopping someone on a "holy" mission.

In consecutive verses, Shlomo HaMelech wrote, "*Al tehi tzaddik harbei* — don't be overly righteous" (*Koheles* 7:16), and then, "*Al tirshah harbei* — don't be overly wicked" (Ibid. v. 17). Which one do you suppose is worse — an overly righteous person, or an overly wicked person? I think that most people would say that they can handle someone who is overly righteous, but not someone who is extremely wicked.

The Blame Game / 171

My rosh yeshivah, Rav Yaakov Yitzchok Ruderman, would say that an overly righteous person is far worse, because you don't have any way of reasoning with him. You stand a chance of striking a chord with even the most wicked person, and you may be able to help him repent. But an overly righteous individual cannot be convinced that his behavior is inappropriate. If you try to get him to mend his ways, he will undoubtedly say, "What are you talking about? This is a mitzvah!"

Not to compare, and *le'havdil*, but this sanctimonious attitude is what leads Arab terrorists to fly planes into buildings and enables them to murder people and send the video to world media. This is why they are able to blow up innocent men, women, and children on buses and in restaurants. In their minds, they are in the employ of God. And when you are doing God's work, no holds are barred.

Be aware of the tendency to rationalize your actions, and especially in ways that make you feel holy.

✥ Defense Mechanism #3: "It's Not My Fault"

The third and final defense mechanism we find Shaul employing is actually the oldest defense mechanism in history, dating back to when the world was but a few hours old: "It's not my fault."

"I was afraid of the people," King Shaul said. "It's not my fault. The people wanted to bring back animals, and I was afraid that they would rebel."

I say that this is the oldest defense mechanism because it was used by the primordial man, Adam HaRishon. When Hashem asked him why he ate from the *Eitz Hada'as* (Tree of Knowledge), Adam answered, "*Ha'ishah asher nasata imadi hi nasna li min ha'eitz, va'ocheil* — the woman whom you gave to be with me, she gave me of the tree, and I ate" (*Bereishis* 3:12).

Perhaps the historical significance of this excuse explains its popularity with men, who for close to six millennia have now been following Adam's lead and saying: "It's my wife's fault."

But the *Sforno* finds further fault with Adam. He writes that not only did Adam try to shift the blame to Chavah, he was actually saying, "It's Your fault, Hashem. You gave me this woman, and look what she made me do."

The repercussions of Adam HaRishon's statement are with us until this very day. Had Adam said that one word, *"Chatasi,"* Hashem would have forgiven him immediately. But he shifted the blame, and Hashem punished him with all the curses — including a curse that is not immediately apparent from the verses in the Torah. Rav Yerucham Levovitz observed something interesting about birds, which actually holds true for all animals. The far end of my backyard borders on a forested area. There is a groundhog that emerges from that forest each March, which I consider a telltale sign that spring has arrived. This groundhog had two babies, and each day, as I'm seated at my desk, they come out of the forest and begin to eat grass. Every five seconds, they lift their heads and look around. Why?

Groundhogs, birds, and many of their counterparts, have predators seeking to attack them, explains Rav Yerucham, and they must constantly be on the lookout. Hashem gave them a survival instinct that makes them run as soon as they sense the slightest sign of danger. If I so much as bang on my desk, the groundhogs run back into the forest.

We, too, have a predator. It is called the *yetzer hara*. Why don't we have that survival instinct?

A survival instinct is necessary for those who have no recourse once they are attacked. We were not given a survival instinct, says Rav Yerucham, because Hashem gave us the power to do *teshuvah*, to repent. As soon as we are attacked and are defeated by our predator, we can do *teshuvah*. But when Adam HaRishon sinned on that fateful first day of creation and, rather than saying, *"Chatasi,"* he blamed his wife and by extension Hashem, he damaged our ability to admit our guilt and say, "I'm sorry. I was wrong."

That damage is a curse, which, like all the other curses that rained down upon Adam, has yet to be rescinded. The mitzvah of *vidui* is about stopping the denial and the rationalization of our mistakes, and not blaming others for our shortcomings. It requires us to be strong enough to stand before Hashem on Yom Kippur and say, "It is *my* fault. I was wrong. I'm sorry."

⇜ "But": At the Beginning or at the End?

The Rambam (*Hilchos Teshuvah* 2:8) rules, based on a Gemara (*Yoma* 87b), that the most important words in *vidui* are, "*Aval anachnu chatanu.*"

Most people would translate these words as, "*But* we have sinned." That translation is incorrect. *Aval* in this context does not mean *but*. It means *indeed*: "Indeed, we have sinned."

I think, however, that we may reconcile this definition of *aval* with the standard definition. A sincere confession of guilt depends on where the word "but" is placed. If it follows the acceptance of responsibility: "I have sinned, but …," "I know I have failed, but …," then it negates all that preceded it. It represents an unwillingness to take responsibility. If, however, it appears *before* the confession, then it is a clear acceptance of guilt. "I know, God, that I have a million excuses for what I did. But *I* have sinned. *I* am wrong."

There are fringe benefits to training ourselves to say, "It's my fault"; it will enhance the relationships that otherwise may tend to weaken during the year.

When a couple has an argument, they often begin to play the "blame game." One says, "It's your fault," and the other retorts, "No, it's your fault," and they continue in this vein until neither of the two is interested in talking. Marriages would be so much better if both husband and wife were strong enough to own up to their failures and say, "It was my fault. I'm sorry."

Let me offer a common example.

A couple is invited to a wedding taking place at a venue that they have never attended. They know that they should leave earlier than usual so that they have sufficient time to find the hall. The husband calls up to his wife, "It's getting late. Could you please hurry?"

She wants to leave, but her *sheitel* just won't cooperate. She *shpritzes*, she pulls, she smoothes … it's just not working. Getting impatient, he yells again, "Could you come down already! We're going to be late."

Finally she comes down and asks, "Do you have the directions?"

His answer will invariably be, "I don't need directions. I can figure it out by myself."

"But the directions are right here," she says, holding them in her hand. "Maybe we should just take them?"

"*I don't need the directions,*" he repeats firmly.

I don't need to tell you that they get lost, and as they search for the hall, they begin to argue. "You took too long with your *sheitel*," he says, "you made me so nervous that I got lost."

"You always insist that you know where you're going," she retorts. "Why couldn't you just take the directions?"

So they miss the *chuppah*.

And they were only invited to the *chuppah*.

They drive the entire way back home in sullen silence. Why? Because neither of the two was strong enough to say, "I'm sorry. It's my fault."

"The inability to admit failure affects us every day of our lives," writes Rav Chaim Shmulevitz. It affects *teshuvah*, it affects marriages, and it affects every aspect of our lives.

This inability may be the primary cause of road rage. Have you ever noticed how you could be driving perfectly — legally and safely — and it is always someone else who does something blatantly wrong, illegal, and dangerous, such as cutting you off. How shameful! You lean on your horn to let him know that he has just done something dangerous. If he is polite, he merely echoes your display of concern, beeping his own horn to show that you were at fault for driving so slowly. The less-polite drivers will react with anything from obscene gestures to actual obscenities shouted out the window. So what do you do? You lean on your horn some more, until your wife says, "Stop! He's going to get out of that car and beat you up."

Doesn't she realize that it is your job to give *mussar* (rebuke) to the dangerous drivers of the world?

Rabbi Dr. Abraham J. Twerski observes that there are four basic necessities for human existence: 1. food and water 2. shelter 3. clothing 4. someone to blame.

This statement is no mere attempt at humor. It is a profound truth. Rabbi Twerski says that he has learned this from his extensive work with alcoholics, who invariably blame others for their addiction. One blames his overbearing boss, another blames his nagging wife. Everyone else is driving him to drink. Shifting the blame releases the alcoholic from the obligation to change. When it is the boss' fault, then drinking is only a normal response.

This is also the reason why the "It's Not My Fault" attitude is the greatest impediment to *teshuvah*. You have no reason to change if you are not at fault.

One of the most glaring examples of the pervasiveness of this attitude was the shifting of blame that took place in the wake of Hurricane Katrina in 2006. The honorable Mayor of New Orleans blamed the federal government, which in turn blamed the governor of Louisiana for not calling in the National Guard; Congress blamed the Bush administration for assigning FEMA (Federal Emergency Management Agency) to oversee the rescue efforts instead of the Department of Homeland Security. The head of Homeland Security shifted the blame to Louisianan officials.

The issue went in circles. No one was willing to take responsibility.

Contrast this with General Dwight D. Eisenhower's sentiments, expressed in a statement drafted before the D-Day invasion. The invasion, which was the largest amphibious invasion in history, was to take place on June 6, 1944. General Eisenhower, supreme commander of the Allied Forces in Europe, drafted a statement to deliver in the event the invasion were to fail:

> Our landing in the Normandy region of France has failed to gain a satisfactory foothold, and the troops have been withdrawn.

But Eisenhower then crossed out the last six words, and rewrote it to read, "And *I* have withdrawn the troops."

A profound difference. Eisenhower realized that he was the commander, and he had to take responsibility. He was willing to say that he was the one who made the wrong decision.

We must learn to take responsibility for our mistakes, first on Yom Kippur, and then throughout the year.

∽§ Are We Sincere?

Vidui turns out to be more difficult than we first envisioned, but the reverse is true for *kabbalah al he'asid* — accepting upon ourselves not to repeat the sins.

A superficial look at this step of the *teshuvah* process leads us to believe that is impossible to achieve. People who have been through twenty or thirty Yom Kippurs know that our resolutions rarely — or, dare I say it, *never* — last. How can we hope to meet the requirement that the Rambam sets forth — that Hashem Himself, Who is aware of our innermost thoughts and emotions, should bear witness that we will never repeat those sins again? Who can honestly say that, in the heat of a battle with their *yetzer hara*, they won't falter again and repeat their sin?

Truthfully, though, *kabbalah al he'asid* is easier than we think. In one of the most encouraging thoughts that I have ever read, Rabbi Yisrael Salanter points out that, as always, the Rambam chose his words in that halachah very carefully. The Rambam did not describe Hashem in this context as the One Who knows the future, but as "the One Who knows a person's innermost thoughts and emotions." The One Who knows the future knows quite well that you may not be able to resist that temptation to sin when tested once again. But the One Who knows our innermost thoughts and emotions is able to see how we *feel* about our sins *on Yom Kippur*. If we can reach a level on Yom Kippur at which we are sincere in feeling that we do not *want* to repeat our sins, Hashem considers us to be complete *baalei teshuvah*.

Similarly, Rav Tzadok HaKohen of Lublin (*Pri Tzaddik, Beshalach* 6) proves that if a person makes a sincere and wholehearted decision at any point to abandon his sinful ways, even if he is later overpowered by his *yetzer hara*, he is still considered a complete *tzaddik* at the point when he reached that wholehearted decision.

Can we not, at least on Yom Kippur, be *tzaddikim*?

Rabbi Nosson Wachtfogel, the *mashgiach* of the yeshivah in Lakewood, once offered a parable to illustrate this point. Whether legend or truth, there are stories of babies who were abandoned in the wild and who were reared by wolves or apes. If we were to find such a feral child, he would undoubtedly act like an animal. He would eat like an animal, sleep like an animal, and behave like an animal. We can attribute that behavior either to nature, and say that the child was born with a genetic predisposition to acting like an animal, or to nurture, and attribute it to the fact that he had lived among animals and had never seen any other form of behavior. If we now take that child and restore him to civilized society, and he begins to behave like an ordinary human, then we can determine that the reason he behaved like an animal is because he was raised like an animal.

For 353 out of 354 days of a (lunar) year, we may be slaves to the *yetzer hara*. Try as we might, we simply cannot shake ourselves free from its seduction. But there is one day a year when the *yetzer hara* has no power over us: Yom Kippur. If on that one day we show Hashem that we can be holy, righteous *tzaddikim*, then it means that essentially we are righteous people.

❧ Be Proactive

The step of *kabbalah al he'asid* is not one that requires us to say, "I'm never going to speak *lashon hara* again." If you have made such a statement in the past, then you know that it is ineffective. The way to make a *kabbalah* for the future is to erect a *geder* (border) to stop you from sinking back into the same behavior. Make a commitment that shows Hashem you are sincere. Take upon yourself, for instance, to learn *shemiras halashon* for five minutes each day.

Similarly, don't say, "I'm going to *daven* better." Say, "Hashem, I want to *daven* better, so I am going to learn from a book or *sefer* that will help me understand the *tefillos*."

Do something to *show* that you are sincere, that you want to improve.

I have a *talmid* who is *kovei'a itim laTorah* (designates time for Torah study), delivers *shiurim*, and has a wonderful, beautiful family. He recently shocked me by admitting that for the past several years, he had fallen prey to the enticements of the Internet. He came to me brokenhearted, feeling horrible about himself. He said that each year during *Yamim Noraim* he would promise himself that this would be the year that he would break free from the clutches of the *yetzer hara*, but, invariably, he would fail. Some years he would last until Chanukah, others until Pesach, but eventually he would lose control and go down that slippery slope once again. When he would slip, he would become so consumed with guilt that it bordered on depression. His wife would ask him, "What's the matter? Am I doing something wrong?" He couldn't tell her. His wife is a pure, *ehrliche* woman, and he could not bring himself to look her in the face and tell her that he was browsing for *tumah* on the Internet.

Based on a decision he made last Yom Kippur, he finally made a *geder*. He went to the IT (Information Technology) professional at his company and told him that he wanted to have his computer blocked from reaching such sites. The IT person complied, and *baruch Hashem*, this person has broken free from his *yetzer hara*.

That is what we all must do. Erect *gedarim*. Set up external controls if internal ones are broken. Do whatever it takes to prevent yourself from sinning.

◆§ Don't Wait Until It's Too Late

Chazal refer to Shabbos as a *matanah tovah* (a great gift). Perhaps the Torah refers to Yom Kippur as *Shabbas Shabbason* because it is an even greater gift, because it can be a lifesaver. It is the one day of the year that we can do a reality check, find the areas that we need to improve, and find ways to do so.

Ashrecha Yisrael — how fortunate we are to have a day each year when we can take stock of where we are going, and whether we are making mistakes, so that we don't reach a day toward the end of life when we suddenly realize that we have been living a lie — as was the case with one Grigory Zinoviev.

Most of you have probably never heard of Grigory Zinoviev, but he is described in a biography written about him as "Lenin's closest collaborator." We know the names Lenin, Stalin, and Trotsky, but there was a person who played a more important role in spreading communism. Grigory Zinoviev was a Jew, but he left the fold at a young age and dedicated his life to the "utopian idea of communism." On Lenin's deathbed, Lenin told him, "Whatever you do, get rid of Stalin, because he will turn on you."

Zinoviev, needless to say, did not follow Lenin's advice, and he formed the Troika (triumvirate) together with Stalin and Kamenev, in order to thwart the aspirations of Trotsky. Zinoviev, Stalin, and Leib Kamenev were thus the top three in the Communist Party, until one fine day, when Zinoviev was imprisoned. He could not believe it. *This must be a capitalist plot,* he thought to himself. *Stalin, the "light of the nation," would never do this to me.*

In his foolishness, he penned letter after letter from his prison cell to Josef Stalin, stating that he was wrongly imprisoned, and begging to be released. Of course none of his letters were answered. Eventually, a show trial was held in which Grigory Zinoviev was found guilty of aiding Trotsky; he was sentenced to death. When he was standing waiting to be executed, the commander of the firing squad came over to him and said, "Stalin did this to you. He imprisoned you, and now he is having you shot."

Imagine how Grigory Zinoviev felt at that moment. He lived for the creation of the Communist Party, he had killed in order to see it succeed — communism was his life. He gave up everything to see it come to fruition. Suddenly he realizes that it is all false.

And then, right before the soldiers pulled their triggers, Grigory Zinoviev uttered his last words on this planet: "*Shema Yisrael, Hashem Elokeinu, Hashem Echad.*"

At that very last moment, he wanted to cling to the truth. Somehow, through it all, he knew that there was a God.

None of us should ever have to face a moment in life when we suddenly find out that we "blew it all."

Never has a man on his deathbed uttered the words, "I regret not spending enough time at the office." But sometimes we live our life without taking stock of what and who we are and what we are doing with our time. That is the purpose of Yom Kippur. If a Jew uses Yom Kippur correctly, and looks himself in the face and admits to his failings, then what happened to Grigory Zinoviev — even on a smaller scale — will never happen to us.

But if there is one thing that is more crushing than finding out at the end of life that your life has been for naught, it is to find that out in the afterlife. We all know that we will face a great Day of Judgment, which the *machzor* describes as such an awesome day that the angels are gripped by fear, and tremble as they call out, "*Hinei yom hadin* — behold! It is the Day of Judgment."

One can barely imagine how dreadful it must be for someone when he finds himself standing before the *Kisei HaKavod* (Throne of Glory) and paraphrasing the words of King Shaul: "*Hakimosi es devar Hashem.* Hashem, I have fulfilled Your will."

Wasn't I a good Jew? Didn't I learn Torah? Didn't I give *tzedakah* (charity)?

But then, to his utter chagrin, the *Ribono Shel Olam* may respond with something to the effect of, "*U'meh kol hatzon asher anochi shomei'a* — what is this racket of the animals that I hear in the background?"

Except that it won't be the sound of animals. It will be the book of the person's life. And Hashem will say, "*That* is your version of *hakimosi es devar Hashem*?"

Then, it will be too late. At that point, one can no longer say *Shema Yisrael* as Grigory Zinoviev did. It is too late for *teshuvah*.

That doesn't have to happen if we use Yom Kippur correctly, if we use this most precious day of the year to review our lives, and look at ourselves and say, "*Aval*, indeed, *chatasi*, I have sinned." I'm wrong. No buts. No denials. No shifting the blame. No rationalizations. Simply, "I'm wrong."

May we be *zocheh* to a *chasimah tovah*, to see *nachas* from our children, to see the long-awaited *geulah* from this long and bitter exile.

It's Never Enough
Striving for More

Marriage: From Caterpillar to Butterfly

The difficulty in addressing an issue as global as marriage is that I have no idea on which audience to concentrate. Should I focus on the portions of the subject matter that apply to single people who are looking toward marriage, or should I address my thoughts to those already married?

Even within the category of married folk, there are still subdivisions: newlyweds, and old hands. One might argue that there is no reason to address the old hands, because they already know all there is to know about marriage. That argument is untrue. At no stage during a marriage is it too late to hear something new, or even to review what you already know, but fail to put into practice. The Talmud equates two things with *Krias Yam Suf* (the splitting of the Sea of Reeds): *shidduchim* (*Sanhedrin* 22a), and *parnassah* (*Pesachim*

118a). Rav Yaakov Kamenetsky points out a distinct similarity between the two. Successful businessmen will tell you that if you want to earn an adequate living, you cannot allow your business to run on autopilot. You must constantly assess and evaluate the day-to-day operation to make sure that it is running in the most efficient and profitable manner. A businessman who rests on his laurels is likely to find that his business is declining and is headed toward insolvency. So, too, does a marriage (an extension of *shidduchim*) need constant attention. If a person does not take care to nurture and recharge his or her marriage — even allowing for the occasional "midcourse correction" — then the marriage may deteriorate or even, *chas ve'shalom*, fail.

It is said that each afternoon, when Rav Shlomo Zalman Auerbach would be driven home from Yeshivas Kol Torah, it was common for one *yungerman* or another to request permission to come along for the ride so that he could consult with the *poseik hador*. Several *yungeleit* noticed that as they drew near to his house each day, Rav Shlomo Zalman would unwrap a piece of cake and eat it. One of the fellows eventually worked up the temerity to ask him why he couldn't just wait until he got home to eat supper. "When a person is hungry, he's not always in good spirits," replied Rav Shlomo Zalman. "I want to be in a good frame of mind when I walk into the house."

I'll point out that Rav Shlomo Zalman had a perpetual smile on his face that melted the hearts of anyone who saw him — and had probably been married for close to 50 years when this story occurred — but he was still concerned that he may not be in perfectly good spirits when he greeted his wife. Clearly, then, no matter the stage we are at in life, we can always seek to enhance our marriages.

In taking into account the diverse audience, I will highlight some general tips on what it is that makes a Jewish marriage successful. I think that these pointers will benefit all adults — whether singles, newlyweds, or those who have already celebrated their golden wedding anniversary.

A Shocking Letter

I would like to paraphrase an excerpt from a letter written approximately two centuries ago; as you read it, try to envision who the letter-writer might be:

> After she went the way of the world, I was overwhelmed by pain and sorrow. I became dangerously weak. I could not eat or drink. My stomach could not hold anything for long. I could barely retain enough food to be required to recite a *berachah acharonah*. I could not sleep, and I had to seek medical care.
>
> I am thankful to Hashem for healing me slightly, but I still cannot pray without my thoughts being disturbed and confused, and I cannot learn even a simple *sugya* in depth.

If I were to tell you of a letter written by a man bemoaning the fact that he cannot eat, sleep, drink, or learn because of something marriage-related, you might guess that it was written by a young man who had recently become engaged and is so overwhelmed by his wonderful *kallah* that he ceases to function. But we know that the person who wrote this letter just suffered the loss of his wife. Who, then, wrote the letter? Some sort of romantic?

The author of this letter is no less a personage than Rabbi Akiva Eiger. Men who attended yeshivah may have blanched when they read that. Rabbi Akiva Eiger is perhaps *the* gold standard among *Acharonim* (Torah scholars from the late 15th century to the present). No work is more discussed and "sweated over" than the writings of Rabbi Akiva Eiger. For him to make the statement that he could not learn after his wife passed away is mind-boggling. I recommend, in fact, that you read the entire letter yourselves (*Igros Rabbi Akiva Eiger* 109), so you can assure yourself that I did not fabricate it.

If Rabbi Akiva Eiger, the giant of giants, could not function after his wife passed away, he must have had a very loving, warm relationship with her. This may not be what we would have envisioned. We think of Rav Akiva Eiger as having been so engrossed in his studies that he barely found the time to notice his wife. Apparently, our view of marriage is warped. There must be something to a Jewish marriage that leads the greatest leaders of our nations to have warm and loving relationships with their wives.

In order to understand the Torah's view on marriage so that we can understand why *tzaddikim* had such warm marriages, let us return to the first marriage in history and examine the reason that Hashem created the institution of marriage.

✥ Why Do We Need Marriage?

When we study the chapters of the Torah dealing with Creation, it almost seems as though Chavah was created as an afterthought. Adam was created alone, and only afterward did Hashem say, "*Lo tov heyos ha'adam levado* — it is not good that man be alone; *e'eseh lo eizer kenegdo* — I will make him a helper corresponding to him" (*Bereishis* 2:18).

In his commentary to this verse, Ramban states that Adam HaRishon must have had a method of procreating even before Chavah was fashioned. All creatures were created male and female in order to procreate. If so, why was it necessary for Hashem to make Chavah into a separate being? Wouldn't it have been more convenient to be self-sufficient — to be able to bear and raise children without the need for another person? Isn't that total independence a utopian dream?

The answer appears in the verse quoted above. *Lo tov heyos ha'adam levado* — it is not good that man be alone. There is something "not good" about being alone. The entire purpose of Creation is for us to perfect ourselves, and one of the most meaningful ways of doing so is by learning to do for others. In the words of Rav Chaim of Volozhin "*Ki zeh kol ha'adam* — for this is the basic principle of mankind: *lo le'atzmo nivra* — he was not created for himself, *rak leho'il le'acheirim* — but to help others, *kechol asher yimtza bekocho la'asos* — as much as is possible for him to do with the strengths he was given."

Had Adam HaRishon functioned on his own, he would have been lacking one of the keystones of humanity and would have been branded *lo tov* for life.

We all entered this world as consummate takers. Anyone who has had a baby or has been in close contact with one knows that babies are the greatest takers. They never worry about anyone else. Their entire focus in life is to be fed, warm, dry, and cuddled, and they have absolutely no interest in how their needs affect you. They couldn't care less whether you had a hard day or whether you haven't slept for two nights. Their motto is, "Feed me; clothe me; diaper me; burp me; love me; take care of me."

And that lasts …

Let's just say that it lasts for a while. A *long* while.

Pardon me for reminding you, but you, too, were born this way. You, too, were once self-centered, self-absorbed, and narcissistic. The *tachlis* (purpose) of life is to transcend that natural inclination toward taking and to become a giver. It is a lifelong endeavor, but if there is one turning point at which we must make the switch from taker to giver, that point is the day of our marriage. Marriage requires us to undergo a metamorphosis — to go from caterpillar to butterfly.

In marriage, we can no longer think primarily about ourselves. The "me" must become "we," and the "I" must become "us." That is the entire purpose of marriage, and that is why Hashem said, "*Lo tov heyos ha'adam levado.*"

This does not mean that a person who never finds his or her *zivug* is doomed. One of the most famous *gabba'ei tzedakah* in Yerushalayim is a man who never married, and he is a giver of the highest degree. But the process of learning to be a giver is far more difficult if one is not married. The ideal situation, which is what Hashem had in mind for each of us, is to marry and have someone to whom to give.

There is a common misconception that one's love for another person increases when he or she receives from that person. The true way to build love is to give unconditionally. As we have mentioned elsewhere, the Hebrew word *ahavah*, love, is related to the word *hav*, to give.

Since giving builds love, we can perhaps understand the inordinate obsession people have for their pets. If children are the hardest thing in the world, pets are the easiest. They don't give you *agmas nefesh* (heartache), they don't need braces, they don't have to be accepted into a seminary, and you don't have to find *shidduchim* for them. But above all, you have to give to pets unconditionally. That is why people are literally in love with their pets. They treat them better than they treat their children.

When I travel, I generally do not make conversation with my seatmates. I exchange pleasantries, and then settle in for a flight in solitude. Once, however, I was flying to Brazil, which is a 10-hour flight. When you are going to spend 10 hours sitting next to someone, you feel that you must make some attempt at conversation. My seatmate turned out to be a cardiac-care nurse who was on her way to a medical conference. She was obviously an intelligent individual. In the midst of an otherwise sensible conversation, she took out her wallet and said — and I'll quote verbatim — "I want to show you the love of my life." She flipped open her wallet and showed me a collage of her three children, lovingly surrounding the most prized member of the family: her dog. "*This* is the love of my life," she said, pointing to the dog — lest I foolishly assume that she was talking about her children.

"What kind of dog is it?" I asked, for lack of a better rejoinder.

"It's a Rottweiler," she said proudly.

I don't know much about dogs, but I do know that you stay far away from Rottweilers. But this was the *love of her life*. Why? Because she had to give so much to it. Now, unlike her children, her dog probably returned her love. It was probably very happy to see her. But that is not where her overwhelming love came from. It came from unconditional giving.

Lehavdil — to make a comparison from the ridiculous to the sublime — this is why Rabbi Akiva Eiger loved his wife so much. Aside from his greatness in learning, Rabbi Akiva Eiger was a perfect *tzaddik*, and as such, gave to his wife unconditionally. It is no wonder, then, that when his wife predeceased him, he felt such an extreme void.

When we look at episodes in the lives of our *gedolim,* we find many other Torah giants whose thoughtfulness and willingness to give to their wives made their marriages so beautiful. I could write an entire book of such stories, but I'll share the two that have had the most profound impact on me.

Rabbi Yosef Dov Soloveitchik was predeceased by his wife, who had suffered greatly from cancer before she passed away. During that period, since the rav himself was not a young man, the yeshivah set up a rotation, in which boys would take turns assisting him in preparing supper and turning in for the night. One night, as the boy who was assisting him was about to leave, Rabbi Soloveitchik asked him where he was going. "I'm going out on a date," the boy responded.

"Why are you wearing sneakers?" the rav asked. "It's not proper to go out in sneakers."

"I only have white socks," the boy responded, "and I don't want to go on a date wearing dress shoes and white socks."

As soon as the words left this boy's mouth, he felt like an utter fool. Rabbi Soloveitchik wore white socks with his dress shoes.

The boy began to apologize profusely for his faux pas, but Rabbi Soloveitchik waved it off, and instructed the *bachur* to go to his drawer and take any of the pairs of black or navy socks stored there.

The boy followed his instructions, and then somehow had the audacity to ask, "If the Rav has black and navy socks, why does he wear white socks with dress shoes?"

Nu, ah gutte kasheh. Listen to the amazing answer.

"Due to my wife's illness," explained Rabbi Soloveitchik, "it is difficult for her to distinguish between the black socks and the navy socks. It is easier for her to pair the white socks, so I wear those."

That is a story of sensitivity, and consideration. Rabbi Soloveitchik *knew* that it was unconventional to wear white socks with dress shoes, and this perhaps even resulted in people looking askance at him, but he did so to spare his wife the difficulty of pairing his dark socks.

If there is one story that is the most astounding, however, it is a story that occurred with Rabbi Yaakov Yisrael Twerski, the Hornosteipel Rebbe of Milwaukee.

Two months before his passing, the Rebbe was diagnosed with pancreatic cancer. From the Rebbe's 50 years of experience visiting sick patients, he understood that his end was near. He summoned his son, Rabbi Dr. Abraham J. Twerski (who is a medical doctor), to discuss his options.

"The doctors suggest that I undergo chemotherapy," the Rebbe said. "*Es iz a brachah levatalah, nein* (it is 'blessing in vain' [i.e. — a waste of time], no)?"

The son nodded in agreement; based on his medical knowledge, his father had already suffered irreversible damage.

"I am going to suffer terribly from chemotherapy, right?" asked the Rebbe.

Rabbi Dr. Twerski nodded again.

"It is not worthwhile to go through it," concluded the Rebbe. "It is not going to help, and I will suffer. I am going to inform the doctors that I don't want chemotherapy."

Painful as it was to confirm his father's analysis, Rabbi Dr. Twerski had to agree that it was the right move.

While this conversation transpired, Rebbetzin Twerski was outside discussing her husband's illness with the attending physician, who told her that chemotherapy was an option. She walked into her husband's room, and, unaware of the previous conversation, she said, "I want you to have chemotherapy."

A moment later the attending physician walked in, and he said, "So, are we going through with chemotherapy?"

"Yes," replied the Rebbe, leaving his son opened-mouthed.

Later that day, Rabbi Dr. Twerski had an opportunity to ask his father why he had changed his mind so quickly.

"We both know that the chemotherapy won't help. We both know that I am going to suffer from it," said the Rebbe. "If I don't try the treatment, however, your mother will not forgive herself. She will always think to herself, 'I should have insisted that he have chemotherapy. I'm sure he would have lived longer if he had done so.'

"I don't want your mother to suffer from such guilt, so I'll do it for her sake," the Rebbe concluded.

We all have times in marriage in which we go beyond the call of duty for our spouses. In many cases, however, our actions are fueled by a "You scratch my back and I'll scratch yours" attitude. Here is a man who knew that there would be no payback. But he was ready to suffer through the horrific physical discomfort of the chemotherapy anyway, just to spare his wife feelings of guilt.

When we read these stories, two thoughts come to mind. One is a feeling that we are far-removed from the greatness and devotion of these *gedolim*. That is true. But it is important to know these stories anyway, because if our aim is to reach a lofty goal, we must aim high. If we set our sights on mediocrity, then mediocrity is the best we will do.

The second thought that might come to mind is that such devotion is the result of 50 years of marriage. Not necessarily.

Rabbi Ephraim Wachsman tells the story of a young man who got engaged and wanted to buy his *kallah* a diamond ring. He came from a poor family, and they simply could not afford the ring. Well aware of his financial situation, his *kallah* told him, "I don't want you to buy me a diamond ring. What does a diamond do for a person anyway?"

"My *kallah* is not going to have a ring like every other *kallah*?" he said. "I *insist* on buying you a ring."

The discussion went back and forth, and finally they came up with a compromise. "Buy me a cubic zirconium ring," the *kallah* said. "For a few hundred dollars you can buy me a rock so large that I will need a sling to hold up my arm. It will look exactly like a real diamond, and no one will know the difference. I'll be happy, and you won't have to put yourself in debt for it."

The *chasan* agreed. But that night, he approached several friends, borrowed a few thousand dollars, bought his *kallah* a real diamond, and presented it to her without telling her that it was real. They got married, and he tutored for a year and a half to pay off the loan for the diamond. When he made the final payment, he told his wife, "Guess what? I didn't tell you, but the stone on your finger is real."

In this case, we are not dealing with someone married 50 years. This was a *chasan*. But it meant a lot to him that his *kallah* should be no less special than all other *kallahs*.

I don't know what happened to this *chasan* and *kallah*, but I think one can safely assume that "they lived happily ever after." If during their engagement they were already so devoted and considerate of each other, it bodes very well for the future. Giving creates a relationship, and this couple was ready to give.

As nice as this story is, it brings us to a point that is worth mentioning when we discuss marriage. Our community has developed a custom of prenuptial giving that has steadily increased over the years. In the past, the *kallah* got a couple of pieces of jewelry, the *chasan* got a *Shas* and a watch, and everyone was happy. Now there is an entire *"Shulchan Aruch"* on what the *chasan* must give the *kallah* and vice versa. But it is not the *chasan* and *kallah* giving to each other as it was in this story. It is the *chasan's* father giving a half-dozen pieces of jewelry to his future daughter-in-law. A father-in-law doesn't need to build much of a relationship with his daughter-in-law. For the relationship they need, it is enough for him to eat at her house after the wedding and compliment her on her lasagna.

The same holds true the other way around. Nowadays, if your daughter becomes engaged before Chanukah, you must buy the *chasan* a towering silver menorah. If you happen to make the wedding after Purim, you must also spring for a *Megillah*, preferably with a silver case.

What does all this giving accomplish? Why do parents have to spend thousands of dollars on these gifts?

A friend of mine recently celebrated the engagement of his son. We were discussing the expenses of the *chasunah*, and I said, "You get off easy. The *chasan's* side pays less than the *kallah's* side."

"No we don't," my friend responded. "Have you taken into account the diamond ring, the pearls, the earrings, the watch, the necklace, and — let's not forget — the custom *sheitel*? That adds up to the price of dinner for 300 people."

Does this enhance our children's marriages in any way? I don't think so. If you want to give your child a great gift, teach him or her what marriage is about. Unfortunately, too many young people are entering marriage thinking about what they can get out of their marriage, not what they can give. Dispel that myth for your children, and you will be doing them the greatest favor. Teach your *chasan* or *kallah* that marriage is about giving, not getting. But giving means giving *of oneself,* and *from* oneself, not spending colossal amounts of their parent's money.

It is important to note that even if someone is approaching marriage with an attitude of "what can I get" for the noblest of reasons — he needs some level of support so he can sit and learn in *kollel*, for instance — it is still wrong. If the *kallah* or her parents want to support a young man so that he can devote himself to full-time Torah study, that is their choice. But a boy should not approach marriage with thoughts of, "What will I be getting? I'm worth a lot." If all of his thoughts are focused on getting, he is unlikely to succeed in marriage, because marriage was created to teach people to become givers rather than takers.

◆§ Marriage: A Second Opinion

I think that there are other reasons why Chavah was fashioned from Adam HaRishon. A spouse plays an important role that can be fulfilled only by a separate party: a spouse provides a second opinion.

One of the basic human traits is that we have a difficult time viewing situations in an objective manner. Our vested interests will taint our view on a matter, even if we try to ignore it. It is important, therefore, to have the input of an impartial second party to help us view our lives properly.

The problem is that we also have egos, we crave independence, and we tend to chafe when people tell us what to do — especially when that person is an outsider. This leads to a situation in which we cannot judge issues in life on our own lest our subjectivity lead us to make a mistake, but when objective observers weigh in with advice, we are inclined to reject their opinion.

Hashem did us a great favor. He provided us with an *insider* who can provide us with an unbiased, loving opinion. A spouse has the advantage of being part of you — as *Chazal* said, "*Ishto kegufo* (one's wife is like himself)," and "*ba'al ke'ishto* (a husband is like his wife)" — but he or she is also objective enough to tell you, "I'm sorry, but you are viewing this issue incorrectly."

The *Netziv* finds an allusion to this idea in the words, "*Lo tov heyos ha'adam levado, e'eseh lo **eizer kenegdo*** — it is not good that man be alone, I will make for him *a helper, corresponding to him.*" Although the term *kenegdo* may be translated as "corresponding to him," the more common translation is "opposite him or opposing him." This leads the Talmud (*Yevamos* 63b) to point out that *eizer kenegdo* seems to be an oxymoron. A wife is either a helper to her husband or opposite him. How can she be both?

The *Netziv* explains that a wife is indeed an *eizer*, a helper, but the help may sometimes come in the form of *kenegdo*, opposing him. It may be difficult for us to hear our spouses tell us, "Honey, you're making a mistake," but the alternative is to stumble through life repeating our blunders or committing even greater ones. On occasion, the *"eizer"* must be *"kenegdo."*

It is important to remember that, like everything else in life, *kenegdo* can be overdone. Have you ever noticed that a salt shaker has several holes, while a pepper shaker has only a few? Food is enhanced by the sharpness of pepper, but only if it is applied in small measure. Criticism, like pepper, must be used sparingly. If you lay it on too thick, it has a negative effect.

☙ Remember the Past

I would like to draw one more lesson from the very first marriage in history, and it is one that we must all incorporate into our marriages if they are to succeed.

As we all know, on the very first day of that marriage, Hashem told Adam that he could partake of the fruit of any tree in Gan Eden except for the *Eitz Hada'as* (Tree of Knowledge). Adam relayed the commandment to Chavah, but before long, the Serpent enticed Chavah into eating from the *Eitz Hada'as*, and she, in turn, gave Adam to eat from the tree. This sin affected the world in the worst possible way, for one of the curses that came upon mankind as a result of that sin was death.

Directly following the verse in which Hashem informs Adam that he would eventually die, as would all of his offspring, the Torah states, "*Vayikra ha'adam sheim ishto Chavah, ki hi hayesah eim kol chai* — The man called his wife's name Chavah, because she had become the mother *of all the living*" (*Bereishis* 3:20).

Have you ever noticed this strange juxtaposition? If we were to name a person who just brought death upon mankind, we might have been tempted to call her *Misah* (death). It may not sound as good as Chavah, but it certainly would have been appropriate given the situation that had just unfolded.

At the moment when all seemed bleak, Adam HaRishon took note of what *chesed* is all about.

The Talmud (*Sotah* 14a) states that the Torah begins with *chesed* and ends with *chesed*. The final verses of the Torah deal with Hashem burying Moshe Rabbeinu. Performing a burial is called a *chesed shel emes*, a true kindness. Where is the *chesed* at the beginning of the Torah? As a result of partaking of the *Eitz Hada'as*, Adam and Chavah were suddenly aware of the fact that they were unclothed, and they became bashful. Although this bashfulness was a result of their sin, Hashem nevertheless performed a *chesed* and made clothing for them. This, says the Talmud, is the first *chesed* mentioned in the Torah.

Left to our own devices, we might have assumed that there was an immeasurable *chesed* that preceded this one. God had no need for us mortals in the world. He created us to enable *us* to reap the reward for our mitzvos. Why doesn't the Talmud consider the creation of mankind the first *chesed* in history?

The creation of Adam HaRishon was indeed a *chesed*, but not a particularly difficult one. Adam was the most perfect being ever created, and he was to perform an important function in the world.

Marriage: From Caterpillar to Butterfly

But when Adam and Chavah sinned, bringing death and destruction to the pristine new world, they felt terrible about themselves. When Hashem showed them that He was willing to look beyond their mistakes and love them and take care of them despite their wrongdoings, that was a tremendous *chesed*.

Adam HaRishon perceived that, and put that form of *chesed* into practice. Chavah had committed the greatest mistake imaginable. No one would ever make such a grave error again. Adam looked at her and said, "You are still Chavah. You are still the mother of all mankind."

If our marriages are to succeed, we must all learn to look beyond our spouses' mistakes. We must learn not to narrow our focus to the present state of affairs, but to look at the totality of our relationships and consider all the good our spouses have done for us.

The Talmud notes that there is an apparent Scriptural contradiction regarding women. One verse states, "*Matza isha matza tov* — One who has found a woman has found good" (*Mishlei* 18:22).

Another verse states, "*U'motze ani mar mimaves es ha'ishah* — I have found more bitter than death: the woman ..." (*Koheles* 7:26).

Is woman good, or more bitter than death?

The answer given is that in past tense, *matza*, woman is good, but in present, *motze*, she can be more bitter than death. How does this explanation answer the question?

Perhaps the Talmud is teaching that if someone constantly dwells on the present, and each time his wife makes even the slightest mistake he places that error under an electron microscope and views it as a catastrophic error, then life with her will be extremely bitter. But if a person is willing to view current events against the backdrop of all the wonderful times spent together, then married life will be good.

Don't dwell on mistakes. Forgive and forget. Remember, no woman will ever make a greater mistake than Chavah did. Even forgetting to mail the mortgage check is not as bad as eating from the *Eitz Hada'as*. (It's pretty bad, but not *as* bad.) Look at the totality of your relationship, and remember that your spouse is the one who has provided you with so much happiness and blessing.

With all the colossal waste of money that goes into making a wedding nowadays, Rav Pam noted that there is one positive aspect of modern-day weddings: the pictures. No, he wasn't referring to the time wasted after the *chuppah* as the photographer artfully arranges all 100 members of each side of the family for portraits with the *chasan* and *kallah* while the rest of the guests languish in the main ballroom. He was referring to the fact that when people were married in prewar Europe, they were lucky if they had one picture of their wedding. My parents had one picture of their wedding, in which they were seated with a group of family members. Nowadays we have a male and female team photographing every second of the wedding.

Rav Pam would ask people, "When is the last time you looked at your wedding album?"

I would take one step back and ask, "Where *is* your wedding album?"

Rav Pam would recommend that people look at their wedding album from time to time to remind themselves of the happiness they felt on their wedding night. Remind yourselves of what you saw in each other and the qualities that are still there — albeit buried under the minutiae of daily living.

✂ Patience for the Future

The Hebrew word for marriage is *nisu'in*, which has its roots in the word *naso*, to carry. In marriage, one must carry — and sometimes it can indeed be a schlep — his or her spouse's foibles and negative traits, along with the idiosyncrasies that so endear us to one another.

In our world of instant communication, with our all-purpose handheld communication devices enabling us to receive all the information we need instantly via email, telephone, and instant messaging, we are no longer used to waiting. In order to succeed in marriage, however, you must have the patience to allow your spouse to change, to grow, and to overcome the obstacles that he

Marriage: From Caterpillar to Butterfly / 199

or she has been born with. People do change, but it takes years. Marriage is not instant. Changing oneself is not instant. You must learn to have patience with the other person's foibles and carry them until they can change.

When I speak to male audiences, they are all able to relate to some of the profound differences that I have found between men and women. For instance:

Men are always hot, and women are always cold.

It takes a man ten minutes to pack. For a five-day trip. It takes women hours and hours!

Every woman must read before she goes to sleep at night. While she reads, her husband is tossing and turning, thinking, "Aren't beds made to sleep in? Why must she read? It's late. I'm tired. *Shut the light!*" (I am not referring to my own marriage, of course. These examples are from anecdotal evidence.)

On the other side of the equation, women wonder why it is so difficult to pick up a pair of socks. And why do men wash only the inside of the pot, not the outside? Why is it so hard for men to learn these things?

The list goes on and on. But that is what marriage is about — learning to have patience to allow the other person to become better, and to schlep around their idiosyncrasies until that happens.

Like everything that is worth having, a happy, successful marriage requires work. But there is not a more worthwhile investment in the world. Nothing is as rewarding as a good marriage.

Statistics show that most American households are now led by a single. How sad. Do you realize how many lonely people that makes for? If you have a successful marriage, you have one of the greatest gifts: a partner for life, a soul mate — someone to give to and to share with. That gift makes any effort that we invest into acquiring it seem like a mere trifle.

Whether you are a single person — may Hashem send your *zivug* speedily — a newlywed, or an old hand at marriage, remember that marriage is about giving, about caring enough to criticize respectfully, about willing to forget and to forego — about willing to make that change from caterpillar to butterfly.

Kiruv: Not Just for Pros

In our times, certain mitzvos seem to have all the "luck," as we witness them being observed on a level that no one could have imagined several generations ago.

Forty years ago, the *kezayis* of matzah eaten at the Pesach Seder was the amount that your father handed you, no questions asked. Today, the *kezayis* we eat is precise, carefully measured to be sure that it is indeed a *kezayis* — and somehow several times larger than anyone could have fathomed an olive-sized piece of matzah could be.

The *esrogim* we use nowadays come with a pedigree. We know from which orchard they came, under whose supervision the field was planted, and so on and so forth.

I would venture to say that a typical bar mitzvah boy today receives a pair of *tefillin* that reaches a far-higher halachic standard than the *tefillin* worn by great Torah leaders of prewar Europe.

And then there are mitzvos being performed today that were not performed at all, or certainly not as frequently, just a few decades ago.

On January 1, 1980, my mother-in-law donated a *Sefer Torah* to Yeshivas Ner Yisrael of Baltimore in memory of her husband, Rav Yaakov Blumenkrantz. That was the first *Hachnasas Sefer Torah* I had ever participated in, and from the enthusiasm of the crowd in attendance it was evident that this was a first for many of them. Today a *Hachnasas Sefer* is no longer a rare event.

Several months before the onset of the *shemittah* (Sabbatical) year of 5768, I noticed an advertisement in the paper stating that I could purchase a small piece of land in Eretz Yisrael for the *shemittah* year, and so, for the first time in my life, I was able to fulfill the mitzvah of allowing a field in Eretz Yisrael to lie fallow during *shemittah*.

Every spring there are advertisements in the Jewish papers from individuals who want to help us fulfill the mitzvah of *shiluach hakein* (sending away a mother bird before taking its eggs or chicks [see *Devarim* 22:6-7]).

With the current renaissance in the observance of formerly uncommon mitzvos, it comes as a surprise that some of the commonplace mitzvos are not performed as frequently nowadays. When is the last time the average adult has fulfilled the mitzvah of *hashavas aveidah*, the mitzvah to return a lost object? I suspect that for many people *hashavas aveidah* went out of style in second grade. Back then it was exciting for us to return a pencil dropped by the person sitting in front of us in class, and proudly announce, "*Hashavas aveidah*."

It would seem that in a day and age in which people will go out of their way to perform *shiluach hakein* and *shemittah*, I should have an easy time convincing you to delve into the relatively easy mitzvah of *hashavas aveidah*. Don't get nervous — I am not about to show up at your door with a trunk full of gloves and scarves and ask you to help me locate their owners. I want to introduce an aspect of the mitzvah of *hashavas aveidah* that deals with something far more valuable than lost articles of clothing.

The Torah mentions the mitzvah of *hashavas aveidah* several times, one of which is in *Parashas Ki Seitzei* (*Devarim* 22:1-2). "You shall not see the ox of your brother or his sheep or goat cast off, and hide yourself from them; *hasheiv teshiveim le'achicha* — you shall surely return them to your brother. If your brother is not near you and you do not know him, then gather it inside your house, and it shall remain with you until your brother inquires after it, and you return it to him."

In his commentary to these verses, the *Ohr HaChaim HaKadosh* writes that "ox, sheep, and goat" are actually references to people who are no more knowledgeable (in terms of Torah knowledge) than animals. When you find such a person, and he belongs to "your brother" — a reference to Hashem, who relates to the righteous as "brothers" — do not hide yourself. Don't turn a blind eye toward the "castaways," the unfortunate souls who have become estranged from Hashem. Return them to your "Brother," Hashem.

Did you ever go to an amusement park or to an event, when suddenly you turn around and realize that one of your children is missing? Do you know the feeling of panic that sets in at such times?

We were at a large hotel several years ago with our married children and our grandchildren, and our 4-year-old granddaughter wandered off into a crowd of approximately 1,000 people. I'll never forget the fright we all experienced, especially her parents. We all knew that she wouldn't be lost forever, and yet the terror that runs through the parents' hearts when their child is missing is not a feeling that you want to experience.

"*Banim atem l'Hashem Elokeichem*," the Torah tells us. "You are *children* to Hashem, your God" (*Devarim* 14:1). Hashem has lost not thousands or hundreds of thousands, but *millions* of His children. Imagine the pain He feels. In the verse *hasheiv teshivim*, Hashem exhorts us, "Please, bring back My children."

In a nearly prophetic statement, the *Ohr HaChaim*, who lived several hundred years ago, explains the verse as follows:

> "*If your Brother is not near you*" refers to the final exile, which is distant in terms of time, when the tribulations of exile will

cause people to feel that they *"do not know Him."* They will stray from Hashem and may be unsure of whether He exists, as we see is the case in our generation.

If the *Ohr HaChaim* bemoans the people lost to Hashem in his times, how would he describe our times?

What does the Torah command us to do in such times? The *Ohr HaChaim* continues his elucidation of the verse:

> *"Gather it inside your house."* Gather those straying, wandering souls into your house — the *beis hamidrash* [study hall] — and teach them Torah and mitzvos. *"It shall remain with you until your Brother inquires after it."* Hashem will eventually gather up these souls, and consider it as if you returned them to Him.

You cannot imagine the debt of gratitude a parent feels toward someone who returns his or her lost child. Out of supreme gratitude, they would literally do anything for the person. Extrapolate once again to Hashem. How must He feel when He sees someone returning one of His lost children, and how willing is He to do anything for that person?

The Talmud states that if a person teaches Torah to the son of an Torah-ignorant person, Hashem grants him the ability to nullify all painful decrees, as the prophet Yirmiyahu said, *"Im totzi yakar mizoleil* — if you shall bring forth an upright person from a sinner, *kefi tihiyeh* — then you shall be like My own mouth" (*Yirmiyahu* 15:19).

Astonishingly, Hashem is so grateful to those who return lost souls to Him that He rewards them by giving them as much power to nullify decrees as He has to make them.

Perhaps this is what Rebbetzin Kanievski had in mind in the following incident.

Four childless women came to Rebbetzin Kanievski for *berachos* to have children. As she is wont to do, the Rebbetzin spent time with each one, discussing their situations and challenges. She asked them how they spend their days, inquired about the medical background of their infertility problems, and then blessed them and advised them accordingly. To one she recommended a specific doctor, to another she advised a specific course of action, and so on.

When she asked the fourth woman what she does, the woman replied that she is *mekarev* people through Lev L'Achim. "In that case," Rebbetzin Kanievski responded, "you need not try any *segulos* or go see any special doctors. You will have a baby." *Im totzi yakar mizoleil, kefi tihiyeh*. Sure enough, nine months later this woman had a baby.

Is this the magic bullet? Will all of your problems disappear if you become involved in *kiruv*? I wish it were so simple. But if you are looking for something to do as a merit for a *yeshuah* (salvation), bringing Hashem's children back to Him is a good place to start.

ৼ Do You Love Hashem?

There is another mitzvah that we can fulfill by bringing back lost souls, and it is one that should not be ignored for even one second.

There is a concept that many are unfamiliar with called *sheish mitzvos temidiyos* — the six constant mitzvos. The *Sefer HaChinuch* is the first to point out that unlike most mitzvos that can be performed only at specific times, there are six mitzvos that we can accomplish every second of the day or night, rain or shine, weekday or Shabbos. One of those mitzvos is *ahavas Hashem*, to love Hashem, a mitzvah we mention at least two times a day in *Shema* in the words, *Ve'ahavta eis Hashem Elokecha* — you shall love Hashem, your God.

Any time of the day or night that you think about the love you have for Hashem, you fulfill a mitzvah *d'Oraisa* (Torah-level obligation). So allow me ask you a pointed question. Do you walk around feeling "in love" with Hashem?

I'm sure that you have told your children, "I love you." I'm sure — or maybe I hope — that you have told your spouse, "I love you." Have you ever said to Hashem, "I love you, Hashem"? In all honesty, it is difficult for us to make that statement, because it seems odd to say it. Let us put the statement aside. When it comes to our children and spouses, we have ways of demonstrating our love, even when we do not express it verbally. Similarly, there are ways that we can demonstrate our love for Hashem even if we feel uncomfortable proclaiming it.

Commenting on the words *Ve'ahavta eis Hashem Elokecha*, *Sifri* states, "*Ahaveihu al habriyos* — make Hashem beloved by others." If it seems that my earlier comparison of love of Hashem to love of our children or spouses was irreverent, listen to the way the Rambam explains this *Sifri*: "Just as one who loves a person will want others to be as enamored with him or her, so too, one who truly loves Hashem will want others to love Him as well."

Who is the prime example of a person who loved Hashem so much that he spent his life sharing his love of Hashem with others? The Rambam concludes that we should follow the teaching of the *Sifri* and make Hashem beloved by others, "Like Avraham, our forefather — as the Torah states, 'And the souls that they made in Charan.'" [These souls were the people who were taught by Avraham and Sarah to recognize Hashem, serve Him, and love Him.]

To bring this concept down to modern terms, I will offer you some contemporary examples, with the caveat that the comparison should not be taken literally in any way, shape, or form.

There is an American concept called "enthusiasts," people who will spend their every waking moment obsessing about something that they hold dear. There are, for example, baseball enthusiasts, computer game enthusiasts, and food enthusiasts. These people devote their lives to their interest, and will convey their enthusiasm to anyone who is willing to listen — and often to those who would much prefer not to listen.

Lehavdil — and I use this comparison only in order to clarify the concept— the Rambam teaches us that Avraham Avinu was a "Hashem enthusiast." He traveled far and wide, spreading the idea of monotheism to the masses, out of his deep love for Hashem. The mitzvah of *ahavas Hashem* obligates each one of us to become a "Hashem enthusiast," and should cause us to want to share our love for Hashem with all who are willing to listen.

A *New* Profession?

In the secular world, there are professions today that did not exist 20 or 30 years ago. Nowadays, we all know that an IT professional is an Information Technology professional. But had someone asked you three decades ago what you do for a living, and you would have answered, "I am an IT professional," he would have said, "What's an *it* professional?"

It would seem that the same is true in the religious world. There is a profession nowadays called "Kiruv Professional" that we don't remember hearing about 30 years ago.

But there are two fallacies in the comparison. First of all, *kiruv* is a profession that is millennia old. Avraham Avinu was a *kiruv* worker, even if he didn't hang a shingle on the entrance to his tent.

The second fallacy is that in the secular world, an engineer is not a dentist, and a lawyer is not a plumber. In our world, however, no matter what you do, no matter how you make a living, you can — and should be — a *kiruv* worker. Avraham Avinu did not make a living from *kiruv*, but that did not deter him. Unlike engineering, dentistry, and law, *kiruv* is something that should not be limited to professionals. All descendants of Avraham Avinu must work in *kiruv*.

The Talmud (*Sanhedrin* 97a) states that the world as we know it will exist for 6,000 years. The first 2,000 will be years of "nothingness (*tohu*)," the next 2,000 will be the years of Torah, and the final 2,000 will be the days of Mashiach.

When did the 2,000 years of Torah begin? An educated guess would probably be that they began when the Torah was transmitted to us at Sinai. A good guess, but incorrect. The Talmud states that the 2,000 years of Torah began when Avraham Avinu began to introduce the existence of Hashem to people around the world.

Kesef Mishneh, considered one of the primary commentaries on the Rambam, asks a question. If we start counting the years of Torah from Avraham Avinu, it would seem that he was the first one to teach Torah. We know, however, that Noach's son and grandson,

Shem and Eiver, had a yeshivah. Why don't we start counting the years of Torah from them?

Shem and Eiver, answers the *Kesef Mishneh*, taught Torah to the students who came to their yeshivah to seek the truth. But they did not venture out into the wide open world and teach Torah to the pagan masses as Avraham did. The era of Torah began only when Torah became available to the masses.

In our day, we have witnessed a renaissance in spreading the truth of Torah. There are organizations urging people to learn *daf yomi*, *Mishnah yomi*, *Mishnah Berurah yomi*, and those organizations are doing important work. But if we keep Torah study in the confines of our shuls and *batei midrash*, then we cannot consider our times an era of Torah study. In order to qualify for that title, we must spread Torah to the masses who are thirsting for it.

◆§ The Rebbetzin's Cholent vs. the Rav's Derashah

I think that we can follow Avraham Avinu's lead in another area related to *kiruv*.

Many people feel a desire to become involved in *kiruv*, but are afraid to take the plunge because they think they will be asked tough questions that they cannot answer: "Prove God's existence" or, "Why did God allow the Holocaust to happen" or, "Why do children die of cancer if God is loving and benevolent?"

They decide that since they do not know the answers to those questions, they had better refrain from inviting these people to their homes.

There are two solutions to that problem. One is to go to a seminar offered by organizations such as Project Inspire. You will be taught how to answer the basic questions that you will be asked.

But the more profound and precise answer is that you don't need to know all the answers. Avraham Avinu did not necessarily succeed in *kiruv* because he knew all the answers. The Talmud relates that Avraham Avinu would invite people into his tent, offer them a good meal and a place to relax, and when they wanted to pay him or to thank him, he would say, "Don't thank me, thank the One Who provides the food."

Today, too, many experts in the *kiruv* field will tell you that the Rebbetzin's *cholent* is often a more convincing *kiruv* tool than the Rabbi's sermon. You may not have the answers to deep theological questions, but you can share a Shabbos or a Yom Tov, and there is nothing more powerful than taking part in an authentic Jewish experience.

I recently read about a new trend developing among busy New York professionals who are constantly on the phone or answering emails, and feel that they need a break from their hectic lives. These professionals have begun to attend weekend getaways in Upstate New York. They head to the mountains, to a little town called Woodbourne, NY, and they spend the weekend in … no, they don't unwind in a *frum* bungalow colony. They spend their weekend in an ashram. They visit a guru who promises to fill their lives with peace and serenity. Here is the schedule of "peace and serenity":

They get up at 4:30 Shabbos morning. (Apparently no one told them about the late *minyan*.) They spend the next two hours meditating, free from their computers, cell phones, blackberries, and other tension-inducing gadgets. They then eat a healthy breakfast of greens and salads, and finally — and I am not making this up — they go out to clean the toilets. And for this pleasure they pay $200. I would tell them to come to my house; I'll pay *them* to clean my toilets.

After such a weekend, these people come back to the office and talk about how invigorating it is, and what a wonderful experience it is. The saddest part of the article was the caption on a picture of the man washing the lettuce for the meals. It identified the man by his first name, which was an Indian name that I cannot remember, and by his last name: Lieberman.

This is overwhelmingly distressing. These people — many of whom are probably as Jewish as this Lieberman fellow — don't have to go all the way up to Woodbourne. They can stop in Monsey, or even stay in Manhattan, and spend a Shabbos with a *frum* family. The fact that they are so desperate that they have to go to an ashram and clean toilets is a tragedy of epic proportions, and it is one that we can all take a part in eradicating.

~§ Just Be Yourself

Sometimes it doesn't even take a Shabbos at your house. You can bring a person back by showing him how a Torah Jew behaves.

There was a fellow in Eretz Yisrael who had to travel from Petach Tikvah to his home in Bnei Brak. He hailed a cab, and after coming to an agreement on price with the driver, he sat down in the passenger seat. As they pulled up to the very first traffic light on their journey, the passenger glanced to his right and saw that his neighbor had pulled alongside him. He deduced that his neighbor was also headed back to Bnei Brak, and he decided that he would rather spend his time discussing Torah topics with his learned neighbor than prattling with the irreligious cab driver.

He reached into his pocket and extracted the full price he had agreed upon for the ride, handed it to the driver, and explained that since his neighbor was going to Bnei Brak anyway, he would like to join him.

"I can't take your money," the cab driver protested. "I drove for less than one block."

"I'm not willing to let you lose out on your fare just because my neighbor happened to have pulled up alongside," the man insisted. "We made an agreement, and you deserve the money."

With that, the man opened the car door and exited the cab before the driver could hand back his money.

"Wait!" the driver called out. "Please give me your name and number."

The man dutifully scribbled his information on a piece of paper and handed it to the driver, and then entered his friend's car just as the light turned green.

One week later, this man received a phone call from the cab driver. "Can my wife and I come to your house? I want to learn about Judaism. If religion makes people so thoughtful and refined, I want a part in it."

ﷺ The Best Sales Pitch: The Torah Itself

Rabbi Uri Zohar is world-renowned for his activism on behalf of Lev L'Achim. But he was once famous for being *the* foremost secular actor and movie director in Israel. In the spirit of the secularists who founded the country, he was virulently antireligious, and actually began to investigate religious Judaism in order to deride it in his movies, but in the process he found truth and became one of the highest profile *baalei teshuvah* in recent history.

Rabbi Zohar was once approached by a *yungerman* for advice. "My irreligious neighbor is showing some signs of interest in religion. He wants to get together with me and study some portion of the Torah once a week. I was wondering what I should start with. Should we study one of *Ramchal's* works on *hashkafah*, or perhaps something more contemporary?"

"What are you learning in *kollel*?" Rabbi Zohar asked.

"*Bava Kamma*," the *yungerman* replied.

"Then take two Gemaros over to his house, and teach him *Bava Kamma*," Rabbi Zohar advised.

"*Bava Kamma*?" the man asked incredulously. "You think that an irreligious man is going to have any interest in the halachic intricacies of an ox goring another ox?"

"Your problem," said Rabbi Zohar, "is that you don't recognize the full power of the Torah. The Torah sells itself; all you have to do is make it available to those who are not able to learn on their own."

Unlikely as it sounds, Rabbi Zohar's advice is upheld by stories that abound in the world of *kiruv*.

An irreligious woman who had become involved in some sort of cult in India called her religious sister in Israel to inform her that she was planning a visit to her guru, and that she could spend a weekend with her in Yerushalayim en-route. The religious sister saw this as an opportunity to introduce her sister to some aspect of the Torah's truth. She searched for a *shiur* by an inspiring *kiruv* professional, but unfortunately none were scheduled for that Shabbos in her neighborhood. The only *shiur* in the neighborhood, in fact, was on the topic of — I kid you not — *hashavas aveidah*. Now, as important as *hashavas aveidah* is, the technicalities of the halachos involved are not noted for bringing people back to *Yiddishkeit*.

With no other options at hand, she decided to take her sister to that *shiur*. The lecturer was well-versed in the intricacies of the mitzvah, detailing for those gathered what constitutes a *siman* (identifying characteristic that might enable the owner to prove that the object belongs to him), when to post signs that they found an object, how to question someone who claims that the object belongs to him, and so on.

As they walked home, the religious woman asked her sister what she thought of it. "Very nice," she said, "but it doesn't speak to me."

On Sunday the irreligious sister left for India, and began a few weeks of "spiritual soul searching" with her guru. One day she was walking and talking with her guru, when he suddenly bent down and picked up a wallet that had been dropped on the street. He opened up the wallet and found a wad of bills that constituted a small fortune. "The gods have sent me a gift," he announced gravely. "This is a gift from the deities to allow us to repair the ashram."

This woman looked at him in shock and said, "But there is a driver's license in there. We can find the owner and return it!"

"No," insisted the guru. "We shouldn't do that. The gods want me to have this."

"That's not what Judaism preaches," she said curtly. "I think I'll head back to Israel."

This woman eventually became religious. The Torah sold itself.

Another case in point: An unfortunate, common scenario in the *kiruv* world is for a husband to become *frum* without his wife following suit, or vice versa. It makes for a terrible dynamic: constant fights, constant compromises, and constant issues. In one such case, the newly religious husband and his irreligious wife were quarreling day after day. Finally, when their child grew to school-age, the husband decided that he would draw a "line in the sand."

"My child is going to a religious day-school," he declared firmly.

"My child is going to a prep school," his wife responded, equally adamant. "I want him to get into a good university."

The man was ready to divorce his wife, but he went to a rav to discuss the situation first. "Should I give in and allow my son to attend a prep school," he asked, "or should I offer her an ultimatum: day school or divorce?"

"*Gadol hashalom*," the rav answered. "It is more important to maintain your *shalom bayis* [marital harmony]. Hire a tutor to teach your son religious studies during after-school hours. Don't break apart your marriage over this issue."

The husband came home from the rav to find his wife bracing for an all-out, final battle. "The rabbi said that peace in the home is more important than anything," the husband said. "You can send him to the prep school."

"If that is what the Torah teaches," marveled the wife, "then I want my child exposed to it."

Once again, the Torah sold itself.

⇜§ Become a Partner

Allowing the Torah to sell itself is another area in which each and every *frum* Jew can succeed in *kiruv*. There are organizations, one of which is Partners in Torah, in which you can enlist to study Torah with a not-yet-religious Jew over the phone. People in Idaho, Wyoming, and Alaska learn with people in Flatbush, Toronto, and Jerusalem. The results are astounding, as illustrated by the following stories.

A Bobover Chassid was in the Independence Savings Bank in Boro Park and noticed a Partners in Torah bookmark lying around. He called up to enlist. The people at Partners in Torah try to pair *chavrusos* appropriately, but somehow the slight detail that this man spoke heavily-accented English — or perhaps it was Yinglish — slipped through the cracks. The Chassid was given the name of a fellow in Westminster, Maryland, a small suburb 25 miles west of Baltimore.

The Chassid calls up one evening and says, "Nee, you want to learn *bechavreeseh*?"

The man says, "What?"

"You know vat I mean," says the Chassid. "Partners — you know… the partners thing."

The guy in Westminster vaguely remembers signing up for Partners in Torah, but can't understand the caller for the life of him.

"*Nu*, vat do you vanna learn?" the Chassid forges ahead. "I'm learning *Buvu Basreh*."

The guy says, "What?"

"I said *Buvu Basreh*. You don't like *Buvu Basreh*? We can learn *Buvu Metziah*. Makes no difference to me."

The guy in Westminster figures that this match-up is obviously a mistake and that he better call the organization to ask for a different partner, but in order to be polite he says, "Actually, I was thinking more along the lines of *Pirkei Avot*."

This time it's the Chassid's turn to say, "What?"

"*Avot. Avot.* You know, Ethics."

"Oh!" exclaims the Chassid. "You mean *Pirkai Oovehs*? Sure, ve can learn *Pirkai Oovehs*."

"*How long do I have to stay on the line to be polite?*" the guy in Westminster is thinking. "*And how do I get rid of him?*"

Meanwhile the Chassid realizes that the time he allotted for the session was up, so he says, "So ven do you vant to learn? Should I call you next veek at dis time?"

Mustering up as much politeness as he can, the guy from Westminster mutters, "Yes."

Ready for the result?

Eleven years later, the Bobover Chassid and the man, now formerly of Westminster, are still learning together week after week. But the man is now fully observant, and has moved to Baltimore.

The Torah sells itself, and can even bridge culture and language gaps.

And finally, the Torah will help you build a relationship with another *Yid* that means so much.

On Sunday, August 29, 2006, Hurricane Katrina made landfall in Louisiana. A fellow named Alan Krilov was standing on his neighbor's roof in New Orleans, watching his world come to an end. He had stayed in the city despite the doomsday predictions, somehow assuming that he would be safe. But when the roof of his house blew off and his home filled with water, he had no choice but to make his way through the water into his garage and retrieve an ancient Coast Guard boat he was relying on for emergency transportation out of the city.

Unfortunately, the boat was of no use. The overpowering winds thrashed it about, until Alan had no choice but to abandon it and climb onto his neighbor's roof. From his perch, he decided to place some phone calls to say good-bye to his nearest and dearest. Call number one was to his parents, who also lived in New Orleans, but had fled before the storm began.

Call number two was to Alex Gans of Scranton, Pennsylvania, who was his Partners in Torah *chavrusa*. "Alex," he said. "I've lost everything. Life is not worth living."

Alex tried to calm him down, assuring him that Hashem was with him and he would be fine. They continued talking until the line mysteriously went dead.

Alex spent that week trying desperately to track down his missing *chavrusa*. He managed to locate Alan's mother and brother, but they, too, had no idea of his whereabouts. By the time Shabbos came around, Alex felt that he had heard the last of his Partner in Torah.

Sunday morning, the telephone rang. It was Alan Krilov, calling from a bus depot. He had been evacuated from that rooftop to a fire station, and from there to a school, then on to an airport runway, and finally to the bus depot, escaping death numerous times. Hashem had indeed been with him, and it is to Alex Gans' credit that Alan hung onto that rooftop and waited for help.

The Torah will sell itself, but moreover, it will enable you to share a relationship built on the most precious commodity on the planet. We have Torah, and they — as of yet — do not. We have Hashem, and they — as of yet — do not. Let's fill that void.

Life, Liberty, and the Pursuit of ... What?

Almost all citizens of the United States can fill in the blank in the title of this essay. We recognize these words from the Declaration of Independence, in which the "Founding Fathers" wrote that they were founding the country to provide its citizen with inalienable rights — among which are the rights to "life, liberty, and the pursuit of happiness."

I find it interesting that the architects of the United States considered the right to pursue happiness as basic a human need as the right to live and be free. Indeed, if you ask average Americans today whether they have as much a right to happiness as they have to life and liberty, they would say that they do. And that feeling is not limited to Americans. Nowadays, happiness has become a nearly universal pursuit — certainly in the Western world, and maybe even in the more moderate countries in the Middle East and Far East.

But whether the founding fathers of the United States were correct in equating these rights — and whether the peoples of the world are correct in making this pursuit a primary focus in their lives — is not my issue. I would like to narrow my focus to the Torah community. I think that if we were to ask parents in *frum* communities what they want most for their children, an overwhelming majority would say that they want their children to be happy. The question I would like to address is whether the pursuit of happiness is a Torah *hashkafah* (outlook) on life, or whether it is one that has seeped into our collective consciousness from the world around us.

Before we can determine whether we should indeed be pursuing happiness — both for ourselves and for our children — we must first define what we are referring to when we discuss "happiness."

∞§ Happiness: A Definition

It may come as a surprise to you that the term *happiness* is one that is difficult to define. Among the synonyms in the dictionary for the term *happy* are: cheer, joy, bliss, and contentment.

If you examine those choices, you will find that they do not do justice to the term *happy* or *happiness*, and certainly do not define the term *simchah*, which is the closest equivalent to happiness in *lashon kodesh*.

As is often the case, perhaps we can narrow our search for the elusive definition of *happiness* by first determining what happiness is *not*.

True happiness is *not*, for instance, what we think of as *fun*. Fun is a wonderful thing. I am not against fun; I like to have fun as much as everyone else. But fun is not a Jewish concept. There is no word in *lashon kodesh* for *fun*. I have heard that there is a word in Modern Hebrew for fun, but those who coined the word were wise enough not to use *simchah*.

True happiness is not related to pleasure-seeking, either. One need not look any further than the "glamorous" people who populate Hollywood to prove this point. Despite the unlimited resources for so-called "pleasure," it would be hard to find a more miserable group of people anywhere in the world. Their marriages and family lives are most often ruined, and their children give them little or nothing to be proud of.

The term *bliss* that often appears in dictionaries under the entry for happiness is also a misinterpretation. *Bliss* best describes a tension-free state of relaxation that is most likely experienced at a beach resort miles from civilization, and I don't think that we want to limit our experience of happiness to such rare occasions. Moreover, *bliss* describes a challenge-free existence, and when we examine the world around us, we find many people with challenges, drawbacks, and stress who are of the happiest among us.

Rabbi Dr. Abraham J. Twerski, the noted psychiatrist, related that he was once sitting in a doctor's waiting room — yes, even doctors have to wait for doctors — and he was bored to distraction. He picked up a magazine and leafed through it, only to find that the most interesting article in the entire magazine was titled "How Do Lobsters Grow?" You have undoubtedly thought about a lot of issues in your life, but how lobsters grow is probably not one of them. Dr. Twerski had as little interest in reading this article as would you or I, but he read it anyway to pass the time.

Why can't lobsters grow like all other creatures? I know that many of you have never seen a lobster. I haven't seen one either — at least not on my plate. But I have seen them in other settings, and they have a hard, shell-like exterior. Lobsters are born with a small shell, and as they grow, they fill the shell and can grow no more. Thus the title, "How Do Lobsters Grow?"

The answer, as I'm sure you are all waiting breathlessly to find out, is that when the lobster feels restricted and confined by its too-small shell, it finds a rock on the ocean bed and it molts, shedding its shell. The lobster remains under the rock in order to protect itself from predators until it grows a larger shell. The lobster repeats this process several times until it is fully grown, at which point it stops molting.

Rabbi Dr. Twerski found a metaphor for life in this article. In his estimation, lobsters are lucky that they do not have psychiatrists

— and I'll remind you that this is coming from a psychiatrist. If a lobster were to visit a psychiatrist and complain about feeling pressure and tension from the shell, the psychiatrist would prescribe Valium, and suddenly the lobster would be at peace, it would feel no need to break out of its shell, and it would not grow to its full size.

Thankfully, there are no psychiatrists for lobsters, and so they teach us an important lesson. If you don't have any tension or stress, and you find yourself in a constant state of tranquility, you will not grow.

Bliss, therefore, does not do justice to the term *happiness*, because growth is *the* vehicle for happiness. Rabbi Samson Raphael Hirsch points out — as he does so often in his commentary on *Chumash* — that there is a phonetic connection between the words *tzamei'ach* (to grow), and *samei'ach* (to be happy). You don't grow from sitting in a hammock on a deserted beach sipping a piña colada while having a servant wave a fan to cool you off. And since you are not growing as a human being, you cannot be happy.

We are now well aware of what *simchah* is *not*. It is not fun, it is not pleasure, and it is not bliss. So what is it?

܀ࡐ Of Soul, Not Body

The Maharal offers us two insights into the essence of true *simchah*.

In *Netzach Yisrael* (23), the Maharal writes that happiness belongs to the *soul*, not to the body. That is why animals cannot feel happiness. They are capable of feeling other emotions, such as fear or bonding with their offspring, but they cannot be truly happy, because they don't have souls. Therefore, contrary to popular belief, if an attempt at achieving happiness is to succeed, it must have something to do with your *neshamah* (soul). A person can spend his entire life chasing the "pot of gold at the end of the rainbow" in the hope that it will provide him with happiness, and he will still come up short, because he is searching for pleasures that stimulate the body, not the soul.

If we think about our own lives, we can see the truth in the Maharal's words. When did you feel happiest? At a son's *bris* or bar mitzvah, or when you walked your daughter down to the *chuppah*. These are spiritual moments, infused with a sense of connection to the continuity of Jewish generations. They touch our soul, and therefore they make us happy.

Western civilization, which is obsessed with fun and pleasure as vehicles for happiness is — pardon the pun — spinning its wheels. Physical stimuli simply *cannot* provide true happiness.

The Rambam (*Hilchos Megillah* 2:17) writes that we are better off spending more money on *matanos l'evyonim* (gifts to the poor), than on the Purim *seudah* or on *mishloach manos*. Why? "For there is no greater and more meaningful *simchah* than bringing happiness to the hearts of poor people, orphans, widows, and converts. *For one who causes these downtrodden people to be happy is akin to the Divine Presence.*"

When you bring happiness to the unfortunate, you become Godlike, and your *neshamah* feels closer to its Source. That is the greatest happiness that a human can experience.

In *Nesiv HaTorah* (18), Maharal adds another point that I think brings us to the crux of the issue. "*Ki hasimchah hi mitzad hasheleimus* — for happiness comes from completion, from feeling fulfilled. *Va'asher yesh lo sheleimus*, **hu** *samei'ach* — and when one feels complete, fulfilled, he is happy.

We can prove this from examining the polar opposite of *simchah*, which is the acute sadness one feels upon the loss of a relative. Maharal identifies that with a lack of *sheleimus*, a feeling that something is missing because the family is no longer complete.

The Maharal goes on to explain that this is why Dovid HaMelech wrote that the Torah and mitzvos are *mesamchei leiv* (make the heart happy). Torah study and mitzvah observance provide a person with the greatest fulfillment, and therefore make him happy.

So we now have a definition of *simchah* — it is the feeling one experiences when he has achieved some measure of *sheleimus*, and he feels close to Hashem. Thus we find great *tzaddikim* who, despite the terrible *yissurim* and misfortune that seem to rain down upon them, are nevertheless in a continuous state of happiness. Nothing seems to bother them. If they miss a plane, they don't become frazzled. Lack of *parnassah*? They say, "*Abi gezunt* — as long as I'm healthy." If they have a health problem, they say, "*Gam zu letovah* — this, too, is for the best." They are happy, because they are *sheleimim*, they are complete and fulfilled.

The *Rama's* first gloss on *Shulchan Aruch* begins with the words, "*Shivisi Hashem l'negdi samid* — I place Hashem before me always." His last gloss on *Shulchan Aruch* concludes with the words, "*vetov leiv mishteh tamid* — a good-hearted person perpetually celebrates." The similarity between these statements jumps out at us, and it seems that the *Rama* was trying to impart an important message. If you are able to keep the entire *Shulchan Aruch* — and you will, if you succeed in placing Hashem before you *tamid*, always — then you will be in the perpetual state of happiness of a *tov leiv mishteh tamid*.

We can say, therefore, that if a person would like to be happy at all times, he must find a way to become *davuk baHashem*, to cling to Hashem. End of essay.

✑ Learning to Feel Complete

Well, not quite. In a perfect world, I could have ended the essay by stating that the true pursuit of happiness comes from clinging to Hashem and becoming *sheleimim*.

The trouble — at least for me, and perhaps for some of you — is that we don't feel this constant *dveikus* (closeness) to Hashem. Life gets in our way. We have to raise children, earn *parnassah*, and cope with the daily grind of life. Our spiritual fulfillment comes sporadically: a few minutes during *davening* when we find ourselves concentrating, or when we spend our designated time studying Torah. But for the rest of the day, we feel somewhat removed.

When I go to the supermarket, for instance, spend half an hour waiting in line, and when I finally get home my wife asks, "Where are the cucumbers?" and I say, "I'm sure I bought cucumbers," but then I search through the bags and I realize that I left two bags at the checkout counter. My wife begins to fret. "I'm not going to be able to make this recipe without the cucumbers, and vinegar, and …"

I must admit that when this happens, I'm *not* happy. Because my wife is not happy. And when the woman of the house is not happy, nobody can be happy.

So I can't end this essay quite yet. Not for my sake, and, I think it is safe to assume, not for your sake either.

I would therefore like to suggest a practical piece of advice that may help us feel more *shaleim*, complete, and therefore be imbued with *simchah*.

I think that the key to happiness for us ordinary folk lies in recognizing how much we have, and *appreciating* it more, thereby feeling more complete.

The first step in this process is to learn to appreciate things that we all take for granted.

The Talmud (*Berachos* 31a) relates that participants at the wedding of Mar, son of Ravina, asked Rav Hamnuna Zuti to sing a song, ostensibly to lend happiness to the occasion. Rav Hamnuna sang the following words, "*Vai lan demisnan, vai lan demisnan* — Woe unto us, we are going to die; woe unto us, we are going to die." End of *niggun*.

I don't advise you to sing these particular lyrics the next time you are asked to speak at a *sheva berachos*. Couldn't Rav Hamnuna have found a less morbid message to deliver to people asking for a joyous song?

Rav Hamnuna was trying to impart an important message: In order to be happy, you must appreciate what you have. If you want to be happy at a *chasunah*, first appreciate the fact that you are alive to be there. We won't always be alive. If you woke up this morning and were able to put your feet on the ground, then that is enough of a reason to be appreciative.

If a person wants to be happy at a child's wedding, the key is not to look for happiness in the color of the gowns and the beauty of the centerpieces. Appreciate the fact that you have lived to see this occasion. Be thankful that you are healthy. Not everyone

Life, Liberty, and the Pursuit of … What

makes it to their child's wedding. The fact that you are alive to witness your child's marriage should, in and of itself, fill you with happiness.

A while back I attended the *chasunah* of a child of a very close friend. I have known this man for over 40 years. We were in yeshivah together, then we lived across the hall from each other for the first 17 of our married years, and we now live across the street from each other. Over two decades ago, he and his wife had a baby daughter who was born without an optic nerve, rendering her blind for life. This couple raised their daughter with the feeling that she could do anything. And she did. This is a blind girl who went to Eretz Yisrael for seminary! Nothing could stand in her way. No one ever dreamed, however, that she would marry.

Lo and behold, this girl *did* get married, to a very fine yeshivah *bachur*. A regular guy. Well, obviously not a regular guy — he had to be special to consider this *shidduch* — but he is a regular guy.

Whether you were invited to the *chasunah* of this girl or not, you came. The entire Baltimore attended. People talk about "bringing a daughter down to the *chuppah*." This was *bringing* a daughter to the *chuppah* in the simplest sense of the word. If you were not crying at that *chuppah*, then you did not have a pulse.

We have been to so many weddings that it has become rote. Smorgasbord, *badeken*, interminable wait for the *chuppah*, an even longer wait for the photographer to finish the photo shoot. Finally the *chasan* and *kallah* enter for the first dance, and then you leave before the main course and get home hungry. Same old, same old.

This *chasunah* was different. The dancing was the happiest, most *lebedike* (lively) dancing that I have ever seen. People stayed all night. Why? Because it was a girl who is blind, getting married. *Halo davar hu*! It was something special!

The truth of the matter is that *every chasunah* should be as special. You've survived to the day that you can walk your child down to the *chuppah*! But we take that for granted.

Let's pare this idea down to a more basic level. The *Anshei Knesses HaGedolah* created a set of *berachos* that we recite each morning to remind us not to take things for granted. When you get up each morning and say the *berachah* of "*Pokei'ach ivrim*," feel thankful to Hashem for the eyesight that He granted you. "*Zokeif kefufim*" — thank Hashem for enabling you to stand up. "*Hameichin mitz'adei gaver*" — be glad that you can walk. If you have ever broken a leg, you would know that you say the *berachah* of *hameichin mitz'adei gaver* differently after your bones heal. At least for a few days, you appreciate the fact that you can walk.

Rav Hamnuna was teaching the participants at that wedding to appreciate the aspects of life that they take for granted, including, or perhaps especially, life itself.

If there is a lesson for us ordinary folk to learn, it is that the secret to happiness is gratitude. We find a linguistic similarity between the words *shachiach* (common) and *shachah* (to forget). The more *shachiach* something is, the more apt we are to forget it.

But when we realize and appreciate what we have, then we have a sense of *sheleimus*, completion. Happy people are grateful people. Ingrates are unhappy, because they never have enough. You need not look further than your own circle of friends to prove this point. You will quickly discover that your happiest friends are those who appreciate what they have and are thankful for it. The unhappy people are those who always expect more, for nothing undermines gratitude more than expectations.

~§ Training Our Children to be Happy

This all brings me to a point that I am guilty of ignoring just as much as everyone else. We love our children dearly, and so we shower them with everything they need and almost everything they want. The problem is that they come to expect it. And the more they expect, the less grateful they are, and ultimately, the less happy they are.

A few years ago, I was in Stamford, Connecticut for a speaking engagement, and after the speech a fellow came over to me and asked, "Rabbi Frand, can I have a word with you in private?"

"Sure," I said. We went off to a corner, and he said, "My name is Stanley Berger. I am a fan of yours. I like your tapes and your books …

"But there is one thing you wrote in your book," he continued, "that really upset me."

"What's the problem?" I asked.

"It's what you wrote in *Parashas Lech Lecha*," he said.

"I know that this is going to shatter your image of me," I responded, "But I don't remember what I wrote six years ago in *Parashas Lech Lecha*."

"You know, the story …" he said, trying to jog my memory.

"Give me some more details," I begged.

He started to tell me the story, which, when prompted, I certainly did remember. The story, which has a documented, historical source, is of a couple named Hiller who lived in the Krakow Ghetto during World War II. When they realized where things were headed, they took a step that many other Jews took. They took their little boy, Shachne, to a childless Polish gentile couple and said, "Please take our child and raise him. If we survive the war, we will come back and get him. If not, here is the name of a relative of ours in Washington D.C. Please contact these relatives and get Shachne to them."

The couple agreed.

The Hillers did not survive the war. This Polish couple raised this little boy as a good Catholic. When he was 10 years old, they took him to the parish priest to be baptized.

"Pardon me for asking," the priest said, "but where have you been until now? Why didn't you baptize him when he was an infant?"

The woman hemmed and hawed, and finally told him the true story. "We want to make sure that this boy gets to heaven," she concluded, "so we decided to keep him and have him baptized."

"Don't baptize him," the priest responded. "You were entrusted with a Jewish child, and he should remain Jewish. Send him to his relatives in Washington D.C. and let them raise him as a Jew."

The name of that parish priest was Karol Wotilla, who later became Pope John Paul II. The Bluzhever Rebbe said something that a layman would not be able to say. He said that the reason Karol Wotilla was accorded the greatest honor available to a Catholic was because he saved a Jewish soul from becoming lost to our nation.

When I realized that this was the story that upset Mr. Stanley Berger, I could not understand what his issue was. "What's wrong with this story?" I asked.

"*I'm* the boy in the story," he said.

"*You're* the boy?" I asked. "But you're name is Stanley Berger, and the boy's name was Shachne Hiller."

"Yes, but my great-uncle and aunt in Washington D.C. adopted me," he explained, "and their name was Berger, so I am Shachne/Stanley Hiller/Berger."

"So what's the problem with the story?" I persisted.

"I don't like the way you denigrated the Polish couple," he said. He took a photocopy of the story out of his pocket, and pointed to a sentence that was highlighted. "Look at what you said."

The offensive line was, "His parents' trust in this couple was misplaced."

"What's wrong with that line?" I asked, flabbergasted. "Isn't it true that they betrayed your parents' faith in them? They didn't do what they had agreed to do."

"You don't realize that these people were *moser nefesh* for me," he retorted. "They could have been shot for harboring a Jewish boy, and they risked their lives to save me. And all you can say about them is that his parents' trust in them was misplaced?"

"Mr. Berger," I said, "You're right. I apologize. I am looking at the situation from the vantage point of a dispassionate third party. You were the recipient of their goodness, and so you look at it differently, and rightly so."

Mr. Berger told me that he sent money to the woman who had hidden him, and that he had flown to Poland several times to visit her, all in appreciation of what she had done for him.

I remember thinking to myself, *"Have I just bumped into a tzaddik named Stanley Berger?"* I know children who don't bother to object when someone says something negative about their natural parents, and will even say derogatory things about them to others.

Why was Stanley/Shachne so protective of his foster parents? Is he a *chassid* in the mitzvah of *hakaras hatov* (appreciation of favors)?

The answer is that Stanley/Shachne realized that *es kumpt em* **nisht.** He felt that he did not *deserve* the favor that the Polish couple did for him. They didn't owe him anything. They had no reason to risk their lives for him. They could have slammed the door in his mother's face and said, "Sorry, find some other fools who will risk their lives for your son."

Unfortunately, we have been raised, and we raise our children, to go through life feeling as though we *owe* them everything. We feel as though parents were placed into the world to provide for their children.

That is the difference between Stanley Berger's attitude and ours. Nothing diminishes gratitude as much as expectations. Conversely, nothing increases gratitude as much as the lack of expectations. We must begin to look at life with Stanley Berger's feeling of *es kumpt mir* **nisht**, nothing is owed to us — not by our parents, and not by the *Ribono Shel Olam*. We must look at all that we have: our lives; our health — more or less; *parnassah*, again — more or less; hopefully, children to bring us *nachas* — and appreciate that Hashem has given us these items as gifts, not because He owes them to us. If we can learn to adopt this perspective on life, then we can be happy people.

Let's return to the question with which we started. Is "*the pursuit of happiness*" a Jewish value? Does the Torah want us to pursue happiness?

The answer is that if we were to fill in the blank in the title of this essay, it would not be with the word *happiness*. We would write, "*And the pursuit of sheleimus*" — the pursuit of trying to achieve a feeling that we are complete. For happiness cannot be pursued as an end in itself. When we feel more complete as a result of *dveikus b'Hashem*, or as a result of our appreciation for all that we have, then we can become truly happy people.

Never Stop Davening

Tefillah, prayer, provides us with one of the greatest anomalies of Jewish life.

We can usually gauge the significance of a mitzvah by the seriousness with which we treat it. The more important something is, the greater the respect we confer upon it.

Bris milah (circumcision), for instance, is considered fundamental to Judaism. Thus we find that even Jews who are extremely distant from *Yiddishkeit* will still insist on having their sons circumcised.

I find that when I am at a supermarket during the weeks leading up to Pesach, I will invariably be approached by someone whose manner of dress leads one to suppose that he or she has no interest in Judaism. This individual will then pop a question like, "Rabbi, are we allowed to use Brussels sprouts on Passover?" Coming from a person who might totally disregard the laws of kashrus throughout the year, this may seem to be a strange question. Somehow, however, the significance of Pesach has not escaped these Jews.

In our own society, in which Torah study is supreme, we refer to one who excels in it as a *masmid*, a *lamdan*, or a great *talmid chacham*. We consider *chesed* fundamental as well, and so we will refer to someone who is constantly helping others as true *baal chesed*.

One thing stands out. *Tefillah*, which stands at the apex of Jewish life, is abused.

Tefillah is an implicit declaration of our belief in Hashem; someone who does not believe would not bother to stand and *daven* to Him. Every single time we *daven*, we reaffirm our belief that Hashem is there, that He can provide all our needs, and that we could not exist without Him. It is an admission, to ourselves and to Him, that we are helpless without Him.

Yet, despite its significance, many of us don't apply the same seriousness to *tefillah* that we do to other mitzvos. You will rarely hear someone complimented as being a "great *davener.*" *Davening* has escaped the pattern of respect-in-proportion-to-significance that we find with other mitzvos.

Truth be told, this is not a new phenomenon. The Talmud (*Berachos* 6b) states that *tefillah* is *omeid berumo shel olam* — it stands at the apex of the world, *u'bnei adam mezalzelin bo* — yet people treat it irreverently.

Perhaps our attitude toward *tefillah* is due in part to the implicit admission of our helplessness. Human beings do not like to feel powerless. This is especially true in Western society, in which the rugged, self-reliant individual is held in high regard.

Perhaps you are aware of a phenomenon called the "I'm-not-asking-for-directions syndrome," which, sociologists have determined, affects only the male segment of society.

Many men refuse to ask for directions, no matter what. They cannot handle the thought of seeming to be helpless in the eyes of the person from whom they seek directions. A woman who asks her husband, "Why don't you ask for directions?" is likely to receive a hurt look in return, followed by the rejoinder: "I don't *need* to ask for directions. Don't you have confidence in me?"

I must tell you that I have been cured of the, "I'm-not-asking-for-directions syndrome."

Our children bought us a GPS system.

But a Jew should not feel self reliant. A Jew should realize that he is helpless without Hashem. One of the basic concepts of *tefillah* is to come before Hashem, as the Ramban (*Shemos* 13:16) puts it, and say before Him, "*Beriyosecha anachnu* — we are Your creations."

We need you, Hashem.

✢ Dashed Hopes? Keep on Davening

There must be something behind the lack of seriousness we have toward *tefillah*. Many of us find it tedious and fruitless. Why is that?

I think it is because we don't believe in the power of our own *tefillos*. And the reason for that may be because we have been disappointed too many times. We have *davened* for sick people who did not survive, for *parnassah* (livelihood) that never materialized, for singles who have yet to marry, for children who gave us grief, and for babies that didn't come.

When you do something over and over again and it doesn't seem to help, you eventually give up. No one is about to stop *davening*, but we begin to treat it as an obligatory exercise that we must absolve ourselves of with minimal discomfort or inconvenience.

How do we deal with this frustrating issue?

The first thing to do is to reeducate ourselves. We must change our outlook on *tefillah*, by coming to the realization that *no tefillah* — again, *no tefillah* — goes unanswered.

That might sound like an inspirational thought I concocted on my own, but it isn't. The entire corpus of Torah *hashkafah* is replete with mentions of this simple fact. *No tefillah goes to waste.*

How can that be, you are probably wondering. *I have davened for so many things that never happened!*

The answer is that your *tefillah* may not have helped for you at that time, and you may never see the results in your lifetime, but I can assure you that somewhere, at some time, it will be applied to someone.

I could provide pages and pages of proofs demonstrating the unanimous recognition of this concept, but I will suffice with one.

We read in *Parashas Vayeira* that prior to destroying Sodom and Gomorrah, Hashem said to Himself, "Shall I conceal from Avraham what I do, now that Avraham is surely to become a great and mighty nation, and all the nations of the earth shall bless themselves by him?" (*Bereishis* 18:17-18).

What does the fact that Avraham is to become a great and mighty nation have to do with Hashem telling him that He was planning to overturn Sodom and Gomorrah?

The Maggid of Dubno characteristically explains these verses through a parable.

Two merchants were traveling on business. One was an elderly man, who had only recently been blessed with his one and only child, and the other was a young man who had several children.

When they reached a certain city, they passed several shops selling beautiful children's clothing. The elderly merchant looked at the clothing and said with a sigh, "I would love to buy something for my son, but I am concerned that it won't fit him properly."

The younger merchant selected a number of garments and went to pay for them. "Aren't you concerned that the clothing won't fit?" the elderly merchant asked.

"Your concern is valid for you," the younger man responded, "because you have only one child. If the garment you purchase doesn't fit him, you will have nothing to do with it. I have several children, and I may still have more. If a garment doesn't fit one, it will fit another."

Similarly, explains the Maggid of Dubno, Hashem knew that if He would share his plans with Avraham, the latter would pray for the salvation of Sodom and Gomorrah. Hashem also knew, however, that Avraham's prayers could not be accepted, because the fate of those two cities had already been sealed. Perhaps it would be better to conceal His plans from Avraham, Hashem said at first, lest he feel that his heartfelt *tefillos* were unanswered.

But then Hashem said, "Avraham is to become a great and mighty nation." If those *tefillos* won't be applied now for Sodom and Gemorrah, then they will be applied later on for Avraham's own descendants.

The inscrutable ways of Hashem are beyond us, and we cannot understand why a *tefillah* does not work for us at the particular moment we utter it. But we must maintain the awareness that no *tefillah* goes to waste.

Lev L'Achim volunteers tell a story that occurred a while back. One day, in a little *shtiebel* in Tel Aviv, nine men had assembled to *daven* Minchah and the *minyan* (a quorum of ten men) was therefore incomplete. One of the *mispallelim* went outside, and in the time-honored tradition of those trying to gather a *minyan*, he shouted, "Minchah! Minchah! Asiri! Ah tzenter! (roughly: we need a tenth man)." To his chagrin, no one was walking down that block except for an irreligious young man who sauntered right past him.

The man ran after him and explained that they were missing just one person, and that it would be a great favor to them if he could sit in the shul for just 10 minutes. "*Lo rotzeh*," the young man responded. "I don't want to."

The man pleaded and badgered until the young man finally acquiesced.

For the first time in his life, this young irreligious fellow heard *Ashrei, Kaddish, Shemoneh Esrei, chazaras hashatz, Tachanun, Kaddish, Aleinu, and Kaddish*. Routine enough for us, but it left an indelible impression on him. He had been offered a study-partnership by Lev L'Achim several times in the past, but he had always resisted. After experiencing this one Minchah, he decided to take Lev L'Achim up on its offer.

To make a long story short, this young man is now fully observant.

The news of him becoming a *baal teshuvah* sent shockwaves through his community, which was known for espousing virulently anti-religious views. "You raised your son on the same hostile rhetoric that we did," his parents' friends noted. "Where did you go wrong?"

"I know exactly what happened," said the boy's father, "and it has nothing to do with us.

"When my family came here from Europe, my father clung to his religion tenaciously. But I had no interest in sticking to the 'old-

Never Stop Davening / 233

fashioned' type of Judaism, and I abandoned it in favor of secular Zionism. I joined this community to ensure that my children would have nothing to do with it, either.

"You know that shul that my son walked into on that fateful day? That was the shul that my father had *davened* in, day after day, *tefillah* after *tefillah*. I am certain that my son was affected by the *tefillos* of my father."

Let's reflect on this story. That *zeide*, that European Jew, must have poured his heart out hundreds — if not thousands — of times in that shul, begging Hashem to make his wayward son have a change of heart. How painful it must have been that his grandchildren had no connection to Judaism. And when he was on his deathbed, he might have thought to himself, "All my *tefillos* were for naught. My children and grandchildren are as secular as ever."

If he thought so then, he now knows the truth. No *tefillah* goes to waste. Sometime, somewhere, for someone, every *tefillah* is accepted. It may not be as overt as it was in this story. It may not help your own grandchild, but it *will* help someone.

✌ Sometimes, A Father Must Say, "No!"

We must be aware that sometimes Hashem answers our *tefillos*, but we do not understand His answer.

On Friday, October 7, 1994, an Israeli soldier named Nachshon Waxman came home to spend Shabbos with his parents in Jerusalem's Ramot neighborhood. On Motza'ei Shabbos, his superiors in the army called him to inform him that the following day, Sunday, he was to head up north, where he and another soldier from his unit would learn to operate a special military vehicle in a one-day course culminating in receiving a license to operate that vehicle.

This was a very prestigious offer. Nachshon left his house late that night to reach the training area in time for the course, and he told his parents that he would be back on Sunday night.

When Nachshon did not come home, his mother, the child of Holocaust survivors, began to be concerned. Knowing of their mother's background, her children knew that she worried about them when they were not home on time, and they would always notify her if there was a delay or a change of plans.

By midnight, Mrs. Waxman began to fear the worst. She notified the military authorities of Nachshon's disappearance, and attempted to trace his movements by speaking with some of his army buddies. All they could tell her was that after completing his course, Nachshon had been dropped off at the Bnei Atarot junction, a populated area from which he could either catch a bus or hitchhike (as soldiers do) to Jerusalem.

On Monday, search parties began to scour the area where Nachshon had last been seen. The army was still apathetic about his disappearance. His superiors were more inclined to believe that he might have taken off for a few days of relaxation in a hotel or resort in Eilat. To Mrs. Waxman, that was inconceivable. She was certain that her son was dead.

On Tuesday, Israeli Television contacted the Waxmans to tell them that they had received a videotape from a Reuters photographer showing Nachshon being held hostage by Hamas terrorists. They said that they would come to the Waxman's home to show them the video before broadcasting it to the entire nation, and the world.

On that video tape, Nachshon was seen held at gunpoint and forced to issue an ultimatum on behalf of Hamas. If the Israeli government would not release Hamas' spiritual leader Achmed Yassin from an Israeli prison, along with 200 other imprisoned Hamas terrorists, Nachshon would be executed on Friday at 8 p.m.

The next four days found the entire country — and Jews worldwide — mobilized on behalf of Nachshon Waxman. Jewish people around the world prayed for Nachshon's release.

On Thursday night, 24 hours before the ultimatum, a prayer vigil was held at the *Kosel*. Some 100,000 people arrived — a people united for the sake of one Jewish soul. Chassidim prayed alongside young men in jeans, Sephardim side-by-side with Ashkenazim, old with young, religious with secular.

On Friday night, the Waxmans sat at the Shabbos table with their eyes glued to the door, hoping that Nachshon would walk through it.

They had no idea that Israeli Intelligence had apprehended the driver of the car in which Nachshon had hitched a ride at Bnei Atarot. That had no idea that he had informed them that Nachshon was being held in a village called Bir Nabbalah, which was under Israeli rule, located just 10 minutes from their home in Ramot. And they had no idea that Prime Minister Rabin had made a decision to launch a military action to attempt to rescue their son.

At the hour of the ultimatum, 8 p.m. on Friday night, General Yoram Yair, not Nachshon, walked through the door to deliver horrific news. The military rescue attempt had failed, and Nachshon had been killed along with leader of the commando unit, Captain Nir Poraz.

On Motza'ei Shabbos at midnight, Nachshon Waxman was laid to rest.

The same amalgam of Israeli society that had come to pray for Nachshon's rescue at the *Kosel* came to attend his funeral.

One of the eulogies was delivered by Nachshon's rosh yeshivah, Rabbi Mordechai Alon. Before he began, he was called aside by Nachshon's father and asked to deliver an important message: the Jewish people should know that Hashem had *not* ignored their *tefillos*. He had listened to their prayers and had collected all their tears. Yet, just as a father would like to always say "yes" to his children's requests but must sometimes say "no," so too our Father in Heaven had heard their prayers, but for reasons beyond our understanding, His answer was "no."

I would like to add just one thought to Mr. Waxman's incredibly strong and faith-filled message.

It may seem to us that Hashem said, "No," but in truth, those *tefillos* helped — we don't know when, we don't know where, and we don't know how — but we can be sure that they helped.

✑ Believe in Your Tefillos

It is extremely important for us to be aware of the power of our *tefillos*, because another rule of *tefillah* is that the more you believe in your *tefillos*, the more effective they are. If you become discouraged and place less hope in the efficacy of your *tefillos*, then they will, indeed, be less potent. This leads to a vicious cycle. The less potent your *tefillos* are, the fewer results they engender. The fewer results, the more discouragement, and the less hope you place in your *tefillos*.

The *Malbim* uses this idea to answer a question on the *haftarah* that we read on the first day of Rosh Hashanah. We read that Channah, the barren wife of Elkanah, would have her husband pray at the Mishkan (Tabernacle) that she would have a baby. One year, Channah decided to go pray herself, and lo and behold, that very year she merited to have a baby, who turned out to be Shmuel HaNavi.

Chazal (*Yalkut Shimoni, I Shmuel* 89) tell us that Channah's visit to the Mishkan took place after 19 years of marriage. Why did she wait so long? And if the reason she waited was because she was relying on her husband's prayers, what changed that year?

The *Malbim* explains that in that fateful year, as we read in the *haftarah*, Elkanah said to Channah, "Why do you cry and why do you not eat? Why is your heart broken? Am I not better to you than ten children?" (*I Shmuel* 1:8).

Channah heard these words, and she heard the unspoken message. She realized that since her husband was consoling her and telling her that she should be content just with him, he must have lost faith in his *tefillos* and had become resigned to her being childless forever. And if he no longer had faith in them, then they would not be effective. Thus she decided to take matters into her own hands and plead her own cause, because she still believed that her *tefillos* would be effective.

We find clear proof that *gedolei Yisrael* believe in the power of *Klal Yisrael's tefillos* in our times too.

In December of 1962, 2 *Kislev* 5723, Rav Aharon Kotler passed away and was brought to Eretz Yisrael for burial.

There was a terrible drought in Eretz Yisrael that year. There is a legend passed down by the elders of Yerushalayim that if an *adam gadol* passes away during a drought, then he should be buried with a wet cloth; he will then beg Hashem for rain. When Rav Aharon was buried, they placed a wet cloth into his grave, and that very night it rained in Eretz Yisrael.

"Look how powerful this *segulah* is," someone commented to Rav Yaakov Kamenetsky. "It took just hours for it to be effective!"

"The rain has nothing to do with a wet *shmatteh*," replied Rav Yaakov. "The reason it rained is because we began to say *v'sein tal u'matar livrachah* [and give dew and rain for a blessing] that night in *chutz la'aretz* [the Diaspora]."

Rav Yaakov knew that *tefillah* is more potent than *segulos*. He knew that it is *tefillah* that really works.

✺ No Atheists in Sloan-Kettering

Interestingly, when the chips are down, we realize that *tefillah* is the only thing that can help us.

When I see someone suddenly begin to *daven* a longer *Shemoneh Esrei* and with greater intensity, I wonder, "What is going on in his life?"

This is a new take on the old maxim, "There are no atheists in foxholes." Or as my son told me, after spending a considerable amount of time with a member of his extended family at Memorial Sloan-Kettering Hospital (a New York hospital specializing in cancer cases), "There are no atheists in Sloan-Kettering."

Irreligious people and even gentiles would approach him and ask, "What can we do to save our relative's life?"

Similarly, a man who is suffering the indescribable pain of having a child abandon *Yiddishkeit* wrote recently that life's challenges offered him a new perspective on *Shemoneh Esrei*:

> The blessing of *mechayei meisim* (Who revivifies the dead) means, "Please bring my son back to spiritual life." *Chonein*

hada'as (Who grants understanding) means, "Please let us understand how to deal with our son." *Rofei cholei amo Yisrael* (Who heals the sick of His nation, Israel) means, "Please, Hashem, heal my son's spiritual malady." *Sim Shalom* (establish peace) means, "Please bring tranquility back to our household."

We all know that life is so tenuous. All one needs to do is to step off a curb the wrong way and he can land in the hospital with a broken ankle. One troubling result on a blood test can change our lives forever.

Yet, when things are going swimmingly, we forget about Hashem. Everything is fine, and we lose touch. One of the ways that He reminds us that He wants to hear from us is to bring a *tzarah* (tragedy) into our lives, either on a personal level, a community level, or even one that threatens world Jewry.

If we were wise, we would not wait for the trouble to begin. We would follow *Chazal's* advice of, "*Le'olam yakdim adam tefillah letzarah* — one should always pray before tragedy strikes" (*Sanhedrin* 44b). We would "keep in touch" when things are going well, so that we don't need a wake-up call from Hashem. We would become better *daveners* before the *yissurim* (suffering) set in.

◆§ Going Straight to the Top

How do we become better *daveners*?

First, there is the tried and true method of studying the halachos of *tefillah* and the meaning of the *tefillos* themselves. Learning about *davening* will make you a better *mispallel*.

Nowadays, there are no excuses not to learn about *davening*. There are so many *sefarim* available on the subject, both in Hebrew and English. In my *shiur*, I started learning a *sefer* called *Rinas Chaim*, by Rabbi Chaim Friedlander. I can say that for me, the first *berachah* of *Shemoneh Esrei* has undergone a transformation, as it has for the young men in my *shiur*, because of the insights that he provides.

Rabbi Shimshon Pincus's *She'arim BeTefillah* is a wonderful work, full of inspiring and uplifting thoughts about *tefillah*.

If you are seeking something in English, there are plenty of titles available at your local bookseller, most notably *Praying With Fire*, Vols. 1 and 2, and *Touched by a Prayer*.

Learn about *tefillah*, and you will become a better *davener*.

Aside from studying *tefillah*, however, I would like to make another suggestion — one that takes less than 10 seconds to implement. Before beginning to *daven*, let us focus our thoughts — for no more than a few seconds — on the awareness that we are about to speak to the *Ribono Shel Olam*.

You may think that this is stating the obvious, but in truth, how many of us begin to *daven* and then wander off into a daydream, oblivious of the fact that we are standing directly before Hashem?

I have not such good news for all of us: The Rambam rules — according to Rav Chaim Brisker's understanding — that one who does not pray with the minimal realization that he is talking to Hashem has not fulfilled the mitzvah of *tefillah* **at all**. Which means that a person can go through an entire lifetime, and never *once* fulfill the mitzvah of *tefillah*.

When you begin *Shemoneh Esrei* with the introductory verse, "*Hashem sefasai tiftach* — Hashem, open my lips, *ufi yagid tehillasecha* — and may my mouth speak Your praises," be attentive to what you are saying.

Anyone who has been in a court of law or has even read a depiction of a court case knows that when a lawyer would like to discuss something with the judge, he must say, "Your honor, may I approach the bench?" *Lehavdil*, this is what we are saying to Hashem with that introductory verse. "I am speaking to the Omnipotent, the most powerful Being in the universe. Hashem, I am speaking directly to You!"

Good businessmen will always try to "cut out the middlemen and go straight to the top." That is what *tefillah* is. It is an opportunity to speak with the One on Top, with no middlemen.

This idea was brought home to me so powerfully one year right before the *Yamim Noraim* (High Holy Days), when I was invited to speak to a group in New Square, N.Y., a Chassidic community near Monsey. Part of the agreement was that I would be permitted to have a private audience with the Skverer Rebbe.

I must tell you something about myself. If there is one thing that I am *not*, it is a Chassid. My parents were Yekkes (of German descent), and I have spent most of my life in a *litvishe* yeshivah. But it was before the *Yamim Noraim*, and the Rebbe is a holy man. It couldn't hurt to get a *berachah* (blessing).

Before I went into the Rebbe, I asked my wife, "What should I ask for?" Then I called my children and asked, "What should I ask for you?"

I went into the Rebbe, and I asked for several *berachos*. Afterward, I said to myself, "Here I was, preparing what I would say to and ask of the Rebbe. I thought about how I would address the Rebbe. Yiddish not being my native tongue, I actually practiced what I would say. Yet three times each day, I go straight to the Almighty. I speak to the *Ribono Shel Olam* Himself. Do I think to myself, 'What should I say? How should I say it?'"

It bothered me for a while, but then I realized that my conduct was in line with the Ramchal's teaching in *Mesillas Yesharim*: "It is difficult for a person to fathom what it means to speak to the Almighty."

We are aware that we are not to try to envision Hashem as having any physical properties. One who thinks of Hashem as having a long white beard is blasphemous.

When you go into a Rebbe, on the other hand, you sit down in front of him, and you see his long white beard, and his piercing blue eyes, and he bends over to listen to you intently, and then he responds with advice and *berachos*. It just seems so much more real and awesome.

But if we remind ourselves when beginning *Shemoneh Esrei* that we are speaking to the most Awesome of all, to the King of kings, then we can transform our *davening*.

☙ Respecting the Audience

There was a man by the name of Yehudah Avner, who was to be the Israeli ambassador to Great Britian. In order to be deemed the ambassador, he had to present his credentials to the Queen of England. He writes the following:

> After practicing the protocol, I was escorted into the queen's chamber by a chamberlain dressed like the Duke of Wellington. I executed the rehearsed choreography with due aplomb, bowing at the door, walking two steps, bowing once more, two more steps forward, bowing once more, and proclaiming, "Your Majesty, I have the honor to present my credentials as the Ambassador of Israel to the Court of St. James."

The entire time, he writes, he was sweating profusely, because he was standing in front of the Queen of England.

It is frightening to stand before the Queen of England — a woman who has *absolutely no power whatsoever*.

It is said that President Ronald Reagan never took off his jacket in the Oval Office, out of deference to the office.

I wish that we could have the same respect for a shul, a place where we meet with and speak to Hashem.

Rav Moshe Feinstein did not *shukkle* (sway) when he *davened*. Not that there is anything wrong with swaying. But when Rav Moshe was in Russia, he was dragged before the communist authorities and was told to stand at perfect attention. He had to stand without moving a muscle. Rav Moshe decided that if that was the way he was forced to show respect for the communists, then that is the way he should be standing before Hashem.

Perhaps if we would learn to treat *davening* and shuls with the awe that we have for a worldly authority, our *tefillos* would become more meaningful.

The Message of a Siddur Unearthed

We are all painfully aware of the fact that in the summer of 2005, the Israeli government decided to surrender the Gaza Strip to the Palestinians, and ordered the evacuation of all the Jewish citizens who had settled there. The people did not leave of their own accord, so the government sent troops to evacuate them by force.

There was an American boy who had made *aliyah* and joined the army several years prior to those events. He had quickly risen in the ranks, and in that summer, he was the officer in charge of a platoon that was ordered to evacuate one of the settlements. The order went against every sinew in his body, and he protested to his commanding officers. "Orders are orders," they replied, "and a soldier is a soldier. You must do what you were commanded to do."

He brought his platoon into the *moshav* that they were to evacuate, entered the shul in which the people had gathered and, together with the rav of the settlement, he announced, "It is time to leave, and leave in peace. Let there not be bloodshed between brother and brother. Let us get on the buses peacefully and leave."

His plea was accepted. In one of the few peaceful evacuations of that summer, the people of that *moshav* boarded the buses. The rav was the last member to leave the shul and the *moshav*, and finally it was time for this soldier to leave as well. But before he got onto the bus, he suddenly stopped in his tracks, reached into his knapsack, and withdrew his personal *siddur*. He opened the front cover and wrote the date of the evacuation. He then knelt and dug a hole in the ground with his bare hands. After a few minutes, he kissed the *siddur*, put it into the ground, covered it with earth, and then stood up.

The rav was watching him, and asked him why he was burying his *siddur*. The soldier explained that he was confident that one day Jews would return to Gush Katif and to this *moshav*. He didn't know when — maybe it would take 10 years, or 20, or 50 — but one day maybe a Jew would find that *siddur* and realize that Jews had been there and had left their hearts behind. That said, the soldier and rabbi embraced and then together, arm in arm, got onto the bus and departed.

Never Stop Davening / 243

One year later, in the summer of 2006, an Israeli soldier, Gilad Shalit, was captured in the Gaza Strip — and he remains in captivity until today, may Hashem bring about his quick release. This same American-born soldier was ordered to take his unit into Gaza under the cover of darkness, and set up a headquarters from which they would launch covert operations. In the morning, this soldier awoke and walked out of his tent to find himself surrounded by utter desolation and destruction. He had no idea where he was, because all the buildings in the settlements had been destroyed. All he saw were mountains of debris surrounding him on every side.

Suddenly, as if possessed, he dropped to his knees and began digging in the dirt at his feet. A few moments later, he felt something in the earth. He reached in and pulled out his very own *siddur*, which he had buried some eleven months earlier.

He stood up and began to shake uncontrollably. "Why?" he shouted. "Hashem, why did you send my *siddur* back to me?"

He called his father in America, and asked him to ask their rabbi what message Hashem was sending him through his *siddur*. Their rav, Rabbi Aryeh Ginsburg of Long Island, wisely determined that it was beyond him to interpret this story, but that he could arrange for the soldier to meet Rav Chaim Kanievski and ask him the meaning.

That Motza'ei Shabbos, the soldier went into Rav Chaim Kanievski, told him the story, and asked him why Hashem had sent his *siddur* back to him.

"What did you do to prevent the expulsion from Gaza?" Rav Chaim asked.

"I *davened* constantly," the soldier responded, "and pleaded with my superiors to ignore the government's directives, all to no avail."

"And after the expulsion, what did you do?" asked Rav Chaim.

"What could I do?" the soldier replied. "It was all over."

"The power of *tefillah* is not to be underestimated," Rav Chaim said. "You should have taken your *siddur* in hand and continued *davening*. Who knows what *Hakadosh Baruch Hu* would have done, if we would have continued to storm the Heavens with our *tefillos*? Instead, you chose to bury your *siddur* in the ground. For you it was over. But Hashem says, 'It's not over. Here is your *siddur*. Pour your heart out again for Eretz Yisrael and for *Klal Yisrael*.'"

By returning that *siddur*, Hashem sent a message to that soldier — and to us: *Never Stop Davening*.

This volume is part of
THE ARTSCROLL SERIES®
an ongoing project of
translations, commentaries and expositions
on Scripture, Mishnah, Talmud, Halachah,
liturgy, history, the classic Rabbinic writings,
biographies and thought.

For a brochure of current publications
visit your local Hebrew bookseller
or contact the publisher:

Mesorah Publications, ltd
4401 Second Avenue
Brooklyn, New York 11232
(718) 921-9000
www.artscroll.com